DAILY THOUGHTS
FROM SCRIPTURE

To Glenn and Margo –

Thanks for your love and friendship over the years! Here is a book that I have really enjoyed and the author is someone who is a bit "familiar" to us. You might recognize his name.

Love,
Chuck and Ellen

DAILY THOUGHTS FROM SCRIPTURE

Selections from the writings of

J. Oswald Sanders

HODDER AND STOUGHTON
LONDON SYDNEY AUCKLAND TORONTO

British Library Cataloguing in Publication Data
Sanders, J. Oswald (John Oswald)
  Daily thoughts from scripture: selections from the writings of
J. Oswald Sanders.
  1. Bible. N. T. Acts – devotional works
  I. Title
  242.5
  ISBN 0–340–53612–8

*Published by Hodder and Stoughton, a division of Hodder and Stoughton Ltd,
Mill Road, Dunton Green, Sevenoaks, Kent TN13 2YA. Editorial Office: 47
Bedford Square, London WC1B 3DP.*
Photoset by Medcalf Type Ltd, Bicester, Oxon.
Printed in Great Britain by Clays Ltd, St Ives plc.

FOREWORD

The readings in this volume are selections from thirty-five of my books written over a period of fifty-five years, which are listed at the end of the book. Many of them are now out of print, but the themes and principles they treat are timeless.

The very generous acceptance accorded to these books by the Christian reading public, and the fact that some of them have been produced in twenty-five languages, would seem to indicate that these readings are worth preserving in the present form.

They are arranged in no special order, so as to give variety. They are all Bible-based, and cover doctrine, devotional material, apologetics, Bible biography, and missionary themes.

As the books were written over so long a period, different Bible translations were used as they appeared. As these and the sources of other quotations have been acknowledged in the respective books, they are not repeated here. The Scripture verses at the head of each reading are normally from the New International Version.

I send these readings forth with the prayer that the timeless truths and principles treated may continue to prove a daily stimulus to those who read them.

J. OSWALD SANDERS

DAILY THOUGHTS FROM SCRIPTURE

January 1

THE TRANSCENDENT GOD

"To whom will you compare me? Or who is my equal?" says the Holy One. (Isaiah 40:25)

Isaiah had a great conception of the transcendence of God. He represents God as sitting above earth's vault. "He sits enthroned above the circle of the earth, and its people are like grasshoppers. He stretches out the heavens as a canopy, and spreads them out like a tent" (v.22).

Such a grand conception is more easily intelligible to our generation than it would have been in ancient times. Astronomers have enlarged our idea of the vastness of space a thousand-fold. From their vantage point above the earth, our spacemen were able to see whole continents at once. From His elevated throne above the circle of the earth, God sees and controls the whole universe.

Creating the innumerable galaxies cost God no more effort than hanging a tent curtain. Small wonder that to Him earth's "inhabitants are like grasshoppers". With a God as great as that, why should His people fear what earth's puny potentates could do? "He reduces the rulers of this world to nothing" (v.23).

FOR WORSHIP:
> *Lord of all being, throned afar,*
> *Thy glory flames from sun and star;*
> *Centre and soul of every sphere,*
> *Yet to each loving heart how near.*
> Oliver Wendell Holmes

January 2

TERRIBLE YET TENDER

Consider therefore the kindness and sternness of God . . . (Romans 11:22)

The prophet Isaiah affirms that in His rule of His people, God will be both inflexibly just and yet considerably tender: "Behold, the Lord God will come with might, with his arm ruling for him. Like a shepherd he will tend his flock, in his arm he will gather the lambs and carry them in His bosom" (40:10,11).

The One who leads His people is terrible in His might, but tender in His attitudes. Though Judge and Ruler of the universe, He tenderly leads His flock in green pastures and by still waters. His mighty arm gathers the tired lambs to His bosom. He rests them in the heat of the day. He adapts His pace to the weakest of the flock. The heart of the Eternal is most wonderfully kind.

A great deal of teaching in Scripture is by paradox, as in this passage. It is quite difficult to hold in the mind at the same time the contrasting qualities of goodness and severity, of loftiness and lowliness, of humility and majesty. Yet those are all ascribed to God in this chapter and elsewhere in Scripture, and are held in perfect equilibrium. God is not a great contradiction. As A.W. Tozer said, "No attribute of God is in conflict with another. God is never at cross-purposes with Himself."

FOR PRAISE: *I praise You, Lord, that there is no conflict in Your divine attributes. I praise You that You are both awesome and approachable.*

January 3

THE SECRET OF BLESSEDNESS

His disciples came to him, and he began to teach them, saying: "Blessed . . . " (Matthew 5:1,2)

It is a popular conception that if only we had wealth, absence of sorrow and suffering, unrestricted gratification of appetite and were kindly treated by all – that would be blessedness indeed. But Jesus' teaching in the Sermon on the Mount reversed this entirely.

The qualities of character and attitudes of which Jesus said blessedness was the reward, are quite different from what one would expect. *The experiences we are most anxious to side-step are the ones most conducive to our joy!* In a day when the emphasis is on activism in religion, it is rather startling to find the Lord giving so high a rating to the passive qualities of character as He does in the Beatitudes (Matt. 5:1–8).

In announcing the manifesto of His Kingdom, it was appropriate that He should have as its keynote, the word BLESSED. It is really an exclamation: "Oh, the bliss of the poor in spirit!" It signifies a deep joy which is independent of the changing circumstances of life, but has the secret of joy within itself. It could be translated: "superlatively happy", "to be congratulated".

The eight qualities presented in the Beatitudes are a description of the one person, the ideal citizen of the Kingdom, in his psychological and spiritual development. There is no thought that the disciple may choose in which of the beatitudes he will specialise.

FOR PRAYER: *Lord, help me to revise my scale of values so that I may qualify for the beatitudes You announced.*

January 4

SPIRITUAL INADEQUACY

"Blessed are the poor in spirit . . . " (Matthew 5:3)

Paradoxically, the superlatively happy person is one who is conscious of spiritual inadequacy. "Oh, the bliss of the inadequate!"

The words "in spirit" provide the clue to the meaning of this beatitude. There is nothing blessed in poverty as such. To be poor in spirit does not mean to be poor-spirited. Indeed, the reverse may well be the case. It is the antithesis of pride and self-sufficiency. A financially poor person is not automatically poor in spirit. He might be just as proud as his rich neighbour.

Insight into the Lord's meaning is afforded by the significance of "poor". Two Greek words are so translated. One means a pauper, the other a beggar. One is poor because of his circumstances. The beggar is often poor because he chooses to be poor. He has nothing, and lives on the bounty of God. Conscious of his need, he looks for help outside himself and gratefully accepts it.

When Jesus said, "I can of my own self do nothing," He evinced this poverty of spirit. Paul did the same when he confessed, "In me, that is in my flesh, dwells no good thing." His conscious inadequacy cast him back on the illimitable resources of God.

FOR THANKSGIVING: *Thank You, Lord, for the enrichment that comes from being bankrupt on Your grace and mercy.*

SPIRITUAL CONTRITION

"Blessed are those who mourn . . . " (Matthew 5:4)

Here again we meet with paradox. "Oh, how happy are the unhappy!" We should be on our guard against two misinterpretations of Scripture. One is that Christians should *never* be a laughing, joyous people. Jesus promises no blessing to the moody and morose. He expects His disciples to be more joyous than their contemporaries.

The opposite mistake is that Christians must *always* be laughing. There is a time for mourning in the sense suggested in this beatitude, for *no one attains full maturity without the experience of sorrow.*

The primary form of sorrow envisaged here is mourning over one's sin and spiritual failure; and who of us has no cause for this? The slowness of our growth in likeness to Christ, the paucity of our spiritual attainment, our bondage to besetting sin, our rebellion against the will of God – these should give us concern. For any or all of these we should experience a sense of sorrow that we have grieved the heart of our Father. Such "godly sorrow works repentance", and results in "the oil of joy for the spirit of mourning".

Paradoxically this mourning is by no means incompatible with rejoicing. "Blessed are you who weep now, for you will laugh" (Luke 6:21). Paul experienced both the sorrow and the comfort of this beatitude – "sorrowful, yet always rejoicing".

FOR MEDITATION:
Repentance is to leave the sins we loved before,
And show that we in earnest grieve
By doing them no more.

January 6

SPIRITUAL HUMILITY

"Blessed are the meek . . . " (Matthew 5:5)

This beatitude is an echo of the former two, for he who manifests poverty of spirit and mourns over his sinfulness will display a meek and lowly bearing.

Meekness is not mere amiability or mildness of disposition. The meek person will be anything but servile and spineless, for *"meekness is not an invertebrate virtue"*. It has nothing in common with the "'umbleness" of a Uriah Heep. But it is the opposite of the haughty and self-assertive spirit.

It is not to be confused with weakness, for "meek" is a very strong word. It implies forces and strength held in check, under strong control. The word was used of breaking-in horses, with the idea of energy controlled.

Reference is made in the Revelation to the "song of Moses and the Lamb". These two are linked together in another significant association. Meekness was an outstanding quality of both, but neither was a milk-and-water character. Both could blaze with righteous anger. Was Jesus "meek and mild" in His treatment of the unholy traffickers in His Father's house of prayer? Yet all the strengths of His character were held on leash. Nietzsche said, "The world is yours if you can get it." Jesus said, *"The world is yours if you renounce it."* The meek inherit the earth.

FOR EMULATION: *Lord, help me to emulate Your lowliness before men and Your meekness under Your Father's disciplining hand.*

January 7

SPIRITUAL ASPIRATION

> *"Blessed are those who hunger and thirst after righteousness."* (Matthew 5:6)

A sense of spiritual destitution creates desire and aspiration. God is presented in Scripture as almost pathetically eager to satisfy the aspirations of the yearning heart.

The Lord uses the elemental instincts of hunger and thirst to convey the idea of passionate desire for holiness. Not mere wistfulness, but passionate craving. These are two of the most agonising and intense of human appetites. This hunger will not be appeased by a light snack, or this thirst quenched by a soft drink.

The righteousness which is the focus of this hunger and thirst is not a merely cold conformity to an impersonal law. It is ethical righteousness, likeness to Christ in outlook and conduct. He is "the Lord our righteousness", so He could have said, "Blessed are those who hunger and thirst *after Me.*"

It is noteworthy that Jesus did not say, "Blessed are those who hunger after *happiness*", which is man's chief object of pursuit, but "after *righteousness*" – a right relationship with God. The truly joyous person has made the discovery that *happiness is a by-product of holiness*.

Then pray for desire, for love's wistfullest yearning,
For the beautiful pining of holy desire.

F.W. Faber

FOR PRAYER:
> I hunger and I thirst:
> Jesu my manna be;
> Ye living waters, burst
> Out of the Rock for me.

January 8

BEATIFIC VISION

"Blessed are the pure in heart . . . " (Matthew 5:8)

The beatific vision is granted only to the pure in heart, for "without holiness no man shall see the Lord". The revelation of God is granted to the mighty in intellect only if it is accompanied by purity of heart.

The vision of God is not a matter of optics, but of moral and spiritual affinity with Him. *Cleanness of heart brings clearness of vision.* Sin fogs the heart and God becomes invisible. There are moral conditions for spiritual vision.

Behind the word "pure" lies the idea of "freedom from alloy, unadulterated". Sincerity and integrity, as opposed to what is false and insincere. Pure gold has no alloy, pure linen no spots.

Throughout this Sermon, Jesus consistently by-passes the external ceremonial purity of the Pharisees and insists on inward purity (e.g. Luke 11:39). Many would seek deliverance from morally impure thoughts and habits, who do not desire God's holiness in every other area of their lives. There is an old Latin proverb: "Unless the vessel is clean, whatever you pour into it turns sour." It is so with the human heart.

But with Christ, the fountain of all purity, dwelling in our hearts, the maintenance of a pure heart is no longer a tantalising mirage but a glorious possibility.

FOR PRAYER: *Lord, if cleanness of heart is the condition of clarity in the vision of God, create in me a clean heart.*

January 9

THE COMPASSIONATE SPIRIT

"Blessed are the merciful . . . " (Matthew 5:7)

It is possible to have a passion for righteousness, and yet to lack compassion for those who have failed to attain it. Righteousness can be cold and hard and unfeeling. In this beatitude Jesus speaks of the bliss of the *sympathetic*.

Mercy can be exercised only to the undeserving. If it were deserved, it would not be mercy, but simple justice. Like meekness, mercy is a distinctively Christian grace, little exhibited among non-Christians, and sadly, too little among Christians as well. Our fallen natures are geared more to criticism and retaliation than to mercy.

It is more than a compassionate feeling, it expresses itself in merciful activity. Pity must graduate from sterile emotion to compassionate action before it is mercy. We must stand in the shoes of the other person, think ourselves into their feelings, and then act appropriately.

The man of compassion does not condone wrong, but is ready to put the best construction on ambiguous conduct.

Our personal experience may well be the rebound of our own attitude, for *it is those who show mercy who receive it*. The person who is reluctant to show to others the mercy of which he has been so lavish a recipient from God, is in a perilous position (Matt. 18:23–35).

FOR ACTION: *Let me today express the mercy I have received in compassionate action for others in need of it.*

January 10

A CONCILIATORY MINISTRY

"Blessed are the peacemakers . . . " (Matthew 5:9)

Our Lord here asserts that the superlatively happy people are those who create harmony, who reconcile people who are estranged, in whose presence discord gives place to harmony, and strife to peace. "Oh, the bliss of the conciliator!"

The significance of this beatitude is often missed. It is not, "Blessed are the *peace-lovers*, the placid, the pacifists." There can be no peaceful coexistence with evil. There is such a thing as a false peace, which Christ said He came to destroy.

Nor is it a peace procured by *evasion of issues*, peace at any price. The peace-maker is prepared to pay the price of his conciliation. He will not compromise with evil. Nor is it for *peace-keepers*, keepers of a peace already in existence. Jesus had in view not a passive virtue but a sacrificial activity.

The *peace-maker* achieves conciliation by allowing his own peace to be broken, and for this there is a notable precedent: "He made peace by the blood of His cross." For us, too, a cross will be involved. It is a ministry that calls for heavenly wisdom, uncommon tact, insight and courage. But patience blended with love will reap a rich reward.

FOR PRAYER:
Lord, make me an instrument of thy peace,
That where there is hatred, I may bring love;
That where there is discord, I may bring harmony;
That where there is sadness, I may bring joy.
                                        Francis of Assisi

UNWAVERING LOYALTY

"Blessed are those who are persecuted for righteousness' sake . . . " (Matthew 5:10–12 RSV)

Even the peacemaker is not exempt from reviling and persecution, as the experience of the Master demonstrated. In our work for Christ we may suffer insult or injury, but even this can carry its freight of blessing.

There is no bliss in the reviling or persecution itself, but in the compensations it brings, or the fruit it bears. Joy in suffering is peculiar to Christianity, and reveals its supernatural origin.

But how can persecution be profitable, or pain pleasant? For Paul said, "I can even enjoy weakness" (2 Cor. 12:10). A clue is found in the tense of the verb in the beatitude. The meaning is not "Blessed are they that *are persecuted,*" but, "Blessed are they that *have been persecuted.*" The bliss is the outcome of a reviling and persecution that is in the past.

But not all reviling or persecution brings blessing.

It must be *for righteousness' sake* — because he will do right, at whatever cost to himself, not because of tactlessness or angularity.

Reviling must be *falsely based*. There must be no just cause for reproach in the life and testimony.

It must be *for Christ's sake* — arising out of the disciple's unwavering loyalty to his Master, and wise zeal for the extension of His Kingdom. This brings its own reward.

FOR MEDITATION: *Father, is the absence of persecution in my life because I have adopted the world's agenda and not Yours?*

CHRIST IS ALL

Christ is all, and is in all. (Colossians 3:11)

Paul compresses into these seven words his comprehensive creed. They enshrine all the excellencies of Christ. J.B. Phillips' happy rendering is: "Christ is all that matters." He directs their attention to Jesus alone as the source of fullness and blessing.

He tells the Colossian Christians that "in Christ *all the fullness of the Deity* lives in bodily form" (2:9). He is the complete embodiment of all there is in God.

He is *the all in all of creation.* "By him were all things created." "All things" here means the whole universe. Ours is a Christocentric universe. He is its nerve centre. The whole creation is designed to reveal Him; the natural shows forth the spiritual.

Christ is *the all in all of providence.* "He is before all things, and in him all things hold together" (1:17). Christ occupies the whole sphere of human life and permeates all its developments. The laws of Nature are formulated and administered by the risen Christ. "In him we live and move and have our being" (Acts 17:28).

He is *the all in all of redemption.* "In whom we have redemption through His blood" (Eph. 1:7). He alone has redeemed us and discharged the debt of our sin, weighing out the ransom price, not in silver or gold, but in crimson drops of precious blood. He nailed the receipted bill to His cross.

FOR PRAISE: *Christ is all that matters.*

CHRIST, THE CENTRE OF EVERYTHING

Remember always, as the centre of everything, Jesus Christ. (2 Timothy 2:8 Phillips)

In the midst of wise counsel to the young pastor, Paul injects this pungent exhortation. Only as he heeds it will Timothy be able to keep his priorities right. The risen Christ is the centre of everything, for Christianity is Christ.

He is central in history, for in a very real sense history is *His story*. Time is divided by His birth. The course of history has been irrevocably altered by His presence on earth. If Christ be omitted, history does not make sense.

Who can deny that *He is central in art*? Traverse the art galleries of the world and note the subject of the greatest paintings. *In literature* He occupies a central role. The great masterpieces of *music* found their inspiration in Him. In *architecture* no structures combine such symmetry, beauty and grandeur as buildings erected for His worship.

He is the centre of *the human race*. In Him alone do we find ideal humanity. We see Him first *in the midst of the doctors* to learn of His Father's world purpose. He is seen *in the midst of sinners*, bringing salvation.

Our final glimpse of Him is *in the midst of the throne* to rule (Rev. 5:6), receiving the homage of the whole redeemed creation. But there is something more wonderful. "Where two or three come together in my name, *there am I in the midst*" (Matt. 18:20).

FOR PRAYER: *Lord, help me to keep You central in every area of my life and activities.*

January 14

SYMMETRY OF CHARACTER

He is altogether lovely. (Song of Songs 5:16)

The character of our Lord was wonderfully balanced, with neither excess nor deficiency. It stands out faultlessly perfect, so symmetrical in all its proportions, that its strength and greatness are not immediately obvious to the casual observer. In the best of men there is obvious inconsistency and inequality, and since the tallest buildings cast the longest shadow, the greater the man, the larger the faults. With Christ it was far otherwise.

Virtue readily degenerates into vice, courage may degenerate into cowardice or rashness, purity may slip into prudery or impurity; but in our Lord there was no deflection: He maintained every virtue unsullied.

In speech as in silence, His perfect balance of character was displayed. He never spoke when it was wiser to keep silent, He never kept silent when He should have spoken.

Mercy and judgement blended in all His actions and attitudes, and neither prevailed at the expense of the other. Exact truth and infinite love adorned each other in His winsome personality. His severe denunciations of apostate Jerusalem were tremulous with His sobs.

The excellences of both sexes coalesced in Him. There is contrast yet not contradiction in His delicacy and tenderness in handling those who deserved such treatment.

FOR MEDITATION: *The character of Christ is one and the same throughout. Its balance is never disturbed or readjusted.*

January 15

FAITH VERSUS SIGHT

We walk by faith, not by sight. (2 Corinthians 5:7
RSV)

One distinctive mark of a mature Christian is that he
walks by faith, not by sight – two principles that are
contradictory and mutually exclusive. Rather than being
a mark of deep spirituality, a craving for outward signs
is evidence of spiritual immaturity. Jesus said in this
connection, "Blessed are those *who have not seen* and yet
have believed" (John 20:29).

Much distress in the lives of some Christians stems
from an unresolved conflict between these two principles.
Sight is concerned with the visible and tangible; faith is
occupied with the invisible and spiritual. Sight is worldly
prudence. Faith is otherworldly wisdom. Sight concedes
reality only to things present and seen. "Faith forms a
solid ground for what is hoped for, a conviction of unseen
realities" (Heb. 11:1, Berkeley). Each principle strives for
the ascendancy, and the believer chooses which will
dominate his life.

The testing circumstances of life afford the opportunity
of adopting one principle or the other as a rule of life and
action. Peter was in large measure governed by sight prior
to his maturing experience at Pentecost. Thereafter faith
became the dominant principle.

It should be noted that faith is said to be "*the confidence*
of things not seen", not *the consciousness* of things not
seen. Before we can feel them, we must exercise faith in
them. *Faith* is the initial act, *feeling* the resulting effect.

FOR MEDITATION: *"What is seen is temporary.
What is unseen is eternal."*

NO SUBSTITUTE FOR FAITH

Without faith it is impossible to please God. (Hebrews 11:6)

The stark absoluteness of the assertion that without faith it is impossible to please God, is almost overwhelming in its implications. *Difficult* to please God? Yes. But surely not *impossible*! But there is no escape from the sweeping assertion.

Since this is the case, faith must be a tremendously important element in our pursuit of maturity. It follows that the person who is weak in faith is also deficient in maturity, and vice versa.

Faith is confidence, reliance, trust. It is the sixth sense that enables one to apprehend the invisible, but very real, spiritual realm. It is confidence reposed in a God who is absolutely trustworthy, utterly reliable; a childlike, effortless trust that is never betrayed.

There is no such thing as faith when considered apart from the object on which it is focused. It is akin to eyesight which does not exist apart from the object of vision. In looking at an object, we do not see our eyesight, only the object of vision. So it is with faith.

The object on which faith relies is *not our faith*, but that which our faith enables us to see. It is our invisible link with God. Jesus alone is the sinner's Saviour. Faith is simply the eye that apprehends Him in that role.

FOR PRAYER: *Lord, since it is impossible to please You without faith, please increase my faith, even at the expense of testing.*

NOT IMPOSSIBLE SAINTS

Elijah was a man just like us. (James 5:17)

The twelve disciples whom Jesus chose to be with Him were "men of like passions" (KJV), men just like us. They were not "impossible saints". They were not theologians or political leaders, just ordinary men who became extraordinary under the moulding hand of the Master Potter. Had He chosen only people who were intellectually brilliant, how could ordinary people be expected to aspire to a similar discipleship? Their humanness brings them into our street.

In order to shape and prepare them for the task of world evangelism, Jesus was willing to restrict His own privacy and liberty, by living in close daily contact with them. He wanted not servants, but friends who would be involved in His programme. "I no longer call you servants . . . I have called you friends" (John 15:15).

They shared with Him the ordinary chores and cares of daily life. Unconsciously, under His gracious tuition, they began to absorb His teaching and imbibe His spirit.

Their imperfections were painfully apparent, but those did not debar them from His fellowship and friendship. If God required perfection before He admitted us into the circle of His fellowship, who would qualify? Quirks of temperament did not disqualify, or Peter with his volatile nature would not have been counted in.

FOR THANKSGIVING: *Lord, thank You that You "know how we are formed and remember that we are dust".* (Ps. 103:14)

January 18

INTO HIS LIKENESS

We . . . are being transformed into His likeness with ever-increasing glory. (2 Corinthians 3:18)

How can transformation into the likeness of Christ be effected? This verse reveals that it is not by "a despairing struggle against that which captivates", but by a steady, consistent "beholding" – a gazing on Christ in all His majesty, glory, love, truth and justice, as those are set forth in Scripture. It is while we are beholding Him that we are being changed into His likeness.

The eye exercises a powerful influence on character. We become like those whom we admire. Alexander the Great read Homer's *Iliad*, and set out to conquer the world. Character and habits are moulded by the manners and habits of those whom we are constantly seeing.

The method employed by the Holy Spirit to effect such radical change, is paralleled on the physical level by the ingestion and digestion of food. We eat our meal and forget all about it. Our gastric juices take over, and without any conscious volition on our part, the food is changed into another form and incorporated into the texture of our physical bodies.

Similarly, as we spend time "beholding the glory of the Lord . . . in the face of Jesus Christ" (2 Cor. 3:18, 4:6), the Holy Spirit not only *reveals* Him to us but *reproduces* Him in us – incorporates into the fabric of our spiritual lives the very virtues and values we see and admire in Christ.

FOR PRAYER: *Lord, grant that I may present no obstacle to Your conforming me to the image of Your Son.*

January 19

VISION, NOT INTROSPECTION

We . . . beholding the glory of the Lord, are being changed . . . (2 Corinthians 3:18 RSV)

Transformation into Christ's likeness begins, not with *subjective* introspection so much as with the *objective* vision of the glory of God as it is manifested in Jesus. That captivating vision is most clearly seen, not in illuminated heavens, but in the written Word of God, illumined by the Holy Spirit. The Word is a mirror that reflects Christ's unique character, perfect manhood, flawless character and redemptive work (2 Cor. 4:6).

The glory of God is not abstract or ethereal; it was actually revealed in terms of human life in the person and work of Christ. The authoritative portrait of Christ is not to be seen on the artist's canvas. That is only his own concept. The face of Christ is seen in the word pictures painted by inspired biographers so vividly in the four Gospels. The Jews of His day saw the face, but missed the glory. Their unbelief shut it out.

God's purpose for His children is not *external imitation* merely, but *internal transformation*. The glory reflected on Moses' face as he descended from the mountain was evanescent and fading. But the glory Paul speaks about is a glory retained and transmitted. "Those who look to him are radiant" (Ps. 34:5).

FOR PRAYER: *You have said, "Those who look to him are radiant." Enable me to keep my eyes fixed on Jesus.*

January 20

"GOD IS TOO SLOW"

Jesus replied, "My time has not yet come." (John 2:4)

On one occasion Phillips Brooks, the famous Boston preacher, was visited by a friend who found him in great agitation.

"What's the matter, Phillips?" he asked.

"Matter enough. I'm in a hurry, and God's not!"

Against the often senseless and furious rush of our times, God often seems unduly leisurely in His intervention in our affairs. We want the answer at once, but God does not always oblige. He refuses to be stampeded into premature action.

Our urgency and impatience stem from the shortness of our vision and the imperfection of our knowledge. God's seeming leisureliness arises from His perfect knowledge of all the facts and His complete control of all the circumstances. Nor does He always offer an explanation of His tardiness. He loves to be trusted. His delay in rushing to the side of Mary and Martha when Lazarus was ill, was not a lack of concern, but a knowledge of what He was going to do.

Abraham, at his wife's suggestion, endeavoured to advance the divine timetable for the birth of his son. Through that single act of presumption and unbelief, the Muslim scourge was unleashed on the world – the most virulent foe of Christianity. God will not be hurried. His delays are not capricious, but purposeful. He is more concerned with our ultimate blessing than our immediate comfort.

FOR PRAISE: *Thank You, Father, for Your assurance: "The Lord longs to be gracious to you . . . Blessed are all who wait for him."* (Isa. 30:18)

"GOD IS NOT FAIR"

You say, "The way of the Lord is not just." (Ezekiel 18:25)

This complaint of the Jews is not without its echo in our own times. Some Christians feel they have been unfairly treated by God. Although they may never have verbalised it, in their hearts they feel resentful and disillusioned.

There is no simple answer to the question of why God intervenes in some cases and not in others. Why, when both men were imprisoned for preaching the gospel, did God allow James to be beheaded, while Peter was delivered and escorted by an angel to a prayer meeting? The only answer is the statement of the Lord to His disciples: "You do not realise now what I am doing, but later you will understand" (John 13:7). That is sufficient for faith.

Asaph the psalmist was mystified as he pondered the seeming prosperity of the wicked, and the trials of the righteous. They prospered, while upright men seemed to experience more than their fair share of trouble. "As for me," he said, "my feet had almost slipped; I had nearly lost my foothold" (Ps. 73:2). But he found the answer when he "entered the sanctuary of God; then I understood their final destiny" (v.17).

It is the end that counts, for there is a life beyond, where every inequality will be remedied.

FOR SELF-EXAMINATION: *"You say, The way of the Lord is not just . . . Is it not your ways that are unjust?"* (Ezek. 18:25)

WHY THE DISCREPANCY?

Inwardly we are being renewed day by day. (2 Corinthians 4:16)

In this paragraph Paul is reviewing his ministry with all the perils it involved and the burdens it imposed. Death was always a possibility. Inevitably, amid the wear and tear of his service and suffering, his body was wearing away.

But that was not the whole story. *A counter-process was taking place* – his inner being was at the same time experiencing daily renewal. "No wonder we do not give up!" he exclaimed.

Now Paul received no favours from God that were not available to his contemporaries and to us. True, he had gifts and abilities far above ours, but God has blessed us equally with him with *"every* spiritual blessing in the heavenlies in Christ"* (Eph. 1:3). Then why the discrepancy between his experience and ours? Why are we so often weak and frail? Is it not because Paul daily appropriated – made his own – his share of the divine provision, while we do not? Why do we not take more from God when He has made such ample provision for our daily needs?

Our Father knows the strains and stresses involved in daily life and service and, to counteract that, promises daily renewal.

FOR PRAYER: *Lord, I claim the fulfilment of the promise, "He gives strength to the weary, and increases the power of the weak."* (Isa. 40:29)

ABSENTEES FROM HEAVEN

There will be no more death. (Revelation 21:4)

In preparing our eternal home, our ascended Lord removes all that would spoil our enjoyment, or cast gloom on our spirits.

What will be absent from heaven?

Tears. "He will wipe away every tear from their eyes" (Rev. 21:4). God will take heaven's handkerchief and wipe away tears caused by sin, pain and sorrow.

Death. "And there shall no longer be any death" (21:4). The king of terrors will never be able to penetrate heaven's gate.

Mourning. "And there shall no longer be any mourning" (21:4) – because of the ravages of sin or the poignancy of bereavement.

Pain. "There shall no longer be any pain" (21:4). The worst thing about illness, for both patients and onlookers, is the excruciating pain that often accompanies it. No pain-killers are dispensed in heaven.

Hunger. "They shall hunger no more" (7:16). What good news this will be to the hungry hordes in Third World countries!

Night. "There shall no longer be any night" (22:5). In heaven the body will no longer be in need of the recuperative process of sleep.

Temple. "And I saw no temple in it, for the Lord God and the Lamb are its temple" (21:22). Buildings will not be necessary, for we will dwell in the immediate presence of God.

Curse. "And there shall no longer be any curse" (22:3). Through the Saviour's cross, the curse has been removed.

FOR PRAISE: *Lord, I praise You for making possible through Your cross the removal of the things that would spoil our enjoyment of heaven.*

BLESSINGS OF HEAVEN

No more death or mourning or crying or pain.
(Revelation 21:4)

After considering the absences from heaven, it is a joyous task to consider its positive characteristics. Here are some.

Glory. "I desire that they . . . be with me . . . that they may behold my glory" (John 17:24). On earth His glory was concealed. Now it is fully manifested.

Holiness. "Nothing unclean and no-one who practises abominations and lying, shall ever come into it" (Rev. 21:27).

Beauty. "Out of Zion, the perfection of beauty, has God shone forth" (Ps. 50:2). In heaven every aesthetic desire and aspiration will be fully satisfied.

Light. "The Lord God will give them light" (Rev. 22:5). God "dwells in light unapproachable", and He will illumine heaven.

Unity. In heaven, the Lord's prayer in the Upper Room, "that they all may be one", will be fully answered.

Perfection. " . . . when the perfect comes, the partial will be done away with" (1 Cor. 13:10). In heaven we will attain full maturity.

Joy. "In Thy presence is fullness of joy" (Ps. 16:11). The climate of heaven is unalloyed joy.

Love. That perennial flower whose petals never fall. "Now abide faith, hope and love . . . " (1 Cor. 13:13).

Satisfaction. "I shall be satisfied with Thy likeness" (Ps. 17:15). In heaven no holy desire will remain unsatisfied. With the devil finally and forever defeated and chained, and our tendency to sin forever removed, we will be able to walk with God in uninterrupted fellowship.

FOR PRAISE: *Lord, I praise You for the glorious prospect of an eternity lived in Your presence and in Your service.*

HEAVEN'S OCCUPATIONS

They serve him day and night. (Revelation 7:15)
They will see his face. (Revelation 22:4)

How shall we be employed in heaven? *Worship and adoration* of the Triune God will be our primary engagement. The twenty-four elders — representative of all redeemed humanity — "fall down before him who sits on the throne, and will worship him who lives for ever and ever" (Rev. 4:10).

Music holds a prominent place in the imagery of heaven, as it did in the worship of tabernacle and temple. No fewer than 288 musicians were employed in the temple services (1 Chron. 25:1–8). Both vocal and instrumental music are cited as adding to the felicity of heaven (Rev. 5:8,9). If earthly choirs can lift us to such heights of aesthetic enjoyment, what will the music of heaven be like?

Service. "They are before the throne of God, and serve him day and night" (Rev. 7:15) — no longer plagued by the limitations of time and space. What endless vistas of possibility open before us as we think of ceaseless service for the One we love.

Fellowship. "They will see his face and his name will be on their foreheads" (Rev. 22:4). In heaven, with all possible causes of discord and dissension excluded, we shall enjoy an infinite extension of the intimacy with God and our fellows on earth.

FOR PRAISE: *Lord, I thank You that You have prepared a heaven where every holy and wholesome aspiration will be fulfilled.*

January 26

CONFESS YOUR SINS

If we confess our sins, he is faithful and just and will forgive us our sins. (1 John 1:9)

It is clearly taught in Scripture that in order to be forgiven, we must confess our sins to God (1 John 1:9). But in order to restore right relationships, *we may need to confess to man as well*. We cannot be right with God when we are wrong with man.

The sincerity of our confession may necessitate an apology being made, a quarrel settled, a debt paid, a relationship terminated. This raises the question of what we should confess, and to whom.

As all sin is against God, obviously we should confess to Him every sin of which we are conscious. Some sins are against God alone, others against our fellow men.

The scriptural principle involved would seem to be that the confession should be co-extensive with the sin. Where the sin is against God alone, the sin need be confessed only to God. There may sometimes be therapeutic value in sharing with a trusted friend.

Where the sin is against another person, confession should be made to the injured party, and need be confessed to no other. Where the sin is against a church or group, confession should be made in an appropriate manner, probably to the leader. There may be cases where public confession is called for, but they would be rare.

FOR THANKSGIVING: *Thank You, Lord, for Your outstretched arms of mercy and forgiveness.*

THERE IS A WAY BACK

If anyone does sin, we have one who speaks to the Father in our defence. (1 John 2:1)

The apostle John took a realistic view of the subtlety of sin and the frailty of human nature when he wrote: ''My dear children, I write this so that you will not sin. But if anyone does sin, we have one who speaks to the Father in our defence.'' For such sin, God has graciously made provision for every contingency in advance in Christ's propitiatory sacrifice.

There was a way back even for the adulterer and murderer, David. Peter did not forfeit his place in the apostolate because he denied his Lord. In each case there was clear evidence of deep repentance and real cleansing.

The gracious provision of a divine Advocate to plead our cause is not to encourage us to keep on sinning. John specifically said he was writing that we may *not* sin, and to save us from despair when we have sinned. God's righteous anger was appeased and His holiness vindicated by the sacrifice of His son. So far as our standing before God is concerned, the blood of Christ answers for all our sins.

> Five bleeding wounds He bears
> Received on Calvary,
> They pour effectual prayers,
> They strongly plead for me.
>> Forgive him, Oh forgive, they cry
>> Nor let that ransomed sinner die.

FOR PRAISE:
> *Christ is our Advocate on high,*
> *Thou art our Advocate within.*
> *Oh, plead the truth and make reply*
> *To every argument of sin.*

THE ESSENCE OF WORSHIP

Worship the Lord your God, and serve him only.
(Matthew 4:10)

Worship flows from love. Where love is meagre, worship will be scant. Where love is deep, worship will be spontaneous and overflowing. As Paul wrote his letters, his contemplation of the love, glory and faithfulness of God caused his heart to overflow its banks in worship and doxology.

But there can be an element of selfishness even in love. True, we should worship God for the great things He has done for us, but worship reaches a much higher level when we worship Him simply and solely for what He is – for the excellences and perfections of His being.

Worship is the loving ascription of praise to God for what He is in Himself and in His providential dealings. It is the bowing of our innermost spirit before Him in deepest humility and reverence.

The essence of worship is illustrated in the return of Scipio Africanus from one of his conquests. As he went, he scattered the largesse of the victor to the crowds that lined the road. Some praised his liberality; others lauded him as their liberator; still others, forgetful of their personal benefits, praised him for his courage and resourcefulness. It was in this last group that the highest element of worship was present.

FOR WORSHIP:
O Majesty unspeakable and dread!
Wert Thou less mighty than Thou art,
Thou wert, O Lord! too great for our belief,
    Too little for our heart.

THE CHIEF END OF MAN

Whatever you do, do it all for the glory of God. (1 Corinthians 10:31)

The maturing Christian has as his or her life objective *the securing of the glory of God*. The Westminster Catechism has its priorities right when its first question, "What is the chief end of man?" has as its answer, "The chief end of man is to glorify God and to enjoy Him for ever."

The first petition of Christ's pattern prayer, "Hallowed be your name," is really asking that God's Person may be honoured and glorified everywhere, by all men. If we pray it sincerely, we will add, "at any cost to me". Every choice we have to make in which the honour and glory of God is involved, will have only one answer from the mature Christian. There is no room for debate.

After He had opened His heart to His disciples in the Upper Room, Jesus offered His moving high-priestly prayer. It reads as though He is reporting to His Father on His earthly ministry: "I have brought you glory on earth by completing the work you gave me to do" (John 17:4). How concise, and yet how comprehensive!

Since the servant is not greater than his Lord, the maturing Christian will experience a growing passion for the glory of his Lord such as gripped Count Zinzendorf, founder of the Moravian Church: "*I have one passion, it is He, He alone.*"

FOR SELF-EXAMINATION: *Is the glory of God the beginning and the end of my service for Him?*

UNRIVALLED LOVE

> *"If anyone . . . does not hate his father and mother, his wife and children . . . he cannot be my disciple."*
> (Luke 14:26)

The word "hate" used here sounds harsh and arbitrary, but it is used in a relative and not in the absolute sense. It means simply "to love less". The unbalanced zealot will find no support here for a lack of natural affection. There is no contradiction between this demand and the command to honour father and mother.

If this passage means anything, it is saying that we cannot be true disciples of Christ unless we love Him more than anyone else. He is claiming *an unrivalled love*. Following Him may at times involve a clash of loyalties – for He indicated that His incoming might be divisive. In the realm of the affections Christ tolerates no rival.

In the times when He spoke these words, becoming His disciple often involved discord within the family and ostracism in society. In Western lands there is usually little family or social cost involved, but in the East, conversion often meant loss of employment. Yet Christ did not scale down His demands. In the world-wide programme on which He was embarking, He wanted associated with Him men and women of quality whose devotion to Him and His cause would not waver before opposition and even persecution.

If there is no such unrivalled love for Christ in our hearts, we may be believers, but He affirms we *cannot* be His disciples.

FOR PRAYER: *Lord, wean my errant heart from the love of earthly things that would intrude and hinder fellowship.*

January 31

STUCK BETWEEN EASTER AND PENTECOST

"You will receive power when the Holy Spirit comes on you; and you will be my witnesses . . . " (Acts 1:8)

This arresting diagnosis of the condition of many Christians is worth careful thought and personal application. It is possible to rejoice in the fact that Christ is risen, without experiencing the enduement with power promised by Christ, and experienced on the Day of Pentecost.

Why the vast discrepancy between the spiritual power wielded by the early Church and that experienced by the Church today? The simple explanation is that we cannot have the fruits without the roots. Early Church achievement was the outcome of early Church enduement.

Pentecost was the necessary complement of Calvary. Like an ellipse, Christian faith and experience revolves around two centres, Calvary and Pentecost. Without Pentecost, Calvary would have failed of its purpose and would have been ineffectual to redeem a lost world. It would have been like perfecting a costly machine, while neglecting to provide motive power.

The great facts on which redemption is based – our Lord's virgin birth, virtuous life, vicarious death and victorious resurrection – had been completed for forty days, and yet nothing happened until the Day of Pentecost. Only then did the machinery of redemption swing into motion.

While there was a dispensational and historical side to Pentecost, it had also personal and practical implications for the disciples – and for us. We know the blessings of Calvary, but have we appropriated and experienced the blessings of Pentecost?

FOR ACTION: *If you have become "stuck" in your spiritual experience, open your heart anew to the Spirit's control.*

February 1

THE HANDS OF CHRIST

He lifted up his hands and blessed them. (Luke 24:50)

Like our faces, our hands reveal much to the intelligent observer. How expressive they are – an index to our character and habits. We can mask our facial expression, but how can we mask our hands?

What has Scripture to say about our Lord's hands?

They were *human hands*. To the beleaguered and frightened disciples in the Upper Room the risen Christ suddenly appeared. Their fears were dispelled when He said, "Look at my hands and my feet" (Luke 24:39). The livid nail marks assured them that He was "this same Jesus" whom they had known.

They were *calloused hands*. He came to earth as a working man and demonstrated the dignity of honest labour. He sweated at the carpenter's bench as did the other men.

They were *stainless hands*. "Who may ascend the hill of the Lord? He who has clean hands . . . " (Ps. 24:3,4). Christ's hands never performed a sinful act.

They were *sympathetic hands*. "Jesus reached out his hand and touched him" (Mark 1:41). Jesus gave the amazed leper the touch of human compassion he had been denied for so long.

They were *wounded hands*. "What are these wounds in your hands?" (Zech. 13:6). How eloquent of His love and mercy were those nail-prints!

FOR THANKSGIVING: *Lord, I thank You that You hold the whole world in Your nail-pierced hands – therefore we need have no fear for the future.*

February 2

THE HEAD OF CHRIST

On his head are many crowns. (Revelation 19:12)

The head is the control tower of the body. From it impulses and messages are transmitted to the farthest limb. It is the dominant part of the body. Our Lord's head is mentioned several times in Scripture.

It was an *anointed head*. In the extravagance of her love, Mary broke the priceless flask of fragrant oils and poured it over His head (Mark 14:3). Her act of love was to Him a green oasis in the desert of human rejection.

His was a *homeless head* at times. "The Son of Man has nowhere to lay his head" (Luke 9:58). There was no bed for Him at the inn. Many a night His head never touched a pillow. He was dependent on the hospitality of others.

His head was *crowned in mockery* (Matt. 27:29). Thorns, symbol of the curse, adorned the brow of the Lord of glory, every thorn a point of fire. All through the ghastly ordeal of crucifixion, His head had remained erect. The curse broke His heart but did not bow His head.

Finally we see His head *in dazzling majesty* — "His head . . . as white as snow" (Rev. 1:14), and crowned with many crowns, the reward of His obedience to death.

FOR PRAISE:
> *O Sacred Head, what glory,*
> *What bliss till now was Thine!*
> *Yet, though despised and gory,*
> *I joy to call Thee mine.*

THE FACE OF CHRIST

To give us the light of the knowledge of the glory of God in the face of Christ. (2 Corinthians 4:6)

How expressive the face is, mirroring as it does the emotions of the soul. It is the index to character and personality. It reveals both weaknesses and strengths.

Our Lord's face differed from all others, because it revealed, not only Himself, but the glory of His Father.

His face revealed *the holiness of God*. Our faces carry the lines of sin, but "in Him is no sin" (1 John 3:5). In His case the transmission of the racial heritage was interrupted by the virgin birth. His face reflected the purity of His heart.

It revealed *the steadfastness of God*. "He steadfastly set His face to go to Jerusalem" (Luke 9:51 KJV). There were many things to weaken His resolve, but He steadfastly held His course.

The sympathy of God was etched on His face. "As he saw the city, he wept over it" (Luke 19:41). What a concept! The sympathy of God was expressed in the salty tears that coursed down His face.

His face manifested *the wrath of God*. "He looked round at them with anger" (Mark 3:5). His face blazed with anger when he cleansed the temple of the rapacious traders.

His face expressed *the gladness of God*. "His face shone like the sun" (Matt. 17:2). His face reflected the joy of God.

FOR PRAYER:
*Show me Thy face — one transient gleam
    of loveliness divine,
And I shall never think or dream
    of other love save Thine.*

February 4

PUNGENT WITNESS

"You are the salt of the earth." (Matthew 5:13)

In the Beatitudes Jesus presents the ideal of the Christian character, and then proceeds to define the role of the Christian in the world. He likens the influence of the Christian to salt. The disciple is *salt in the midst of earth's corruption*.

He did not tell the disciples that they were to be salt, or carry salt, or scatter salt. He said, "You *are* salt." He was speaking not of an activity — but of an influence. Though often unseen and unnoticed, the Christian exercises a potent influence in society.

Salt is the foe of insipidity. The disciple who walks in close fellowship with Christ will not be pale and insipid in personality. His speech, though "always with grace", will be "seasoned with salt", and therefore not insipid, but pungent and aseptic. He will have moral courage to check unsavoury or critical talk. There will be a "tang" about him that evidences the difference Christ makes in a life.

Salt is the foe of corruption. It destroys germs and fights harmful bacteria. It imparts its own wholesomeness to whatever it touches. Just as salt arrests physical decay, so the influence of the disciple arrests corruption in society. Without the salt of Christianity, civilisation would have collapsed long ago.

FOR PRAYER: *Lord, so often my life is isolated from men and women in need of help. May my life have more of the salt quality.*

February 5

RADIANT WITNESS

"You are the light of the world." (Matthew 5:13)

If salt stands for pervading influence, then light stands for luminous radiance. Both salt and light make their presence felt, and are indispensable to normal living. If salt signifies internal worth, light stands for external witness.

Israel had disappointed God in her function as "a light to the nations" (Isa. 49:6). He now delegates this responsibility to the disciples He has chosen. They had kindled their torches from the Light of the world, and now in turn are to be light to the nations of the world.

Theirs was only a borrowed light – He *was* the Light; they were luminaries. He was the Sun, collectively they were the moon, reflecting the Sun's light. Only by constant contact with the Light, could they fulfil their role as luminaries in a dark world.

Jesus said they were "the light", not "the lights" of the world. It was as a group, not as individuals, that they functioned. His Kingdom can do without rugged individualism. Rather are His disciples to be fellow-servants and fellow-workers, following the directions of the same Master.

Many Christians fail to master this fundamental principle, with the result of the fragmentation we see on all sides. Light is to *illuminate* and *guide* and to *warn* of dangers. It is to be *diffused*, not concealed or hidden under the bed of laziness or the bushel of business.

FOR THANKSGIVING: *Thank You, Lord, for giving me the privilege to reflect Your glory in my life. May the mirror not distort the image.*

SET ON THE SKYLINE

"A city on a hill cannot be hidden." (Matthew 5:14)

It may be that as Jesus spoke, He pointed out some city on a nearby hill. A city is an aggregation of houses. Jesus is not speaking of an isolated house, but of a community. *Christianity knows nothing of solitary religion.* The lighted house is multiplied until it becomes an illuminated city that cannot be concealed – a growth symbolic of the irresistible, on-going witness of the ideal church.

Christians are set on the skyline. Like their Master, they cannot be hidden. The Church is to be a landmark in a spiritual as well as a physical sense. Failure in this respect has resulted in the minimal impact the Church is making on society in our day.

Like John the Baptist, the church at Antioch was "a burning and a shining light" in the darkness of contemporary heathenism. So luminous was its witness that at the peak of its spiritual power it was said that of every two citizens, one was a Christian. Small wonder that the Lord of the harvest chose this church from which to launch His world-wide missionary enterprise.

Our good works ought to be noticed by men so that God can be glorified in them. But that must never be the inspiring motive.

FOR PRAYER: *Lord, by Your indwelling Spirit, enable me to so live today, that others may see that Christ lives in me.*

THE GATE IS NARROW

"Enter through the narrow gate . . . that leads to life." (Matthew 7:13)

The narrow gate is not the gate to heaven, as is often thought. It is the entrance to "the way that leads to life". It would appear to signify conversion, which is the necessary prelude to entering the Kingdom of God. Entering the wide gate, then, would be the choosing of the world with its allurements rather than the Kingdom with its apparent restrictions and disciplines. Jesus challenges His hearers to make a crucial choice.

The broad way is attractive to those who tread it, because they are free to do exactly what they like. It is the way of self-indulgence.

The narrow gate may smack of sacrifice and self-denial, and this is not welcome to the worldly and materialistic. It is not easy to pass through, for Jesus said *"Strive* to enter . . . "It involves moral effort and conflict. But while it is not all glamour and excitement, *the end is glorious*. Though entry may be difficult, the narrow way on the other side is in reality ever broadening, leading on to abundant and eternal life.

On the other hand, the wide gate, though easy to enter and the broad way alluring, ushers the traveller into the narrow defile of "destruction", which begins now and climaxes in eternal separation from God. So, *"Enter through the narrow gate."*

FOR ACTION: *"Since we know what it is to fear the Lord, we try to persuade men."* (2 Cor. 5:11)

February 8

THE HIGHWAY OF HOLINESS

"Prepare the way for the Lord, make straight paths for him." (Matthew 3:3)

In Isaiah 40:3,4, the prophet stressed what Israel must do if God was again to be revealed in their midst. "Make smooth in the desert a highway for our God."

In the east, a victorious general, on returning from his conquest, was accorded the victor's triumphal march. History records titanic feats of engineering in making roads through the trackless desert for the conquering hero. Every low place was filled, every high place reduced, every uneven place levelled, every rough place smoothed, so that the conqueror would enjoy unimpeded progress.

This custom illustrates a contemporary spiritual principle. If God is to reveal Himself to His people in special blessing, there must be prior spiritual preparation; such a sense of sin and repentance as would make it possible for the Holy Spirit to work in power among them.

Anything crooked in the life must be straightened, any stumbling-blocks removed. Low levels of spiritual living must be raised, and rough elements of character smoothed. Areas of neglect must be remedied and relationships adjusted.

This is something for which we alone are responsible, but the Holy Spirit will co-operate with us to this end.

FOR PRAYER:
> *The dearest idol I have known,*
> *Whate'er that idol be,*
> *Help me to tear it from its throne*
> *And worship only Thee.*

February 9

THE PATH TO GREATNESS

"Whoever wants to become great among you must be your servant." (Mark 10:43)

Like his Master, the maturing Christian *will prefer serving others to being served by others*. He will emulate the Lord who said, "Even the Son of Man did not come to be served, but to serve" (Mark 10:45).

True spiritual leadership springs not from ambition to rule but from a passion to serve. This exotic grace is not native to most of us. But the Master equated it with greatness when He said, "Whoever wants to become great among you must be your servant."

This was one of the most revolutionary and unwelcome concepts Jesus introduced into the religious world of His day, and it is little different today. Now, as then, most of us want to be masters, not servants; leaders, not followers.

His view of the Kingdom was a community of people serving one another and the needy world outside. Unlike in earthly realms, our status in His Kingdom is to be judged by the number of people whom we serve, not by the number who serve us.

It was in this context of servanthood that Jesus said, "I have set you an example that you should do as I have done for you. I tell you the truth, no servant is greater than his master" (John 13: 15,16).

FOR MEDITATION: *"A great leader is seen as servant first, and that simple fact is the secret of his greatness."* S. Greenleaf

HOLINESS, NOT MERE HAPPINESS

Make every effort . . . to be holy; without holiness no-one will see the Lord. (Hebrews 12:14)

To the maturing Christian, *holiness will be more attractive than mere happiness*. It seems that in some Christian circles, the pursuit of happiness has become almost pathological.

In a recent letter the writer made this assessment of the contemporary scene: "Ours is a very self-centred culture. Self-fulfilment and self-advancement have become our chief goals. The leading question of our faith seems to be, 'How can I be happy and satisfied?' As a result there is shallow conversion and superficial commitment."

The mature Christian has discovered that true happiness is a by-product of holiness. A consuming desire to be holy is clearer proof of sanctification than is an itch for thrilling and exciting experiences.

God wants His people to be joyous, for "the fruit of the Spirit is joy". But true joy, lasting joy, comes only along the pathway of holiness.

Our Lord was the most joyous Person on earth, because He was the holiest. Of Him it was said, "You have loved righteousness and hated wickedness; therefore God has set you above your companions by anointing you with the oil of joy" (Heb. 1:9).

When we make holiness the object of our pursuit, joy is thrown in as a bonus. *We are happiest when we are holiest.*

FOR MEDITATION: *If happiness is a by-product of holiness, is that why Satan has made the idea of holiness unattractive to Christians?*

February 11

THE IDOL SELF

"If anyone would come after me, he must deny himself and take up his cross and follow me." (Mark 8:34)

An infant is self-centred, and so also is an immature believer. The current emphasis on loving oneself sounds rather strange when placed alongside Christ's emphasis on denying oneself, and tends to be another manifestation of spiritual infantilism. The mature person is self-forgetful, and spends his or her love on others.

The story is told that when Mahmoud with his all-victorious armies laid siege to Guzurat in India, he forced his way into one of the costliest shrines of the Brahmins. They prostrated themselves before him, offering vast ransom if only he would spare their god, for, they claimed, the fortunes of their city depended on him.

After a pause Mahmoud replied that he would rather be known as the breaker than the seller of idols, and struck the image with his battle-axe. It proved to be hollow and had been used as the receptacle for thousands of precious gems which, as the image was shattered, showered down at the conqueror's feet.

Such an idol is self. For Mahmoud to have spared it would have meant the loss of untold wealth. If we deliver the idol self to destruction by Christ, there will be showered on us spiritual enrichment beyond our power to receive.

FOR MEDITATION:
This cruel self, Oh, how it strives
And works within my breast,
As if it were not safe to trust
And enter into rest.

February 12

LOVE MORE THAN EMOTION

Love the Lord your God with all your heart and with all your soul and with all your strength. (Deuteronomy 6:5)

Because love is central in His own nature, it is not surprising that God requires it to be central in man. God loves us with all *His* heart and He longs for reciprocity.

The *heart* is the seat of our *emotional* natures and includes the mind. The degree to which our emotional natures are involved may vary with different temperaments, but there must be some degree of emotional involvement. Not everyone can rise to such heights of rapturous devotion as Frederick W. Faber:

> O Jesus, Jesus, dearest Lord,
> Forgive me if I say,
> For very love, Thy sacred name
> A thousand times a day.

We are to put not only *intellect* but emotion into our worship. A cold heart cannot worship.

The *soul* is the seat of our *volitional* nature. Genuine love for God is more than a pleasing stirring of the emotions. It will involve the whole strength of our moral natures. God's love moved Him to make an infinitely costly sacrifice. The will must be engaged.

The *strength* of our *physical* natures will also play its part. We are to love God with "all our being's ransomed powers". We are to worship with zeal and intensity. God desires the love of the whole personality.

FOR PRAYER: *Lord, I have no reservoir of love in my heart to draw upon, but I believe Your Word: "God has poured out his love into our hearts by the Holy Spirit."* (Rom. 5:5)

February 13

LOVE ESSENTIALLY UNSELFISH

"God so loved the world that He GAVE . . ." (John 3:16)

It is unfortunate that the word "love" as it is commonly understood today has been sadly debased. The romantic and erotic aspects of love dominate television and modern literature, and the higher aspects are paid scant courtesy.

In its essence, love is "the self-imparting quality in the nature of God that moves Him to seek the highest good of His creatures, in whom He seeks to awaken responsive love". Since this is so, love is basic to our knowledge of and intimacy with God. Love is grounded in the nature of God and is the highest expression of His character. We are mature only to the degree that we are mature in love.

Love is more than sentiment, it is an activity. It must express itself, sacrifice itself, pour itself out on another. It is essentially outward-going and unselfish.

God's love moved Him to selfless, sacrificial action. "This is how God showed his love among us: he sent his one and only Son into the world that we might live through him" (1 John 4:9).

Paganism does not produce selfless love. The Japanese language had no word to express Christian love; another word had to be coined and filled with new content to express that essentially Christian grace.

FOR PRAYER: *Father, help those of us who are husbands to "love our wives just as Christ loved the church and gave himself up for her".* (Eph. 5:25).

February 14

THE SEEKING SAVIOUR

"Here I am! I stand at the door and knock. If anyone hears my voice and opens the door, I will come in and eat with him, and he with me." (Revelation 3:20)

The above words were addressed to the church at Laodicea, and down the ages their message has echoed with hope to successive generations.

Their primary application was to a church which had, to all intents and purposes, excluded the very Christ who had formed it. The words enshrine a truth which we are apt to forget. We are told that everywhere men are seeking after God, and books are written about man's quest for God.

This is not the biblical outlook. "There is no-one who seeks God" (Rom. 3:11). *It is not man's quest for God, but God's quest for man.* The initiative is always with Him.

The first question in the dawn of history was God's: "Adam, where are you?" God did not leave Adam to find Him. He took the initiative, and has done so ever since. He came "to seek and save the lost". *He makes the first approach*, and man's quest for Him is the initial response to that approach.

In the parables of Luke 15, it was the shepherd who sought the sheep. Did the coin seek the woman? Was it not the father who through the years kept watch to welcome his returning son? The text demonstrates the attitude of God towards all men in all ages.

FOR MEDITATION: *The distinctive glory of Christianity is its concept of a seeking God.*

February 15

OUR MOST PRECIOUS COMMODITY

Redeeming the time . . . (Ephesians 5:16 KJV)

Time is one of the Christian worker's most precious commodities, for one's use of time determines not only the amount, but the quality of one's work.

Time is not given, but purchased. Some such thought is behind Ephesians 5:16: "Buy up the opportunities." Time is opportunity and it becomes ours by purchase. There is a price to be paid for its most strategic employment. We exchange it in the market place of life for certain occupations or activities. We should exchange it only for things of the greatest value.

Time is a stewardship for which we must render account. The value of our contribution to our generation will depend on how strategically we use it. Each moment is a gift of God, therefore it should not be wasted. Because it is our most valuable possession, we should develop a critical conscience in this area.

Time can be lost as well as redeemed, and it is a solemn thing to remember that it can never be recalled. *Time cannot be hoarded.* It must be fully spent each day. *It cannot be postponed:* it is now or never. If not used productively, time is irretrievably lost.

It is reassuring to remember that everyone has been entrusted with exactly the same amount of time, and that God's plan leaves sufficient time for the fulfilment of all His will each day.

FOR ASPIRATION:
> *No trifling in this life of mine,*
> *Not this path the blessed Master trod;*
> *But ever hour and power employed*
> *Always and all for God.*

THE INFALLIBLE WORD

All Scripture is God-breathed . . . (2 Timothy 3:16)

The convictions of a leader concerning the Bible will affect profoundly the nature of his leadership. One who has mental reservations about the absolute inspiration and authority of the Scriptures, will inevitably have only a tentative note in his handling and application of divine truth. Here, as elsewhere, Paul sets the standard.

His only Bible was the Old Testament, and even before his conversion he treated it as the oracles of God. In his training, he would commit large tracts to memory, a worthy habit. Too many Christians have never read the Bible through, even once.

In his letters Paul did not give the slightest hint that he entertained any doubts of the divine origin and inspiration of Scripture. He had to face, as his Master had done, the same textual problems as we meet today. But there is not a scintilla of evidence that these problems gave him any concern. We are in good company when we take the same stand.

Paul's confidence in the authority and integrity of Scripture is expressed in these unequivocal terms: "All Scripture is God-breathed and is useful for teaching, rebuking, correcting and training in righteousness." He shared his Lord's conviction: "Until heaven and earth disappear, not the smallest letter, not the least stroke of a pen, will by any means disappear from the Law until everything is accomplished" (Matt. 5:18).

FOR MEDITATION: *The convictions of a spiritual leader concerning the Bible will affect profoundly the nature of his leadership.*

February 17

SOLVING DOUBTFUL MATTERS

"Everything is permissible for me" — but . . . (1 Corinthians 6:12)

From time to time we are each confronted by perplexing problems to which there is no easy answer. Scripture suggests questions to ask ourselves in such a case:

Is it beneficial and helpful? "Everything is permissible", Paul writes, "but not everything is beneficial" (1 Cor. 10:23). So in areas of concern and uncertainty, it is important to consider: If I take this course, will it tend to make me a better and more mature Christian? Will it make my life more profitable to God and to my fellow men? Is it beneficial?

Is it constructive? Does the pursuit of this activity edify and build up the Church and fellow Christians? "Everything is permissible — but not everything is constructive."

Will it tend to enslave me? "Everything is permissible for me — but I will not be mastered by anything." Even things quite lawful in themselves can exercise an undue influence, occupying too much of our time, and thus holding us back from God's best for us. An undue amount of secular reading, or an excessive amount of television viewing, for example, can vitiate our appetite for the Word of God. We have to choose our priorities carefully, even in the area of lawful things.

Will it strengthen me against temptation? There is no use praying, "Lead us not into temptation" if we voluntarily walk right into it.

FOR ACTION: *If we act according to these principles, we will discover a new and joyous liberty.*

February 18

JUST LIKE US

A man just like us. (James 5:17)

Elijah was a man just like us, and in the apostle Paul God provided us with just such another. True, he was a man of towering spiritual stature, but he was also a man who knew failure as well as success. Even as he cried out in his despair, "What a wretched man I am! Who will rescue me from this body of death?" he also exulted, "Thanks be to God – through Jesus Christ our Lord" (Rom. 7:24,25).

These, and similar outpourings of his heart, bring him into our street. He was not "an impossible saint", but a fallible man just like us – someone who can speak to our need.

In our Lord we find inspiration from a real Man who never failed or sinned. In Paul, we find encouragement from a man who fell and rose again. "A perfect man reveals what the ideal is; a man defeated and finally victorious discloses what, by the grace of God, we may become . . . We need Jesus on the one side of us and Paul on the other, if we are to walk in triumph along the difficult and perilous way."

We more readily grasp spiritual principles when we see them embodied in flesh and blood, than when formulated as mere academic propositions. In the letters of Paul we see reflected in his autobiographical glimpses, an illustration of their truth.

FOR THANKSGIVING: *Lord, I thank You, that unlike in human biographies, in the Bible You did not omit the delinquencies of the characters.*

GOD'S PLAN IS HARMONIOUS

IN ALL THINGS *God works for the good of those who love him.* (Romans 8:28)

The events of life are not unrelated. They work into a preconceived pattern. The physician's prescription is compounded of a number of drugs. Taken in isolation, some of them would be poisonous and would do only harm. But blended together under the direction of a skilled pharmacist, they achieve only good. William Barclay renders the verse, ''We know that *God intermingles all things for good* for them that love Him.'' The experiences of life when taken in isolation may seem anything but good, but blended together, the result is only good.

In adverse circumstances, unbelief queries, ''How can this be working for good?'' The answer is, ''Wait until the Great Physician has finished writing the prescription.'' Who cannot look back on life to see that things which seemed disastrous, proved in the ultimate to be blessings in disguise? The artist blends colours which, to the unskilled eye, seem far removed from his objective. But wait until he finishes the picture. Life has been likened to an elaborate tapestry:

Not till the loom is silent
   And the shuttles cease to fly,
Will God unroll the pattern
   And explain the reason why
The dark threads are as needful
   In the Weaver's skilful hand,
As the threads of gold and silver
   For the pattern He has planned.

FOR MEDITATION: *With our God, ''accidents are not accidental, and adversity is not adverse''.*

February 20

GOD'S PLAN IS ACTIVE

In all things GOD WORKS *for the good of those who love him* . . . (Romans 8:28)

The heart that loves God discerns Him busily at work in even the most heartbreaking and unwelcome happenings of life. All things are turning out for the best because God is at work in them, transmuting bane into blessing and tragedy into triumph.

His operation is not always immediately discernible. Indeed, it often seems as though He is doing nothing. Carlyle, meditating on the enigmas of life, in the anguish of his heart said, "The worst of God is that He does nothing!"

But God is often active when all seems most still. God's greatest works in the natural world are carried on silently and unnoticed. Under His invisible control the stars maintain their predestined courses, the restless ocean keeps within its appointed limits. We should never, in impatience at the seeming inactivity of God, take things into our own hands and try to be our own providence.

The daily happenings, whether tragic or joyous, are the raw material from which God is weaving the design of life. As Browning put it, "Machinery just meant, to give thy soul its bent." Introduce God into the events of life and order emerges out of chaos. No conceivable circumstances could better prosper God's plan, or further our highest good.

FOR MEDITATION: *"God is too kind to do anything cruel, too wise ever to make a mistake."*

GOD'S PLAN IS BENEFICENT

We know that in all things God works for the good of those who love him, who have been called according to his purpose. (Romans 8:28)

This sentence, interpreted in its context, can bring unlimited cheer to the Christian in the midst of testing. With Paul it was a matter of profound conviction. No room for question here – *"We know!"* He had unwavering confidence in the overruling providence of God. He believed that "God makes everything turn out for the best."

For him *this conviction rendered complaining unthinkable*, since every event was planned or permitted by God. It made possible his counsel of perfection, "In everything give thanks." It turned sighing into singing. It was a practical embracing of this truth which enabled him and his companion to sing in prison at midnight, even when their plans seemed to have miscarried (Acts 16:25).

To him it mattered little whether physical conditions were propitious, so long as he knew that he loved God and was called according to His purpose. Everything, whether seemingly adverse or advantageous, would certainly turn out for the best. The important question is, do we share Paul's joyous assurance?

What is the "good" which God promises? It may not always, at first sight, seem "good, acceptable and perfect" to us. Sometimes His providences seem disastrous from a materialistic viewpoint. *The "good" which God promises is spiritual rather than temporal*, and some time may elapse before we discern its true beneficence.

FOR EMULATION: *Let us ask and answer Job's question: "Shall we accept good from God, and not trouble?"* (2:10)

THE INITIATIVE IS OURS

Be transformed by the renewing of your mind.
(Romans 12:2)

Forming a new habit often involves breaking an old one, and this is no light task. The established pattern of the years will not be easily changed. We will need the powerful aid of the Holy Spirit if we are to break totally with sinful habits of the past.

We, as did the Christians at Philippi, can cultivate new habits of thought that will oust the former habits that led to sin. Every temptation comes to us by way of our thoughts. These, if evil, must be replaced with wholesome thoughts which are in keeping with the mind of Christ. Hence Paul's exhortation: "Whatever is true, whatever is noble, whatever is right, whatever is pure, whatever is lovely, whatever is admirable – *think about such things*" (Phil. 4:8).

The initiative is ours! We choose what thoughts fill our minds. Because this is commanded by God, it must be possible for us to conform. We can, for example, cultivate new habits of speech. If we have been in the habit of embroidering the truth, or telling untruths, or making insincere or inaccurate statements, we must resolutely form the habit of abjuring these things and become scrupulously truthful and strictly honest in our speech. We are commanded to "put off all falsehood" (Eph. 4:25), and to "put on the belt of truth" (Eph. 6:14). We must persevere until this becomes habitual.

FOR MEDITATION: *"The most advanced Christian life needs a perpetual renewal and repetition of past acts of faith. It cannot live in the past."*
Alexander Maclaren

THE FINAL ASSAULT

"This gospel of the kingdom will be preached in the whole world as a testimony to all nations, and then the end will come." (Matthew 24:14)

On the first recorded occasion when Christ mentioned His Church, He stressed its invincibility: "The gates of Hades shall not overcome it." In this uncertain world, one thing is certain – there is going to be staged a *final assault* on the strongholds of Satan that will result in his final defeat, and the glorious coronation of our Lord.

> He shall reign o'er all the earth,
> He who wore the crown of thorn,
> Whom they deemed of little worth,
> Whom they met with hate and scorn.

History is not moving along purposelessly; it is moving, not to termination but to consummation – with its goal achieved. We are not moving to a cosmic Dunkirk but to certain victory.

There is *no lack of audience*. Never before have non-Christians been so open to receive the gospel message. There is no lack of *potential missionaries*, but all too few share Paul's ambition to preach the gospel where Christ has not been named (Rom. 15:20). There is *no lack of money*. The Church is very rich if it would release its wealth for this purpose. The apostles had little money, but they "turned the world upside down".

The lack is of committed men and women willing to live in unsettled and uncomfortable situations, and adopt a simple life style, in order to reach the lost for Christ.

FOR PRAISE:
> *He shall reign o'er all the earth,*
> *He who wore the crown of thorn.*

February 24

POSSIBLE BECAUSE COMMANDED

" . . . to the ends of the earth." (Acts 1:8)

These were our Lord's last words before His ascension, and they expressed what was nearest to His heart. His Great Commission envisaged nothing less than world conquest.

But is this command possible of fulfilment? No previous generation has achieved it. Is it just a beautiful mirage that recedes as we approach it? *Because Jesus commanded it, it is possible.* He never hinted that it could not or would not be achieved.

This present generation is in a more favourable position to achieve this goal than any before it. Today we have almost *total mobility*. The world has become a global village. Better *training facilities* are available than ever before. In the realm of *linguistics*, new techniques have greatly facilitated language acquisition. The *perils of disease* that decimated the early missionary force have been largely eliminated. There are greater resources of *trained men and women* than ever before in history. Radio, TV and other *electronic media* have brought the whole world within range of the gospel. No previous generation has had such resources.

Our generation is without excuse if we continue to hoard the bread of life. True, the task has increased enormously, but so have our resources. Some generation will be able to say, *"Mission accomplished!"* Why should it not be ours?

FOR MEDITATION: *"I do not ask if the task is compassable, only, is it commanded?"* John Wesley

February 25

THREE MEN WHO PRAYED TO DIE

"Kill me, I pray you." (Numbers 11:15 KJV)
"O Lord, take away my life." (1 Kings 19:4 KJV)
"O Lord, take my life from me." (Jonah 4:3 KJV)

It is claimed that in our day there are more cases of mental disorder than ever before. Even among Christians, depression and despondency are increasingly common. Scripture tells of those men of God who were so depressed that they prayed to die.

Moses had achieved great things for God. Under his leadership a million slaves had become an organised nation. Again and again he had experienced God's miraculous intervention. But Israel's continued rebellion became more than he could endure, and he asked to die.

Elijah, fresh from the dramatic victory on Mount Carmel in which he was God's instrument in national revival, suddenly wilted and fled from the woman he had so recently defied. Under his lonely juniper tree, he prayed for death.

Jonah, after his craven flight and submarine adventure, repented, and delivered God's message to Nineveh and saw the city repent. In strange disillusionment, he considered death better than life.

A diagnosis of these cases reveals that in each there was *a physiological cause*. Their physical and nervous systems were overtaxed. There was a *self-centred reason*. After great success they turned their eyes inward in self-pity. There was *a spiritual cause*. Each had an unjustified sense of failure. In not one case did God answer their prayer. Instead, He dealt with them in tender compassion and restored them to fellowship with Himself.

FOR MEDITATION: *Is it not significant that each of these men was an outstandingly successful prophet? What is the message?*

A DAUNTING STANDARD

"Be perfect, therefore, as your heavenly Father is perfect." (Matthew 5:48)

The word frequently translated "perfect" in the King James Version, is often, and correctly, rendered "mature" in many modern versions. Our English word "mature" is defined as "a state of full development".

The Greek word Paul uses, *teleios*, has a special technical meaning, and signifies "an end, a goal". It combine dual ideas — the full development of one's powers, and the attainment of some goal or standard.

This word can be used of our Lord in the absolute sense, for during His life on earth all His powers reached their full development. He completely fulfilled His Father's will and attained the standard of perfection which that implied. He also attained the goal for which He came to earth — the redemption of a world of lost men and women.

However, when the term is used of man, it is not absolute, but relative, as of a child compared with an adult. The word "perfect" in the New Testament does not hold out the promise of moral perfection on earth. Scriptural perfection or maturity has always another summit ahead for us, for as the poet Coleridge said, "Beyond what is found in Christ, the human race has not, and will not progress."

So it remains for us to "continue progressing towards maturity".

FOR MEDITATION: *The word "perfect" here does not imply "sinlessly" perfect. It suggests completeness, and maturity as sons of God.*

WHAT SPIRITUAL MATURITY IS NOT

> *Not that I have already obtained all this, or have already been made perfect . . .* (Philippians 3:12)

In our pursuit of spiritual maturity, there are negative factors to be considered as well as positive.

It is not an ageing process. Grey hairs and maturity are not necessarily wedded. Because we are ageing, we should not of necessity conclude that we are progressing in maturity. One's hair may turn grey, but one's reactions to people and circumstances may be anything but mature.

It has been well said that it is the *intensity* of our years and not their *extensity* that is the true measure of our maturity, for that is an attitude to life. Our age is beyond our control, but whatever our age our attitudes can be changed by the power of grace and a holy purpose. It is our attitudes and not our arteries that determine the quality of life.

It is not automatic as a result of mastery of the teaching of Scripture. Of course that is an essential element, but of itself it cannot produce maturity. Accumulation of biblical information is of immense value, but *it is only as the principles of Scripture are worked out in daily obedience that spiritual growth is advanced*. Bible study can be a merely intellectual exercise that leaves the life unchanged.

FOR MEDITATION: *Love is the mark of maturity and proves that we are mature sons of the Father, and not mere infants.*

PROGRESSIVE MATURITY

*Let us leave the elementary teachings about Christ and
go on to maturity.* (Hebrews 6:1)

The attaining of spiritual maturity takes time; but time
alone is no guarantee of growth. Maturity sometimes out-
runs time. Do we not sometimes remark of a child, "She
is very mature for her age"? Or of another, "Will he never
grow up?"

Maturity, whether physical or spiritual, does not always
progress at a constant pace. This is especially so in the
adolescent stage. It is the natural outworking of the
growing process of the soul, and is organic, not
mechanical.

All growth is progressive, and the more complex and
delicate the organism, the more time it will take to reach
maturity. But one attains that objective not merely after
a certain lapse of time, but after the laws of spiritual
growth have been obeyed.

Physical growth is determined by observance of the
laws of nutrition and health. Spiritual growth is
spontaneous when the soul is fed consistently from the
Word, breathes the pure air of prayer and cultivates
fellowship with the people of God. On the other hand,
growth can be stunted if we fail to provide congenial
spiritual conditions. An anointed ministry grows out of
the soil of a consistent devotional life.

FOR ASPIRATION:
*Lord, lift me up, and let me stand
By faith on heaven's tableland,
A higher plane than I have found.
Lord, plant my feet on higher ground.*

February 29

STAGES OF MATURITY

I write to you, dear children . . . I write to you, young men . . . I write to you, fathers . . . (1 John 2:12,13)

There are three stages of maturity in normal human life – dependent babyhood, independent adolescence, and adult maturity. A similar progression is seen in our growth in Christian maturity. At conversion, the new life enters as a *babe-life*. ''Like newborn babes, crave pure spiritual milk'' was Peter's counsel (1 Pet. 2:2). This embryo life is fragile and requires loving care and nurture in the dependent stage. Gradually the child will progress to solid food as it moves on to adolescence.

Next comes the *independent stage*, when the young believer has found his or her feet and becomes impatient of restraints. As in physical adolescence, this is sometimes a rather tempestuous period, when the sanctity of old institutions is challenged and the wisdom of age questioned. The young person wants to step out on his own. Provided it is kept within limits, this is a normal development, but the life must be brought under the Lordship of Christ and the control of the Holy Spirit if it is to attain full maturity.

The third stage is that of *progressive maturity*. Adult maturity is attained, but there is endless scope for growth. Paul says we are to ''grow up into Christ in everything'' (Eph. 4:15), every part of life finding its centre and goal in Him.

FOR SELF-EXAMINATION: *Am I showing a degree of maturity commensurate with the number of years I have known Christ?*

THE LACKING LEADERSHIP

"We too are only men, human like you." (Acts 14:15)

The strong, sure, charismatic leadership so desperately needed in our confused age seems to be conspicuously lacking. One citizen, disturbed by prevailing conditions, and his nation's inability to find a panacea for their ills wrote: "The critical juncture found none but second-rate actors on the political stage, and the decisive moment was neglected because the courageous were deficient in power, and the powerful in sagacity and resolution."

That sounds strangely contemporary, yet it was written a century ago by Friedrich Stiller. Have things changed essentially? Our Lord's graphic words are proving true: "On the earth, nations will be in anguish and perplexity at the roaring and tossing of the sea" (Luke 21:25).

World conditions have worsened immeasurably since this statement was made, but the same appraisal of the situation would be appropriate. *Each generation has to meet and resolve its own leadership problems*, and we today are facing an acute crisis in leadership in many spheres. Crisis succeeds crisis, but our leaders come up with few solutions.

The Church has not escaped this dearth of authoritative leadership. Her voice which once sounded a call of hope to beleaguered humanity, is now strangely muted, and her influence in the community minimal. The salt has lost its savour, and the light its radiance.

We need to pray desperately for authoritative spiritual leaders.

FOR EMULATION:
> *I saw a human life ablaze for God,*
> *I felt a power divine*
> *As through a vessel of frail clay*
> *I saw God's glory shine.*

March 2

SPIRITUAL LEADERS NOT SELF-MADE

Remember your leaders . . . Consider the outcome of their way of life and imitate their faith. (Hebrews 13:7)

Spiritual leadership is a blending of natural and spiritual qualities. Even the natural qualities are not self-produced but God-given, and therefore reach their highest effectiveness when employed in the service of Christ and for His glory.

Personality is a prime factor in natural leadership. The spiritual leader, however, influences others not by the power of his own personality alone, but by that personality irradiated and empowered by the Holy Spirit. Because he or she permits the Holy Spirit undisputed control, His power can flow unhindered through them to others.

Spiritual leadership is a matter of superior spiritual power, and that can never be self-generated. There is no such thing as a self-made spiritual leader. He is able to influence others only because the Holy Spirit is able to work through him to a greater degree than in those whom he leads.

It is a general principle that we can influence and lead others only so far as we ourselves have gone. The person who is most likely to be successful, is one who leads, not by pointing the way, but by having trodden it himself. We are leaders only to the extent that we inspire others to follow us. One way we can test our leadership is to look behind us, and see who is following!

FOR THANKSGIVING: *Father, I thank You for those godly men and women whose lives have influenced me to follow You. Help me to follow their faith.*

March 3

NEEDED, LEADERS OF QUALITY

I searched for a man . . . who should stand in the gap before me for the land. (Ezekiel 22:30 KJV)

The supernatural character of the Church demands a leadership that rises above the human. Such leadership has always been in short supply.

The overriding need of the Church, if it is to discharge its obligations, is a leadership that is authoritative, spiritual and sacrificial.

Authoritative, because people love to be led by one who knows where he is going and inspires confidence. They follow one who shows himself wise and strong.

Spiritual, because a leadership that is unspiritual, that can be fully explained in terms of the natural, although ever so attractive and competent, will result only in sterility and spiritual bankruptcy.

Sacrificial, because modelled on the life of One who gave Himself a sacrifice for the whole world, leaving us an example that we should follow His steps (John 13:5).

The Church has always prospered most when it has been blessed with strong spiritual leaders who expected and experienced a touch of the supernatural in their service.

The lack of such men and women is a symptom of the malaise that has gripped it. In a world aflame, the voice of the Church has sunk to a pathetic whisper. It is the binding duty of those in leadership to face up to the situation, and do all in their power to see that the torch of truly spiritual leadership is passed on to the younger generation.

FOR PRAYER: *"Do not forsake me, O God, till I declare your power to the next generation."* (Ps. 71:18)

March 4

AN HONOURABLE AMBITION

To aspire to leadership is an honourable ambition. (1 Timothy 3:1 NEB)

Paul's affirmation that to aspire to leadership is an honourable ambition will not be accepted by all Christians without a measure of reservation. Should it not be the office that seeks the man, rather than the man the office? *Is it not perilous to put an ambitious man into office?* Is there not more than a modicum of truth in the claim that ambition is "the last infirmity of noble minds"?

Was Shakespeare not expressing a profound truth when he made Wolsey say:

Cromwell, I charge thee, fling away ambition:
By that sin fell the angels; how can man then,
the image of his Maker, hope to win by 't?

We cannot deny that there are ambitions that warrant these strictures, but there are ambitions that are noble and to be cherished. In appraising an ambition, it must be remembered that in Paul's day, conditions were much different. We think of the honour and prestige that accrue to those in Christian leadership in our day. But then the leadership positions, far from being coveted, often involved great dangers. Hardship, contempt and rejection were often its rewards. It was the leaders who drew the fire in times of persecution.

When read in the light of these conditions, Paul's statement does not seem so fraught with danger as might at first appear.

FOR EMULATION: *Paul declared, "It is my ambition to bring the Gospel to places where the very name of Christ has not been heard."* (Rom. 15:20 NEB)

March 5

TEACH US TO PRAY

*When he finished [praying], one of his disciples said
to him, "Lord, teach us to pray." (Luke 11:1)*

As His disciples heard the Lord in prayer, they could not
help but discern the depth of intimacy that existed
between Him and His Father. Aspiration after a similar
experience was kindled in their hearts, and they asked
Him, "Lord, teach us to pray just as John taught his
disciples." Jesus gladly responded, for was not this the
very road along which He had been leading them?

In replying to their request He said, "When you pray,
say, 'Father'." A sense of the true fatherhood of God in
all the richness of that relationship, cannot but kindle
worship – the *loving ascription of praise to God for all that
He is, both in His person and His providence.*

Jesus thus impressed on His students the important
principle that in prayer God must occupy the supreme
place – not we ourselves, or even our urgent needs.

What a wealth of meaning is compressed into that
single word, *Father*, as it fell from the lips of Jesus. If God
is not accorded chief place in our prayer life, our prayers
will be tepid and pallid. It is significant that in the Pattern
Prayer, it is half completed before we mention our own
needs. When God is given His rightful place, faith will
be stimulated.

FOR MEDITATION: *Satan dreads nothing but prayer.
His great concern is to keep the saints from
praying.*

March 6

PRAYER AND THE PROMISES

*Every promise of God finds its affirmative in him, and
through him can be said the final amen, to the glory
of God.* (2 Corinthians 1:20 Phillips)

A promise by God is a pledge by God. It provides the
warrant and forms the basis for the prayer of faith. The
validity of a promise rests on the character and resources
of the one who makes it. The character and fidelity of God
vouch for the credibility of the promises He makes.

It is entirely with such promises that the prayer of faith
has to do. As we claim a promise of Scripture, the Holy
Spirit imparts the faith to believe that its terms will be
fulfilled in the context of our prayer. With God, promise
and performance are inseparable.

But promises must be distinguished from facts. We
accept a stated fact of God's Word. When God proclaims
a fact, faith *accepts* and *acts* on it. When God makes a
promise, we *comply* with its conditions, and *claim* its
fulfilment. The function of prayer is to turn God's
promises into facts of experience. Through faith, the
patriarchs obtained the fulfilment of God's promises, and
turned them into personal experience.

The prayer of faith has its basis neither in outward
circumstances nor inward feelings. It springs from the
naked promise or affirmation of the Word of God, for
faith proceeds only from a divine warrant.

The prayer of faith is the power that converts promise
into performance.

FOR PRAISE: *I praise You, Father, that with You
there is no equivocation, but promise and
performance are inseparably linked.*

March 7

WHY UNITED PRAYER?

Peter was kept in prison, but the church was earnestly praying to God for him. (Acts 12:5)

That *unity begets strength* is a principle of grace as well as of nature. A number of Christians uniting in prayer for a given person or objective brings special power into operation. Their unison demonstrates that oneness which God delights to see and honour (John 17:11).

Both Scripture and contemporary experience indicate that *there is a cumulative power in united praying*. Faith is infectious, and infection spreads where numbers congregate. Unbelief thrives more readily in isolation. Only with great difficulty can a fire be kindled with a single stick.

Jesus suggested that there was an intensification of prayer force in united praying. "If two of you on earth agree about anything you ask for, it will be done for you by my Father" (Matt. 18:19). It was at a united prayer meeting that the mighty power of Pentecost was unleashed. It was the prayer of the whole church that secured Peter's release (Acts 12:5). The missionary enterprise had its birth in a united prayer meeting of church leaders (Acts 13:1–4).

"The prayer of a righteous man is powerful and effective," wrote James (5:16). But Scripture and experience combine to teach that the united prayers of many such people, avail yet more.

FOR MEDITATION: *"No great spiritual awakening has begun anywhere apart from united prayer — Christians persistently praying for revival."*

March 8

PRAYING FOR MISSIONARIES

On him we have set our hope that he will continue to deliver us, as you help us by your prayers. (2 Corinthians 1:10–11)

"Strive together with me in your prayers to God for me", pleaded the great missionary apostle. Despite his great gifts of nature and of grace, we search in vain for any sign of conscious adequacy. "Who is sufficient for these things?" he asks (2 Cor. 2:16). Small wonder if his weaker successors crave the intercessions of God's people. But what shall we ask of God for them?

Dr Northcote Deck, a veteran missionary, wrote: "There is nothing more profitable, more priceless, that you can ask for us than that, in spite of physical weakness, frequent infirmities and the care of multiplying converts, *we may be enabled to remain on our knees,* for there is a praying in detail to be done if the infant churches are to grow and prosper." Here is a subject for intercession.

Note in these verses (2 Cor. 1:8–11) the juxtaposition of the hard-pressed missionary's extremity and his deliverance. "We were under great pressure . . . you help us by your prayers." Our prayers may be instrumental in delivering missionaries from "unreasonable and wicked men" (2 Thess. 3:2 KJV). Closed doors swing open on unwilling hinges as we lay hold on God (Col. 4:2).

Paul asked the Ephesians: "Pray for me that whenever I open my mouth, words may be given me so that I will fearlessly make known the mystery of the gospel" (Eph. 6:19).

FOR EMULATION:
Because you prayed –
God touched our weary bodies with His power
And gave us strength for many a trying hour.

March 9

DOORS AND ADVERSARIES

I will stay on at Ephesus until Pentecost, because a great door for effective work has opened to me, and there are many who oppose me. (1 Corinthians 16:8,9)

When a door of service opened to Paul, adversaries were not excuses but opportunities; they were not excuses for seeking an easier sphere, but an opportunity to rout Christ's enemies and bring more territory under His imperial banner. He laid hold of adverse circumstances, and brought them under tribute.

It would be difficult to find a more apt description of the missionary situation in the world today than these words. There have always been adversaries, but today they are more numerous and complex. When persecution failed to halt the early Church, Satan caused the Judaisers to carry the day. When paganism in Rome was overthrown, he injected a mixture of truth and error into the Roman and Greek churches. When the gospel was capturing Africa, he interposed Islam between heathenism and Christianity.

But the last word is not with the devil. Never in the history of the missionary enterprise has there been such a wide-open door as today.

Paul set an inspiring example. The massive difficulties of the situation, far from daunting him, constituted an irresistible challenge. "I will stay on at Ephesus," where the hostilities were most fierce. He did not seek safety in flight, but attacked the adversaries and routed them.

A difficulty is more than a test of our powers. It is a possible addition to our resources.

FOR PRAYER: *Lord, I would pray for courage and faith for those who are bravely witnessing for You in the midst of many adversaries.*

March 10

A DEFLATING VISION

I saw the Lord, seated on a throne, high and exalted . . . "Woe to me," I cried, "I am ruined."
(Isaiah 6:1,5)

The vision of God inevitably results in a vision of oneself and a sense of unworthiness and defilement. The beatific vision deflated Moses. It caused Daniel to see the corruption of his supposed virtues. It blinded Saul. It threw John on his face.

We tend to shrink from a preacher whose message has a subjective edge to it, because it *downgrades our self-image*. When Isaiah saw the Lord, how did the vision affect him?

The collapse of his complacency. "Woe to me, I am ruined." He was no profligate and was probably the holiest man in the nation. But when he came into the dazzling purity of God's presence, he could only cry, "Unclean!"

The unveiling of his unworthiness. "I am a man of unclean lips" – and therefore disqualified as God's messenger. Before he could pronounce God's judgement on the nation, he must first pronounce judgement on himself.

A new sense of his identification with Israel. "I live among a people of unclean lips." He realised his solidarity with his people, and that he was jointly responsible for their sins.

God's remedy was seared lips, and an assurance that his guilt was removed and his sin atoned for (6:1–7).

FOR MEDITATION: *To be a true messenger to our nation and generation, we must embrace the truth of our solidarity with them.*

March 11

HEAVEN'S PRESCRIPTION
FOR DEPRESSION

*He came to a broom tree, sat down under it and prayed
that he might die.* (1 Kings 19:4)

A man who is not capable of depression, has little capacity
for exultation. But despondency can strike God's servant
at most unexpected times. The moment of victory can be
the moment of danger. It was so with Elijah.

He was fresh from a drama in which he had filled the
leading role. He had been God's instrument in over-
throwing Baal worship. He had seen the nation on its face
acknowledging Jehovah to be God. Was this not cause
for exultation? But suddenly he wilted. His courage failed,
and he fled from the woman he had defied. There was
a threefold background to his despondency.

A physiological cause. Think of the emotional stress and
strain of his lone encounter on Carmel; the physical drain
of his run to Jezreel; his flight from Jezebel. He was
exhausted.

A personal cause. His self-esteem had been struck a
shattering blow. He felt God had let him down.

A spiritual reason. He was a true man of God. He longed
for national revival. But the fair promise of Carmel had
largely vanished once the rain fell. He felt that he was
all alone in his zeal. He prayed that he might die.

God's prescription for his overwrought servant – two
long sleeps; two meals baked in heaven''s kitchen. Then
the assurance that he had seven thousand colleagues, and
after that a recommissioning. God understands our
frailty.

FOR MEDITATION:
*Yet in fallen Israel there are hearts and eyes
That day by day in prayer like thine arise.
Thou knewest them not, but their Creator knows.*

NO SIN IS SIMPLE

Against you, you only have I sinned and done what is evil in your sight. (Psalm 51:4)

The dark stain on David's life is a beacon light to people in all ages — a warning that a godly man or woman can, in a moment of time, sully the achievements of a lifetime.

Could he have foreseen the tragic consequences of that lustful look, he would gladly have plucked out an eye to avoid them. His sin left indelible marks on his family and home. More serious still, he lost the smile of God. The dove of peace flew from his heart. His throne lost its stability, his testimony was tarnished.

The comprehensive nature of his sin appears on closer examination. His breaking of the tenth commandment led to his breaking the seventh. Soon, in order to break the eighth, he broke the sixth and committed murder. He broke the ninth by bearing false witness against his neighbour, and brought dishonour on his parents, and thus broke the fifth. There is no such thing as a simple sin. It is always complex.

The bright spot in the sordid affair was that the enormity of his sin was matched by the depth of his repentance. How men react after they have been sifted by Satan, is a revelation of their true character.

For a whole year David remained in stubborn unwillingness to confess his sin. Not until Nathan confronted him did his defences crumble. Then followed the greatest confession chapter in the Bible — Psalm 51.

FOR ACTION: *When we have failed, let us not, like David, delay in making confession and receiving forgiveness.*

THE MID-LIFE TEST

They will run and not grow weary. (Isaiah 40:31)

Middle life has its own peculiar testings in both physical and spiritual realms. They may not be as volcanic as in youth, but what they lose in intensity they gain in subtlety. Many who soared like rockets in youth, have descended like burnt-out sticks in middle life.

There are usually obvious advantages when we attain this stage of life. Our powers are at their zenith. Important life decisions – career, friends, marriage, family – have been made. Ideally, status and influence have been attained, and financial circumstances are easier.

But there are counterbalancing dangers. Often at this stage there develops a loss of fervour and a waning of personal devotion to the Lord. A lukewarm sense of duty replaces ardent love. Instead of transmuting the vanishing enthusiasms of youth into an absorbing life purpose, life becomes insipid and anaemic. We are tempted to ease up on self-denial and to yield to softening ease. Often unrealised ideals of marriage and home life are accepted as inevitable.

Caleb passed the test of youth with flying colours (Josh. 14:6–15). His mid-life experience could have embittered him. Despite his faithfulness to God, he had to join his unbelieving fellows in an aimless forty-year trek in the desert. Instead of being resentful, he retained his integrity and survived the long test without losing spiritual stature. On the middle mile we need the grace of patience.

FOR PRAYER: *Lord, grant that in middle life I may not lose spiritual momentum.*

March 14

CONSIDER HIM

Fix your thoughts on Jesus . . . (Hebrews 3:1)
Let us fix our eyes on Jesus . . . (Hebrews 12:2)

Two different Greek words are used in these sentences. One signifies the prolonged, concentrated gaze of the astronomer. The other means to reckon up, to compare or weigh. Taken together in their context, these words are an exhortation to fix our minds consciously on Christ, comparing His testings and sufferings with our own. We will find in the exercise a panacea for our spiritual maladies.

It will deliver us from self-pity – a spiritual disease to which we are all too prone. Too many are vocally sorry for themselves and feel that life has given them a raw deal. "Consider him who endured . . ." (12:3). Was He misunderstood, badly treated, unappreciated? Compared with His, our trials are trivial.

It is an antidote for discouragement. "Consider him, so that you will not . . . lose heart" (12:3). Discouragement is one of Satan's debilitating weapons. Christ was despised, rejected, maligned. His ministry was not conspicuously successful, yet *He endured.* Consider Him, and take heart again.

It will prove a stimulant for lethargy. "In your struggle against sin, you have not yet resisted to the point of shedding *your* blood" (12:4). Have we grown lethargic in the battle against sin? Never for one moment did Jesus relax in His warfare with Satan. Consider Him, and take fresh courage.

FOR PRAISE: *Lord, I thank You for displaying a humanity so attractive and a deity so perfect to be the home for my thoughts.*

BEHOLD THE MAN

Pilate said to them, "Here is the man." (John 19:5)

Never in human history were physical frame and nervous system called on to endure such unremitting strain as that imposed on our Lord during His three years of public ministry which climaxed in the cross. Only a physically perfect constitution could have supported such unceasing activity and expenditure of nervous force.

When on one occasion it was reported that "Jesus realised that power had gone out of Him" (Mark 5:30), we are given an indication of *the cost at which His ministry was exercised*. The physical effort alone was prodigious. His recorded journeys during the three years – and only a small part of them is recorded – cover over 2,500 miles, travelled on foot. He was usually thronged with crowds, and always preaching teaching and healing.

What better preparation could there have been for such a demanding programme than His work as carpenter. Those silent years He recognised as part of His preparation for ministry. They were invaluable in building up the physical and nervous resources that would be so heavily overdrawn in coming days that He would stagger under the weight of His own cross.

This example helps us to appreciate the nobility of honest labour. We, too, can welcome the hidden years of preparation for ministry.

FOR PRAISE: *O Lord, I praise You that though You were a GENTLE-man You were none the less a gentle-MAN.*

THE SUFFERING CHRIST

> *Christ suffered for you, leaving you an example, that you should follow in his steps.* (1 Peter 2:21)

Our Lord was the Prince of sufferers. Here, as in all else He was pre-eminent. We tend to conceive of His sufferings mainly in the realm of the physical. But so intense were His spiritual sufferings, that physical pain could have been almost a relief.

He was *a sinless sufferer*. Note the juxtaposition of the two thoughts: "Christ suffered for you . . . He committed no sin." His sinlessness added to the poignancy of His sufferings, for suffering can mean much or little according to the nature of the person. To a sensitive musician, discord causes exquisite pain. Christ's powers had not atrophied, nor had sin done its ugly work. It is the holy person who feels sin most keenly.

He was *a sensitive sufferer* — the essence of refinement and sensitivity. How He must have suffered when denounced as a liar, glutton, drunkard, blasphemer, in league with the devil! These verbal barbs pierced more deeply than the crown of thorns.

He was *a silent sufferer*. "When they hurled their insults at him, he did not retaliate" (v.23). He harboured no spirit of revenge. Like an aromatic leaf, the crushing released only fragrance.

FOR PRAISE: *I thank You, O Lord, for Your silences. Had You spoken to justify Yourself, You could not have justified me.*

THE CRUCIFIED CHRIST

Golgotha. Here they crucified him. (John 19:17–18)

Christ was as unique in His death as in His birth. In a picturesque statement, Martin Niemöller said, "The cradle and the cross of Christ were hewn from the same tree." The incarnation was with a view to the crucifixion.

Christ's death was *the only death that fulfilled millennia of prophecy*. It was foreshadowed in meticulous detail in the Jewish sacrificial system and in the prophetic Scriptures. In His tragic hours on the cross, no fewer than thirty-three Old Testament prophecies were fulfilled.

He was the only Person to whom death was not inevitable. "I lay down my life of my own accord" (John 10:17,18). No-one took it from Him, death was deliberately chosen. He was not dragged to the cross, but drawn by quenchless love.

To Him alone, *death was not the result of sin*. As He committed no sin, the wages of sin – death – were not His due. This left Him free to assume the burden of the world's sin, and provide deliverance from its bondage.

His was *the only death accompanied by miracles*. It was appropriate that a life replete with miracle should conclude with a series of miracles. The miraculous darkness was no eclipse. The rending of the veil "from the top to the bottom" was no human achievement. The mighty earthquake which opened the graves was no natural occurrence. All were conclusive evidence of His power over death.

FOR WORSHIP: *Lord, I pause in wonder that the mightiest event in history is compassed in three words — "they crucified Him".*

THE RISEN CHRIST

Christ died . . . he was raised again the third day. (1 Corinthians 15:3–4)

Two important things about Christ emerge from this passage. First, *He was truly man* because He died. Death is characteristic of mankind. In this fact lay the necessity of the incarnation. *He was also really God* because He rose from the dead. Man cannot rise from the dead. Because He was infinite, His death was of infinite value, and made expiation for the sins of the whole world.

He rose again the third day, under the circumstances recorded in the Scriptures. It was a *bodily resurrection*. When the women and Peter and John looked into the tomb, it was empty except for the grave clothes, still lying in the folds that had encased Him. The butterfly had flown, leaving an empty chrysalis.

Muslims glory in the *full coffin* of Mohammed in Mecca. Christians glory in the *empty tomb* in Jerusalem. We have a living Christ, they have a dead prophet.

How can the resurrection be explained? His body must have been removed by human or superhuman hands. If human, it must have been by friends or foes. His foes would not, and His friends could not, for the tomb was sealed, and a guard of sixty soldiers watched to ensure that it was not rifled. The only alternative is that "God the Father raised him from the dead" (Gal. 1:1).

> You ask me how I know He lives
> He lives within my heart.

FOR PRAISE:
> *Christ is risen: Hallelujah!*
> *Risen our victorious Head;*
> *Sing His praises, Hallelujah!*
> *Christ is risen from the dead.*

March 19

THE ASCENDED CHRIST

While he was blessing them, he left them and was taken up into heaven. (Luke 24:51)

The ascension of our Lord directs attention to the fact that He is not only risen, but *enthroned*. It is that event in which the risen Christ finally and visibly withdrew from His disciples and passed into the heavens – a fitting climax to His unique life. It was the necessary complement to His resurrection.

He did not vanish out of sight as He did at Emmaus, leaving a question as to whether there might be further appearances. It took place in broad daylight as they were looking on. He was really and finally gone. He ascended bodily, and carried His glorified human body into heaven.

He left them *with hands outstretched in blessing*. As soon as His nail-pierced feet left the earth, He commenced His ministry as our Advocate and Intercessor. They exchanged His physical presence for His spiritual omnipresence.

His ascension imparted *the assurance that His death was effective* and that all God's claims against sinful men had been met.

It was *the necessary prelude to the coming of the Holy Spirit*, as the Lord had promised (John 7:39). Now the way was open for the Pentecostal effusion. By the ascension, the local Christ became the universal Christ, whose personal presence was mediated by the Holy Spirit.

The ascension reversed man's verdict on the Son of God.

FOR MEDITATION: *What was the significance of the ascension to the Lord Himself?*

March 20

THE RETURNING CHRIST

"I will come again." (John 14:3 RSV)

The return of Christ is the denouement towards which the Church has been looking for centuries. It is not only the object of her anticipation, but an admonition to very practical Christian duties. A careful study will reveal that it is linked to every great doctrine and ethical duty.

It sounds *a call to consecration*. "Behold I come like a thief! Blessed is he who stays awake . . . " (Rev. 16:15). We are to be punctilious in keeping the garments of the soul stainless and pure.

His return carries with it *the assurance of reward*. "Behold I am coming soon! My reward is with me" (Rev. 22:12). There is a tendency to regard the reward motive as a commercialising of Christianity, but it played a prominent part in the thinking of the early Church. Paul frequently refers to it, as did his Master. In any case, rewards are not *given*, they are *earned*.

The second advent is *an encouragement to continuance*. "I am coming . . . Hold on to what you have, so that no-one will take your crown" (Rev. 3:11). The Lord urges us to hold fast what we already have, lest our reward be taken by someone else. "Run in such a way as to get the prize" (1 Cor. 9:25).

There may still be years before He comes. Let us fill the days with worship and sacrificial service.

FOR MEDITATION: *When Jesus said, "This gospel of the kingdom will be preached for a testimony to all nations, and then shall the end come," does this not lay a responsibility on us to complete the task?*

March 21

THE UNCHANGING CHRIST

Jesus Christ is the same yesterday and today and for ever. (Hebrews 13:8)

> Change and decay in all around I see:
> O Thou who changest not, abide with me.

No-one can doubt that we live in a changing world. The rate of change is so rapid that we find difficulty in keeping pace with its kaleidoscopic movements.

At the centre of our unstable world stands the *unchanging Christ*. All that He was in the past, He is in the present and will be in the future.

Jesus Christ, *the same yesterday*, will care for all our yesterdays – the past that sometimes haunts and paralyses us. He is able to cleanse us from all the guilt and defilement of past years. We must not allow Satan to revive what God has forgotten.

Jesus Christ, *the same today*, will take care of all our todays. He who delivers us from the tyranny of the past, will dissolve the perplexities of the present. And how insoluble they often seem! Cares of family, health, finance, age – as the Great Physician, He can help our physical problems.

Jesus Christ, *the same for ever*, is well able to care for all our tomorrows, and to dispel the uncertainties of the future. There are fears that assail us at every stage of life. Fear of the future can cripple us in meeting the demands of the present. But in the midst of life's uncertainties stands One who is utterly dependable.

FOR PRAISE: *Father, I praise You for Your assurance that, "I the Lord do not change."* (Mal. 3:6)

GOD – SOVEREIGN CONTROLLER

The king's heart is in the hand of the Lord; he directs it like a watercourse wherever he pleases. (Proverbs 21:1)

The leading truths of divine providence are set out in vivid terms in the Book of Esther, in the deliverance God gave to His people and the retribution that came to the wicked Haman. Here are some of the lessons:

God is controller of all human acts. No-one can deny responsibility for his actions on the grounds that he is held in the grip of necessity, for God never does violence to the free will with which He has endowed man. God's sovereignty and man's liberty co-exist in such a way that while God does not coerce man, He overrules his actions for the highest good of all.

God is frequently an unseen actor. While the name of God is absent from the Book of Esther, His hidden activity is everywhere discerned. So although God does not work ostentatiously, He is none the less active.

God's timing of events is perfect. Follow the time factor in the story. While God may not be before time, He is never late. When the hour struck on God's clock, the wicked man was punished.

God's retribution is strangely exact. What issue could be more fitting than the exact reversal of the wicked Haman and the virtuous Mordecai?

God's providence leaves no room for chance. All is foreseen, foreordained or permitted. All proceeds under His superintendence.

FOR MEDITATION: *Before an emergency arises, God in His providence has made adequate and perfectly timed provision to meet it.*

WORTHY WORSHIP

> . . . *the light of the knowledge of the glory of God in the face of Christ.* (2 Corinthians 4:6)

A difficulty confronts the person who desires to worship God in a more worthy and meaningful way. How can God be really known so that He can be truly worshipped? To some believers God seems so unreal and far away that attempts to worship seem almost a farce. What are the means by which worship may be stimulated and become the spontaneous expression of the heart? One important step is to make sure we are on praying ground, and that there is no cherished sin between us and God.

God has granted a partial revelation of Himself in the wonders of nature. "The heavens declare the glory of God" (Ps. 19:1). From nature we learn something of His mighty power and transcendent beauty and infinite wisdom, but little of His love and mercy.

Only in the face of Jesus Christ can we see the full blaze of "the light of the knowledge of the glory of God", for in Christ all the fullness of the Deity lives in bodily form (Col. 1:19). No worship is acceptable to God which ignores or excludes Christ. It is through Him that we have access to the Father. To worship Christ is to worship God who has revealed Himself in Christ.

> In Thee most perfectly expressed
> The Father's glories shine,
> Of the full Deity possessed,
>   Eternally divine.

FOR MEDITATION: *Worship can be wordless. The Psalmist urged, "My soul, be thou silent unto God."*

March 24

WORSHIPPING BY THE SPIRIT

It is we who are the circumcision who worship by the Spirit of God, who glory in Christ Jesus, and who put no confidence in the flesh. (Philippians 3:3)

All attempts to worship other than through the enabling of the Holy Spirit are unacceptable to God. Jesus asserted that "God is spirit, and his worshippers must worship in spirit and in truth" (John 4:24).

It is the Third Person of the Trinity who strikes the strings of our human spirits and produces the harmony of spiritual worship, where once there was the dissonance of worldly activity. Andrew Murray wrote: "There is a worship which is satisfying to the flesh, because it is in the power of what the flesh can do, and a worship of God which is in the Spirit. It is this worship Christ came to make possible in us by giving us . . . God's Holy Spirit."

Not all worship is in the Spirit, for the flesh knows no modesty and will intrude into our most sacred hours. We must deliver the flesh to the cross and cast ourselves on the Spirit whose delight is to help us in our weaknesses.

Paul's prescription is, "Be filled with the Spirit" (Eph. 5:18). The Spirit-filled believer will discover that worship becomes delightfully spontaneous, for the Holy Spirit, ungrieved, will be able to present God to the mind for contemplation in a hitherto undreamed-of way. He will also illumine to heart and mind that God-revealing Word which He has inspired.

FOR PRAYER: *Father, when I pray, may I not forget or ignore the help your Holy Spirit promises to give.*

March 25

CONTRASTING COVENANTS

By calling this covenant "new", he has made the first one obsolete. (Hebrews 8:13)

The writer has been contrasting the Old Covenant of law with the New Covenant of grace. The Old showed what man ought to do, but provided neither the disposition nor the power to do it. It demanded what it could not give. The New, on the contrary, gives all it demands.

The *Old* finally proved to man that he could not by himself keep God's law – a disillusioning revelation. The *New* was given to demonstrate what God can and will do in spite of our weakness, when we cast ourselves upon Him.

The *Old* was a system of human endeavours of works and ceremonies. The *New* was vital, springing from an inner Source.

The *Old* consisted of cold precepts whose key words were, "Thou shalt. Thou shalt not." The *New* was spontaneous. Obedience now could be not duty but delight. The key word was not "Thou shalt", but "I will".

The *Old* was written on stone tablets. The *New* was inscribed "on tablets of human hearts" (2 Cor. 3:3). Under its terms the desire and ability to do God's will are incorporated into man's inmost being. "I will put my laws in their hearts, and I will write them on their minds" (Heb. 10:16).

All that the Old Covenant demands, the New provides. Every defect in the Old, occasioned through the weakness of human nature, finds its remedy in the New, through the enabling Holy Spirit.

FOR PRAISE: *Through our union with Christ, we inherit the spiritual fulfilment of every promise made to Abraham's seed.* (See Gal. 3:29)

March 26

CAUTIONS IN GUIDANCE

"If anyone chooses to do God's will, he will find out . . ." (John 7:17)

We should beware of claiming infallibility in matters of guidance, although we may be confident that we have followed God's will. We are fallible creatures, and are prone to spiritual pride. Such expressions as, "The Lord told me to do so-and-so," should be avoided. Many criminals have used this expression. If it is true, the outcome will demonstrate that God did indeed tell us.

Even a direct answer to prayer, if our wills are biased in a certain direction, does not necessarily *by itself* indicate divine approval. Of Israel it was said, "He gave them their request, but sent leanness into their souls" (Ps. 106:15). Such guidance must be tested.

If our decision has been influenced by frustration or failure, we should be doubly careful before acting on it.

The voice of prejudice should not be confused with the voice of God. This is more frequently done than we may think. In his zeal in persecuting the Church, Paul was convinced that he was obeying God.

We should never be ashamed to own that we have mistaken our guidance when we have taken a wrong turning. It would be dishonouring to God to persist in attributing to Him a course of action which does not have His seal of approval. Even when the need seems most urgent, we should refuse to be hurried into decision before the green light appears.

FOR MEDITATION: *God's guidance will never contradict the principles of His Word.*

GUIDANCE IS INDIVIDUAL

I will instruct you and teach you in the way you should go; I will counsel you and watch over you. (Psalm 32:8)

In His guidance of our lives, God does not treat us as robots but as intelligent, responsible beings; not dealing with men in the mass, but having personal transactions with each. Since each person is distinctive and unique, *God has as many methods as He has men and women.* No detail of heredity or environment, of temperament or talent is left out of account.

Among young people especially, there is a tendency to indulge vain regrets that they are not like someone they admire, or to envy others who have gifts or advantages that are denied to them. Instead of setting about to discover and exercise their own distinctive talents, they try to reproduce some human model. This is a denial that God has a plan for each life.

The circumstances of each life are not accidental. They are designed by an all-wise Father, who has the highest interests of His children at heart. When this is understood and accepted, no detail of life is unimportant. Life is a long and romantic voyage of discovery. Trial and suffering are seen in a new light.

Had Philip delayed for one hour when God summoned him to leave Samaria and go to the desert, and argued the point, his path would never have crossed that of the Ethiopian minister of finance, and Ethiopia would have missed that early opportunity of hearing the gospel.

FOR ACTION: *Never dig up in unbelief what you have sown in faith.*

DUTY TO GOD AND SOCIETY

"Give to Caesar what is Caesar's, and to God what is God's." (Matthew 22:21)

The Pharisees and Herodians laid plans to trap Jesus, so they posed a question which they thought demanded a clear "yes" or "no" answer (vv.16,17). The Lord's masterful answer "hoisted them with their own petard".

When He asked for a coin, they produced a denarius on which was imprinted Caesar's image and inscribed with his name. In theory at any rate, God was King in Israel. Would Jesus declare Himself for the Jewish zealots who refused to pay the Roman tax, or for the collaborators with Rome?

If He aligned Himself with the former, they would charge Him with disloyalty to Caesar. If with the latter, He would lose favour with the crowd who hated the tax.

It seemed that Jesus was caught in a cleft stick, but His answer completely routed them: "Give to Caesar what is Caesar's and to God what is God's." This is a statement of an important principle. *The Christian has a dual responsibility* – first to his God and then to his country, but God must come before Caesar, and religion before politics.

By his astute answer, Jesus turned the tables on His enemies and exposed their deceit. He taught in the clearest terms that while we do have civil and national responsibilities, observation of them does not absolve us from our higher spiritual responsibilities to God.

FOR ACTION: *"Seek first His Kingdom and His righteousness, and all these things will be given to you as well."* (Matt. 6:33)

NO GATE-CRASHERS IN HEAVEN

*The king . . . noticed a man who was not wearing
wedding clothes . . . "Friend," he asked, "how did
you get in here without wedding clothes?"* (Matthew
22:11,12)

The details of this parable (vv.1–14) are true to oriental
custom. An initial invitation to a marriage feast would
be sent out, followed by a second as the hour drew near.
The symbolism of the marriage of the believer to Christ
appears in Romans 7:1–4, and again in Ephesians
5:23–32, where Christ is represented as loving the Church
as His bride. *The marriage supper of the Lamb* (Rev. 19:7–9)
is in the future, but this parable deals with the present.

The king sent messengers to invite guests to honour
his son, but the invitation was variously received. To the
first call, their attitude was indifferent and frivolous (v.3).
Some made light of it and followed their usual vocations
(v.5). Others were hostile and even killed his servants
(v.6), bringing judgment on their own heads (v.7).

The king was determined to have guests, so his
servants importuned both good and bad to come (v.10).

On entering, the king discovered a guest without the
required wedding garment, which was provided by the
host, and had him ejected (v.13). The guest's neglect was
culpable because he had failed to avail himself of the
provision freely made, and elected to appear in his own
garments.

*There is an absolute requirement for entrance into God's
Kingdom.* We must be clothed in Christ's righteousness,
imputed to us upon repentance and faith (Phil. 3:9).

FOR SELF-EXAMINATION: *There are garments of
mind and heart-reverence, expectation,
penitence. Do we often go into God's presence
without these garments?*

March 30

WHAT REALLY DEFILES

"What goes into a man's mouth does not make him 'unclean', but what comes out of his mouth, that is what makes him 'unclean'." (Matthew 15:10)

No wonder the Pharisees were shocked! Christ's revolutionary statement cut the very ground of their teaching from under their feet. If Jesus was right, then their whole religious system was wrong, a thought not to be tolerated.

They had probably vented their displeasure on the disciples, who voiced their concern to Jesus (v.12). Quite unconcerned, Jesus said in effect that the corrupt doctrine of these blind guides was doomed, and would ultimately be destroyed. The inevitable issue of their teaching is graphically depicted in verse 14.

Even the disciples did not fully grasp the Lord's meaning, and Peter asks for explanation. By a very simple illustration Jesus made His meaning clear. The real source of defilement is not what or how a man eats, but what comes out of his heart — that is spiritually defiling, for sinful words and acts spring from evil thoughts of an evil heart.

Christ's list of the sources of soul-pollution (v.19) commences with "evil thoughts". Then follow violations of the sixth, seventh, eighth and ninth commandments of the Decalogue. We cannot stop evil thoughts being injected into our minds, but we are under no obligation to extend hospitality to them.

It would be a revealing exercise to take Galatians 5:19–21, check our lives by it, and "put off" any of the sinful acts of which we find ourselves guilty.

FOR ACTION: *Take one of the lists of sins (Gal. 5:19–21 or Matt. 15:19) and check your life by it.*

NONE GREATER THAN JOHN

"Among those born of women there has not risen anyone greater than John the Baptist." (Matthew 11:11)

Jesus was warm in appreciation but sparing in eulogy. His "well done" was bestowed only on those who had done well. Yet He bestowed on John an eulogy such as He gave to no other. It has been said that if the worth of praise is measured by the lips from which it fell, then *no one was so praised as John*.

The tremendous stature of this austere man is not given the prominence in our preaching and teaching that it deserves.

In ancient times every king or high official has his *kawass* or forerunner, who preceded him to announce his coming. It was this office that John fulfilled for Christ. He was great not only in personal character, but in dignity of office. He was greater in having a more privileged position. He prepared for Christ's coming by calling the apostate nation to repentance, and enforcing the ethical demands of the law.

The statement, "Yet he who is least in the Kingdom of heaven is greater than he," is difficult. It obviously does not mean greater in intellect or nobility of soul, or in devotion. But he is *greater in privilege*. One suggestion is that, as a child on a hill can see further than a giant in the valley, so he who is least in a higher dispensation has advantages over him who is greatest in the lower one.

FOR SELF-EXAMINATION: *For what qualities of character could God eulogise me?*

April 1

AN EXPEDIENT DEPARTURE

"It is for your good that I am going away. Unless I go away, the Counsellor will not come to you." (John 16:7)

From our vantage point, it is not difficult to grasp the expediency of our Lord's departure, with the resulting gift of the Holy Spirit. But to the disciples it must have seemed incomprehensible. In what possible way could the spiritual presence of the Holy Spirit be preferred to the physical presence of the human Jesus? *How could Christ's absence from earth enrich them*?

In His earthly life Jesus was geographically limited by His body. He could not be in two places at once. When He was in Nazareth, Jerusalem was denied His comforting presence. At best His disciples' contact with Him was only occasional and His influence on them from without.

In contrast to this, when the Paraclete was given, they would exchange Christ's physical presence for His omnipresence. The Holy Spirit does not know the limitations of a human body, but is equally accessible to all God's people everywhere. Moreover, His is an internal, not an external influence.

Not until Jesus breathed on them and said, "Receive the Holy Spirit" (John 20:22), did the apprehensive disciples realise the joyous significance of their Master's enigmatical statement, "It is for your good that I am going away." No longer would they need His visible and bodily presence among them. They would have something better. The Divine Comforter had come to stay.

FOR THANKSGIVING: *Father, I thank You for the presence of the Holy Spirit on earth, mediating to us the presence of Christ.*

April 2

THE REVEALER OF CHRIST

"The Spirit of truth . . . will testify about me. And you also must testify . . . " (John 15:26)

The ministry of the Spirit is Christo-centric, therefore the test of any professed movement of the Spirit, whether in personal or corporate experience, is the place it gives to Christ. If it glorifies man or unduly magnifies some spiritual experience, it lacks the distinctive hallmark of the Spirit.

The function of the telescope is not to reveal itself, but to reveal the glories it brings into the range of vision. The ministry of the Spirit is to conceal Himself behind the scenes, and give prominence to Christ. As the Spirit of Christ, it is His delight to unveil His glories.

There is no rivalry within the unity of the Godhead. Each Person delights to serve the Other. Christ's passion was to glorify the Father. "I seek not my own glory," He said. His work had reached its zenith when He said, "I have glorified you on earth" (John 17:4).

The Spirit, in turn, is jealous for the glory of the Son. He cannot bear to see in a believer a cooling love for Him. The Spirit's primary concern is to glorify Christ, and to secure the acknowledgment and practical manifestation of His Lordship in our lives. We cannot see a person in a dark room, but let someone touch the switch and he stands revealed. Such is the Spirit's ministry.

FOR MEDITATION: *The purpose of the Holy Spirit in revealing the glories of Christ to us, is to kindle the desire to be like Him.*

THE GRAVITY OF SIN

*"He will convict the world of guilt in regard to sin
. . . because men do not believe in me."* (John 16:8,9)

A jury may convict of *crimes*, offences against man.
Conscience may convict of *sins*, acts of sin, but it is of
sin in the singular that the Holy Spirit convicts. To the
world, sin is an outward act, the breach of some law,
which is unfortunate but not necessarily culpable, so long
as it does not outrage local conventions.

"I don't see why God should be so hard on my
peccadilloes," said a man of the world. His outlook is
common. Christ's definition of sin differs radically from
that of society. He goes straight to the very heart of sin,
and affirms that the primary mission of the Paraclete is
to convince unregenerate men and women that the one
damning sin is failure to believe in Himself. Sin became
a new thing with His advent. "If I had not come and
spoken to them, they would not be guilty of sin. Now,
however, they have no excuse for their sin" (John 15:22).

To the non-Christian, unbelief in Christ seems a trifling
matter altogether out of proportion to the magnitude of
the results Scripture says accrue from it. But trivial though
it may seem, *unbelief is the parent of all sin*, and the Spirit
will present to the heart incontrovertible evidence that
this is so. The reception and believing of this evidence
will lead to eternal life, its rejection will lead to inevitable
judgement.

FOR MEDITATION: *The sinfulness of sin is seen in
the deep conviction that gripped holy men of old
when faced with God's holiness.*

THE WIND OF THE SPIRIT

"The wind blows where it pleases . . . So it is with everyone born of the Spirit." (John 3:8)

The literal meaning of the Hebrew word *ruach*, and its Greek equivalent *pneuma*, is "wind, breath". The Spirit is referred to under this figure in three connections.

His vivifying power is prominent in the vision of the valley of dry bones when through His agency the dry bones were transformed into a mighty organised army. (Ezek. 37:7–10).

In the discourse with Nicodemus, it is *His regenerative work* which is compared to the unpredictable and irresistible motions of the wind. "You hear its sound, but you cannot tell where it comes from or where it is going. So it is with everyone who is born of the Spirit."

The "sound like the blowing of a violent wind" that came from heaven, accompanying the descent of the Holy Spirit, indicated *His mighty yet unseen power*. The wind was heard but not felt. It was not a reality but a symbol. The literal translation would be, "a sound of a mighty blast borne along". It was an entirely supernatural sound, and not due to ordinary physical phenomena. So is the working of the Holy Spirit. His operations are like the secrecy and sovereignty of the wind.

> Come as the wind, with rushing sound
>   And Pentecostal grace,
> That all of woman born may see
>   The glory of Thy face.

FOR MEDITATION: *The symbols used of the Holy Spirit are impersonal, but they symbolise His personal activities in the world and in the Christian.*

April 5

THE FIRE OF THE SPIRIT

"He will baptise you with the Holy Spirit and with fire." (Matthew 3:11)

In Isaiah's prophecy the Holy Spirit is termed "the spirit of burning" (4:4 RSV), and of Christ it was prophesied, "He will baptise you with the Holy Spirit and with fire."

As an emblem of the Spirit, fire, the mightiest and most terrible of human forces, represents *the presence of the Triune God*. The climax of this representation was when "what seemed to be tongues of fire" rested on the disciples at Pentecost. These tongues of fire were symbols of aggressive Christianity. There was no actual fire. "They saw what seemed to be tongues of fire."

Fire symbolises also *the power of the Spirit*. John contrasted his cold baptism of repentance with the fiery baptism which the disciples of His Successor would receive. Just as the fiery sun is the source of power in the solar realm, so the Holy Spirit is in the moral and spiritual realm. The fire of the Spirit produces burning zeal and incandescent love in the hearts of those who yield to His influence.

As the Spirit of burning, *His purifying influence* is in view. Since He is the Spirit of holiness, He cannot tolerate sin in the believer whose body is His temple. His purging work aims to consume everything that is out of harmony with His divine nature.

> Come as the fire, and purge our hearts
>   Like sacrificial flame.
> Let our whole life an offering be
>   To our Redeemer's name.

FOR MEDITATION: *God reveals the purpose of the fire: "I will thoroughly purge away your dross, and remove all your impurities."* (Isa. 1:25)

CLOTHED WITH POWER

"Stay in the city until you have been clothed with power from on high." (Luke 24:49)

These were among the last recorded words of our Lord to His disciples. Just before His ascension He assured them, "You will receive power when the Holy Spirit comes on you" (Acts 1:8).

Without this divine empowering, one may have formed a definite purpose to engage in personal evangelism, possess a knowledge of Scripture, be very tactful and prayerful, and yet not be successful in winning men and women to Christ. With it the value of all training will be immeasurably enhanced.

From a study of the biographies of great men and women who have been singularly successful in this ministry, there emerges the fact that in almost every case there came a crisis, a new and more complete surrender to the Lordship of Christ, and a new enduement of the Spirit that equipped them for the task. They discovered that the Holy Spirit Himself was their power for service.

Observe the tremendous transformation evident in Peter's life after he had been so endued. He preached with a passion, a logic, a fearlessness and a convicting power to which he was previously a stranger. His words now left saving impressions on the minds of his hearers. We should seek and appropriate this enduement, without which our most earnest endeavours will prove abortive.

FOR MEDITATION: *Before Pentecost, the apostles made a minimal impression. After Pentecost, they "turned the world upside down". What is the message for us?*

THE MAN WHO MISSED DEATH

By faith Enoch was taken from this life, so that he did not experience death. (Hebrews 11:5)

"Enoch made a habit of walking with God." This familiar figure of speech pictures a close walk with God, reminiscent of the holy familiarity enjoyed by Adam and Eve in paradise. He had not always walked with God, and it appears that the transforming experience was in some way connected with the birth of his son, Methuselah. God can use the cradle as well as the casket to awaken a sense of the reality of the eternal.

Enoch's intimacy with God over a period of three hundred years assures us of three things:

An unbroken walk with God is possible *in the midst of an unholy environment*. Jude's four times use of "ungodly" (Jude 14–15) affords a glimpse into the contemporary world of Enoch. Yet in this context, "Enoch pleased God."

His walk with God was *his own free choice*. He was not pressured into it. It was not God who walked the way Enoch was going, but the reverse.

His walk took him *in the same direction as God*. "Can two walk together except they be agreed?" asked Amos. Had Enoch not fully accepted God's will, the walk would have been of short duration. Jude's brief paragraph indicates how deeply Enoch had embraced God's viewpoint.

Small wonder that there was an unusual ending to the story. "By faith Enoch was translated that he should not see death."

FOR MEDITATION: *Am I imitating Enoch in his walking with God, or am I unconscious of His presence in my daily walk?*

April 8

A PSYCHOLOGIST'S DESPAIR

[Isaac said] "Who is it?" Jacob said to his father, "I am Esau your firstborn." (Genesis 27:18,19)

The warped character of Jacob provides an appropriate background for the display of God's grace, and for the revelation of His attitude towards the weakest of His children. If God chose only the strong, the noble, the brilliant for His service, the majority of us Christians would be disqualified. When Paul wrote: "God chose the foolish things ... the weak ... the lowly ... the despised ... so that no one may boast before him" (1 Cor. 1:27–29), he could have been justifying God for His choice of Jacob to be progenitor of the Chosen Race.

Jacob was no callow youth but a middle-aged man when he filched Esau's birthright. He was past middle life when he cheated him of his blessing. He was a mature man who had persisted in his duplicity for half a lifetime. Psychologists would affirm that it was almost impossible for his character to be radically changed at such a late hour.

But *God is not the prisoner of His own psychological laws.* He does not despair of us even when we despair of ourselves. His patience is never at an end, His resources never exhausted.

He stooped to associate Himself with one of the least attractive of the race, whom He addressed as "thou worm Jacob" (Isa. 41:14), and of him He made Israel, a prince, having "power with God and men" (Gen. 32:28).

FOR PRAYER: *Lord, deliver me from the Jacob qualities in my character, and change me as You changed him.*

April 9

A GOSPEL OF RECOVERY

God said to Jacob, "Go up to Bethel . . . and build an altar there to God who appeared to you when you were fleeing from your brother." (Genesis 35:1)

There is no fundamental difference between one man and another — it is only the incidence of temptation that is different. Most have the common experience of failure in the face of temptations such as pride, ambition, money or sex. The same flaw of character pursues them through life like a bloodhound.

To such the devil brings *a message of despair*, that the future can never be better than the past. But in the typical life of Jacob, God is preaching *a gospel of recovery*. The laws of heredity are not the highest laws. The laws of psychology are not unbreakable to the God who made them.

The God of Jacob is the God of the second chance to the Christian who has failed. But the second — or twenty-second — chance does not necessarily avert the temporal consequences of past sin and failure; but even that failure can be a stepping-stone to new victories. God wastes nothing, even failure; it can have an important educative value.

The supreme lesson of Jacob's unhappy story is that *no failure need be final*. No failure puts the possibility of victory out of reach. When God has saved and apprehended a man or a woman, He pursues them with undiscourageable perseverance, with the sole purpose of blessing them.

FOR PRAISE: *I praise that the Hound of Heaven has pursued me with relentless feet, and saved me from a spoiled life.*

UNDISCOURAGED PERSEVERANCE

The potter formed it into another pot, shaping it as seemed best to him. (Jeremiah 18:4)

God's educative dealings with Jacob afford a glowing example of His undiscouraged perseverance with an unlovely character. Though there was little in Jacob to merit it, God lavished on him an unwearied but uncompromising love. Through all the shady and despicable actions that debased his life, that love was unabating, but never condoned or tolerated his sin.

For many years Jacob was allowed to pursue the path he had chosen, learning the bitter lessons of human independence, and the costliness of "going it alone". At last, he manoeuvred himself in to the final crisis God had been preparing for him.

Jacob's life illustrates not so much the perseverance of the saints, as the perseverance of God. But for the latter the former would be impossible. Though the nation of Israel baulked and thwarted Him at every turn, He persisted in His disciplines until His purpose of blessing for all families of earth was realised through them.

God knows no unfinished task. Paul confirmed this in glowing words: "Being confident of this, that he who began a good work in you, will carry it on to completion" (Phil. 1:3). Christian experience, too, is replete with evidence of the tenacity and patience of God's everlasting love.

The work began when first your prayer was uttered,
And God will finish what He has begun.

FOR MEDITATION: *God's grace and mercy are so magnificent that we could presume on them instead of being humbled by them.*

April 11

THE TEST OF PROSPERITY

The Lord was with Joseph and he prospered. (Genesis 39:2)

The story of Joseph's elevation from a prison cell to the most responsible position in the world of his day, reads like a romance. The King made him ruler of Egypt. The gift of his signet ring marked the bestowal of legal authority. The linen garments were those worn by the nobility. Less than thirty years old, Joseph had risen as high as he could go. *He found that godliness did pay.*

Not every man can carry a full cup. Sudden elevation often leads to a sudden fall. Would Joseph survive the test of prosperity? Though still young, his trials had developed a maturity, a poise, a stability which only tested faith can impart. His moral and spiritual equilibrium remained undisturbed. The disciplines of the hidden years had not been wasted. He resisted the temptation to pride and arrogance. It was a different sin he was fighting, less volcanic and more subtle, but still a sin against God.

Now at last he could see the unfolding of the hitherto hidden plan of God. The links in the chain of providence became clearer. His spirit had been tempered in the fires of testing. He now possessed strength for his great task. He saw the hand of God in it all, and expressed it when he said to his brothers: *"You intended to harm me, but God intended it for good"* (Gen. 50:20).

FOR SELF-EXAMINATION: *Has prosperity changed my set of values and dulled the edge of my witness?*

April 12

THE TEST OF ALLUREMENT

She spoke to Joseph day after day. (Genesis 39:10)

Sexual attraction is perhaps the strongest lure of mankind. It is both test and temptation – it makes or breaks a man or woman.

At the age of twenty-seven, Joseph was in the full flush of youthful virility. Suddenly he found himself facing the most subtle yet volcanic temptation of his life. The circumstances were exquisitely difficult for virtue, and tragically easy for moral licence. It seemed as though everything had conspired to make sin easy and resistance next to impossible.

He was a slave living in a polluted society. The amoral wife of Potiphar was greatly attracted to this handsome and intelligent young man and used all her seductions to lure him into immorality. Herself a slave to sin, she craved to drag another down with her.

The temptation gathered strength because it was *totally unexpected* and came from an unexpected quarter. There was *favourable opportunity*, no other men in the house. It was repeated daily.

Here was a wonderful chance of advancement from his menial position. Joseph shut his eyes to worldly advantage and clung to moral principle. To his temptress he said, "How could I do such a wicked thing *and sin against God*?" (v.9). He gained final victory by taking to his heels and escaping from the zone of temptation. The lesson is, *"Kill the serpent, don't stroke it."*

FOR PRAYER: *Father, in this polluted world, keep me from adopting its agenda and accepting its standards.*

April 13

THE TEST OF AMBITION

Abram said . . . "I will accept nothing belonging to you, not even a thread or the thong of a sandal."
(Genesis 14:22–23)

Abraham was subjected to a succession of tests in God's training school, one of which is faced by most who desire to be the best for God.

The test of worldly ambition. Many who have survived other tests, have succumbed to this one. Genesis 14 records a battle of eastern kings. It was no mere tribal squabble, but a battle on a considerable scale. Abraham's nephew Lot and his family were carried away with the people of Sodom. When Abraham heard this, he assembled his 318 servants and set off in pursuit of the marauding armies. In a daring night attack, they routed the unsuspecting army and rescued the captives.

Here was a unique opportunity for Abraham to gratify his ambition. He had conquered four kings, and under ancient customs of war he would have been allowed to retain all persons and property he had captured. But the man of faith refused to capitalise on the victory, which was not his but God's. He firmly renounced both prestige and possessions which were rightfully his.

"I have raised my hand to the Lord God most High, Creator of heaven and earth, and have taken an oath that I will accept nothing belonging to you . . . so that you will never be able to say, 'I have made Abraham rich'" (vv.22–24).

This detachment from worldly ambition brought an immediate response from God – the promise of the longed-for son (15:1,4).

FOR ACTION: *Check the motivation of your ambition and see if it is genuinely Christ-centred.*

April 14

A MAN OF FAITH AND FAILURE

Now there was a famine in the land, and Abram went down to Egypt to live there for a while because the famine was severe. (Genesis 12:10)

This man of faith was a man of failures too — very far from perfect. While the flaws in his character are to be neither condoned nor emulated, they do afford encouragement to one who desires to be of service to God and man even though conscious of his own frailty. They give assurance that God is willing to use ordinary men and women in His service.

Abraham's life was marred by ignoble falls. His faith was sometimes chequered with doubt. The treasure was there, but in an earthen vessel. God was able to use him because these failures were incidental and not fundamental to his life. If he stumbled from the pathway of faith, God drew him back; and he always responded.

His failures were in four areas. The first, *through unexpected adversity*. When famine threatened, instead of trusting God, he went down to Egypt. The second had its source in *ties of kinship*. He was told to leave his kindred, but he did not obey. The third stemmed from *craven fear*. He stooped to deceit and falsehood to protect himself. The fourth, the birth of Ishmael, arose from *God's protracted delay* in giving the promised son.

It is significant that *each failure was in the very quality which later became his strong point*. Abraham teaches that there is always a way back from failure.

FOR ENCOURAGEMENT: *God can use even our failures to make us more dependent on Him.*

April 15

UNDER SEALED ORDERS

By faith Abraham, when called . . . obeyed and went, even though he did not know where he was going. (Hebrews 11:8)

Abraham's spiritual development proceeded in stages. A graph of his life would not be unlike our cost-of-living index — mounting sharply, a short dip, and then mounting to a still higher point. But there was overall advance. So it is with the line of growth of a soul. In Abraham's case, the points of sharp progress were the outcome of a fresh revelation of God under a new name which revealed some new facet of His being.

His obedience to God's call was the expression of his faith in Him. So sure was he of God's trustworthiness, that he responded without hesitation or argument. The absoluteness of his faith was staggering. He went out, not knowing where he was going. Faith never knows where it is being led, or it would not be faith. *True faith is content to travel under sealed orders.*

His initial step of obedience lengthened out into a walk of faith and blessing. God's call does not come only to the young. Abraham was over seventy years of age when the call came. Ties of home and kindred are more easily severed in adventurous youth than in the maturity of age, when ease and security are so attractive. Abraham boldly ventured on God and left the results to Him. He may be calling the reader to some such step of faith.

FOR MEDITATION: *God's call to service does not come only in youth. Is He calling me to some new step of faith?*

April 16

WHEN JESUS COOKED THE BREAKFAST

When they landed, they saw a fire of burning coals there with fish on it, and some bread. (John 21:9)

We are here presented with an entirely normal and natural breakfast scene, set on the seashore. And yet it was unique in history – a divine COOK!

When the disciples reached the shore with their huge catch of fish, they discovered that Jesus had lit a fire to warm them and a meal to refresh them. Ever after they would remember the morning when their breakfast was cooked by the risen Lord of glory. Fish was already cooking when they arrived, but He used some of their miraculous haul to supplement what He had prepared.

Despite their monster catch, the net was not torn. The gifts of God exceed what we can receive, yet they never burst the vessel we offer. If we want a spiritual application of the event, we could adopt William Barclay's suggestion that the net stands for the Church. There is room in the Church for all men and women of all nations.

In the Franciscan chapel by the Sea of Galilee which commemorates this incident, the altar is a natural slab of rock in the form of a low table, called the Table of Christ. Beside the church a flight of steps leads to a beach where a boat could be dragged on to the sand. In some such place, Jesus cooked the breakfast.

FOR EMULATION: *The Lord of glory stooped to perform menial tasks. Why should I have reservations when asked to do the same?*

April 17

COMMISSIONED AND ENDUED

"As the Father has sent me, I am sending you . . ."
He breathed on them and said, "Receive the Holy
Spirit." (John 20:21,22)

The disciples had heard that Jesus had risen, but they had not seen Him in His resurrection body. Paralysed with fear of the religious leaders, they cowered behind closed doors.

Suddenly Jesus appeared and took His appropriate place in their midst. It requires no vivid imagination to picture the effect on the disciples.

His first words were calculated to allay their fears: "Peace be with you." He then confirmed their feeble faith by presenting tangible and visible evidence of His true identity and the continuing nature of His humanity. "He showed them his hands and side" (v.20). There, before their eyes, were the incontrovertible marks of His crucifixion. Note that the record makes it clear that it was the *actual body* of Christ, not only the Spirit of Christ that appeared to them. It was a physical resurrection.

Jesus then commissioned each for service in the most personal terms (v.21). He now sent them in the same manner, for the same purpose and with the same empowering.

Next, Jesus performed a significant symbolic act. "He breathed on them and said, 'Receive the Holy Spirit'" (v.22). He gave them a foretaste of Pentecost, an experience that helped them through the waiting days until the full outpouring came. *He breathed out* – imparted – the Spirit. *They must breathe in* – appropriate – the Spirit. This has been termed the Johannine Pentecost.

FOR MEDITATION: *The primary purpose of the enduement of the Spirit is for witness to Christ (Acts 1:8), not for personal enjoyment.*

April 18

THE DOUBTER BELIEVES

"Unless I see the nail marks in his hands . . . I will not believe." . . . *Thomas said to him, "My Lord and my God!"* (John 20:25,28)

The Scripture record depicts Thomas as having a marked tendency to doubt and despondency, but coupled with a deep devotion to Christ (John 11:16; 14:5). His nature was set in a minor key. It *would* be Thomas who was absent when the Lord appeared! Good things always happened to other people. Do you know people like Thomas?

But we must be fair to him. Was he not simply demanding evidence that others had already been granted? It has been said that he was a disbeliever rather than a real doubter. He did not absolutely refuse to accept the fact of the resurrection, but demanded incontrovertible evidence of it.

The Lord's next appearance a week later was especially for Thomas. That Jesus knew what Thomas had said is clear from the invitation He extended (v.27). How gracious He was to condescend to His disciple's defective faith.

Thomas discerned in the Lord's words the implication of His deity. His doubts were quelled, and he did not accept the invitation. Instead, he burst out in his magnificent confession: "My Lord and my God!" He was as whole-hearted in his belief as he had been in his disbelief. He was completely satisfied with the evidence.

It is striking that it was Thomas the doubter who finally made the most complete confession of Christ's deity.

FOR MEDITATION: *The Lord will meet and satisfy the honest doubter, but will not tolerate unbelief.*

April 19

THE GENUINE VINE

"I am the true vine . . . you are the branches." (John 15:1,5)

In the Old Testament, Israel is called a "choice vine" (Isa. 5:2). But her abject failure to realise the divine ideal led the Master to claim that He alone was the true, the genuine vine. The vine functions through its branches, which He identified as believers.

It must be borne in mind that in this parable, Jesus was speaking of fruitfulness, not salvation. The wood of the vine is notoriously useless except for one purpose – bearing fruit. If it fails to do this, removal is inevitable.

So failure to abide in Christ is the cause of fruitlessness, and results in the branch being cast out and burned. Failure to abide does not result in loss of salvation, but it does mean a wasted life (v.6). But note that for a maximum yield even the fruitful vine requires pruning.

What does it mean to abide in Christ? It involves keeping in unbroken contact with Him, keeping the channel of communication open, constantly depending on and trusting Him.

Bishop Ryle paraphrases it: "Cling to Me. Stick fast to Me. Get nearer and nearer to Me. Roll every burden on Me. Cast your whole weight on Me." If the aperture through which the sap flows becomes blocked, the fruit-producing liquid cannot get through. The secret of our Lord's incredibly fruitful life was His unbroken contact and fellowship with His Father.

FOR PRAYER: *Lord, may I not shrink from the pruning knife whose radical cutting produces more fruit.*

April 20

AN ENACTED PARABLE

[Jesus] took off his outer clothing, and wrapped a towel around his waist. After that, he poured water into a basin and began to wash his disciples' feet. (John 13:5)

In the act of washing His disciples' feet, a very menial service, Jesus portrayed His whole career in a single act. Its significance is highlighted by the fact that He did it in the full consciousness of His Deity (v.3). He was not too great to condescend to the lowliest service for His own.

The symbolism is clear. As He now rose from supper, laid aside His garments and girded Himself with a towel, so He had risen from heaven's lofty throne, divested Himself of His robes of majesty, and in His descent to earth littered space with the glories He laid aside.

He wrapped Himself with the towel of our humanity. Just as He poured cleansing water into the basin to wash His disciples' dirty feet, so He was soon to pour His cleansing blood into the basin of the cross, to purge our defiled hearts. He did it because He loved His men and because He had taken "the very nature of a servant".

Loyal but impulsive Peter saw the incongruity of what was taking place, and refused to permit such an outrage. He said, "You shall never never wash my feet!" How like Peter we are! We would rather remain dirty than humbly confess our sin and allow Jesus to cleanse us. Peter had to learn that continued fellowship with Christ involved a daily cleansing.

FOR EMULATION: *"I have set you an example that you should do as I have done for you."* (John 13:15)

April 21

NEVER! NEVER!

"I give them eternal life, and they shall never perish; no-one can snatch them out of my hand." (John 10:28)

The Lord had told the Pharisees that they did not believe because they were not His sheep (v.26). Then He outlined the characteristics and privileges of those who were His sheep. They are sensitive to His voice and obedient to Him. They experience eternal life and are assured of eternal security (vv.27,28). But because of their obdurate unbelief, the Pharisees knew nothing of this.

The Lord's assurance, "They shall never perish," brings the utmost comfort to the genuine believer. Had He not promised eternal life to His sheep? He then asserted that the promise carries with it the most inclusive assurance. "They shall *never, never* perish," is the sense of the Greek construction. In English a double negative is a positive, but *in Greek it becomes a stronger negative*. They will never, never, be banished from God's presence.

The voice of the verb in "They shall never perish" gives the sense, "They shall not destroy themselves." No man can snatch us out of Christ's hand. And "No one can snatch them out of my Father's hand" (v.29).

How secure we are! We can rest in Paul's inspired and assuring words: "Neither death, nor life, neither angels nor demons . . . nor any powers . . . will be able to separate us from the love of God that is in Christ Jesus our Lord" (Rom. 8:38,39).

FOR PRAISE: *The Good Shepherd not only leads and provides in the present, but also keeps and protects till the end.*

April 22

GOD'S TIMETABLE

"The right time for me has not yet come; for you any time is right." (John 7:6)

In spite of their living in the presence of a perfect life, the Lord's brothers failed to see in Jesus the promised Messiah. They credited him with power to work miracles (vv.3,4) but utterly misunderstood His mission.

They suggested that He was too modest and should "promote" Himself more. It was one thing for Him to dazzle the credulous Galileans, but He should make a name for Himself by convincing the sophisticated people of Jerusalem. He would never establish His prestige by hiding His gifts in a corner (v.4).

Jesus answered their cynical challenge by asserting that He would reveal Himself when the time was ripe. He never allowed anyone to interfere with His timetable. "My time" signifies "the appropriate moment". His timetable had been planned by His Father, and there was an appropriate moment for every action.

His brothers' movements were undisciplined and had no spiritual motivation, but He would choose the right moment to go to Jerusalem. His objective was not personal aggrandisement, but to do God's will at God's time. There was no duplicity in His answer: "You go to the Feast. I am not yet going . . . because for me the right time has not yet come" (v.8). He would depart at God's time, not theirs.

FOR SELF-EXAMINATION: *Are we equally careful to discover and keep God's timetable?*

April 23

CHRIST THE CHARMER

"No-one ever spoke the way this man does." (John 7:46)

The winsomeness of Christ's character and the forceful-ness of His teaching rendered neutrality concerning Him impossible. People were compelled to take sides for or against Him.

The officers sent to arrest Him found themselves powerless to stretch out a hand to take Him – a strange experience for them. They were charmed and over-awed by His gracious words and deportment. Surely this must be more than a man! "No-one ever spoke the way this man does," they said with bated breath.

Never had they seen such a blending of majesty and humility. But when they offered the Pharisees this strange reason for not arresting Him, the rulers were enraged. In scorn they suggested that Jesus had cast a spell over them.

With biting sarcasm they asked whether any Pharisee had succumbed to His charms (v.48). They were too clever to yield to His wiles! Only ignorant fools would be so credulous. They vented their spite on the crowds. Ignorant rabble!

The bigotry and arrogance of the supposed religious leaders were never more evident than in this vitriolic tirade – *and all because Jesus was charming*, because there was the ring of deity in His words. Their denunciation of the crowds who flocked to hear Him, only revealed their own spiritual bankruptcy.

FOR ASPIRATION:
> O Jesus, Jesus, dearest Lord,
> Forgive me if I say
> For very love Thy sacred name
> A thousand times a day.

April 24

A PESSIMIST'S PREDICAMENT

> *"Sir, I have no-one to help me into the pool when the
> water is stirred . . . someone else goes down ahead of
> me."* (John 5:7)

The Pool of Bethesda was a famous mineral spa to which
the sick and crippled, lured by its reputed curative
properties, resorted in great numbers. The pool was fed
by an intermittent spring, and this gave rise to the belief
that an angel periodically stirred the waters. Among the
unfortunate people was a pessimistic paralytic. Thirty-
eight years of frustrated hopes had reduced him to a state
of chronic pessimism.

At the pool it was a case of every man for himself, and
someone else always reached the pool ahead of him at
the propitious moment.

The Lord's first words were a challenge to his will. "Do
you want to get well?" The question sounded almost
cynical, but the Lord discerned that the man had lost all
hope. The Great Physician knew His case. The paralytic
was as hopeless psychologically as physically, and the
Lord moved healing into the realm of the will. In His
radiant presence, hope revived and faith was rekindled.

Jesus said, "Pick up your mat and walk!" To his
amazed delight the man discovered that Jesus was able
to restore his atrophied muscles. When his will was linked
to Christ's power, he received strength.

The man's condition finds its counterpart in those
whose wills have been paralysed by sin.

FOR WARNING: *Undue pessimism can easily
develop into actual unbelief. No pessimist makes
a good leader.*

April 25

CHAIN REACTION

The first thing Andrew did was to find his brother Simon and tell him, "We have found the Messiah." (John 1:41)

When two of John the Baptist's disciples perceived that Jesus and not John the Baptist was central in God's purpose, they left John and followed Jesus (v.37). As with most of us, Andrew and John followed Jesus because someone had been a faithful witness. It proved characteristic of Andrew that his first impulse was to share what proved to be the greatest discovery of the ages (v.41). He had to search for his brother, and each time we later meet him in the Gospels, he is bringing someone to Jesus (John 6:8,9; 12:20–23). It has been suggested that Andrew's finding Peter, who later became leader of the apostolic band, was as great a service to the Church as any man ever performed.

When Jesus met Peter, He subjected him to searching scrutiny. His discerning eye saw in the loving, impulsive and volatile fisherman, qualities of character and potential for service unsuspected by others. His play on Peter's name was not a joke, but both appraisal and prophecy (v.42).

Cephas was the Aramaic equivalent of *Peter*. The Greek word *petra* signifies a massive ledge of rock, not a pebble or stone. In calling Peter "Mr Rock", Jesus was assuring him that though he was now fickle and unstable, under His moulding hand, he would develop a rock-like character. And he did!

FOR CHALLENGE: *Have I been as diligent in bringing my relatives to Christ as was Andrew?*

April 26

MULTI-RACIAL AND SUPRA-NATIONAL

> *In the church at Antioch there were prophets and teachers: Barnabas, Simeon . . . Lucius . . . Manaen . . . and Saul.* (Acts 13:1)

One of the distinctive characteristics of the Church at Antioch which set the world on fire was that it was both multi-racial and supra-national. It was a church which in many ways was a prototype for the centuries ahead.

Christians of our day are probably perforce more sensitive to racial issues than those of any era since the first century. The world has become a global village. Widespread racial ferment throughout the world has thrown into stark relief both the justified resentments and the unwarranted arrogance of various segments of the human race. Unfortunately the Church has not emerged with a stainless record in this respect. The Antioch church accepted the revealed fact that "from one man God made every nation of men, that they should inhabit the whole earth" (Acts 17:26).

The cosmopolitan stance of this church was reflected in its leadership. Barnabas hailed from Cyprus. Simeon and Lucius were black men from Africa. Manaen was of Hebrew or Edomite stock. Saul came from Tarsus in Cilicia.

With such racially representative leadership, the old Jewish exclusiveness had little chance to rear its ugly head. They were determined that no differences of national status or culture would be allowed to mar their unity in Christ. We may well emulate their example in our churches.

FOR SELF-EXAMINATION: *Are there remnants of unwarranted racial prejudice and national superiority lingering in my heart?*

April 27

THE PERIL OF COMPROMISE

Certain men came from James . . . But when they arrived, [Peter][7] began to . . . separate himself from the Gentiles because he was afraid of those who belonged to the circumcision group. (Galatians 2:12)

It was not long after Pentecost before Satan launched his attack on the infant Church. The apostles were thrown into prison, James was executed, and Christians experienced opposition from all quarters. Nevertheless the Church grew and flourished.

A little later in history the adversary changed his tactics and substituted subtle compromise for open opposition. The Church succumbed to the new popularity accorded to it, and little by little lost the keen edge of its witness. It became popular to be a Christian; Christianity became the national religion and the Church lost its distinctive message.

The greatest danger in our western churches comes not from persecution, for that might well do us good, but from the temptation to compromise with Satan and the world. Compromise means to gain something by making concessions – often of principle. For example, I say, "If you will give me such and such, I will not press such and such a point." But a compromise always means that something has been given away – and usually something important.

Many Christians are trying to discover the golden mean between two extremes – worldliness on the one hand and surrender to God on the other. But Scripture concedes no middle path between worldliness and full consecration to Christ, for they are mutually exclusive.

FOR PRAYER: *Lord, give me wisdom in making decisions lest unwittingly I am led into compromise.*

April 28

A MISSIONARY MAGAZINE

*They gathered the church together and reported all that
God had done through them.* (Acts 14:27)

In essence, the New Testament is the record of a
remarkable missionary movement. The Book of Acts is
simply a missionary magazine, embodying, under the
guidance of the Holy Spirit, the philosophy and history
of mission. It is full of typical scenes and experiences that
were to be repeated down the centuries. It reports failures
as realistically as successes.

Almost all the writers were themselves *missionaries
living under a totalitarian regime*, and the last book was
penned in a concentration camp. The pressures and
stresses that are being experienced by Christians in many
lands in our own day, were all too familiar to the early
Christians.

Because of the exclusive claims of Christianity, the
Church must of necessity be missionary in character. If
as it claims, Christianity is the only true religion, then
it must be self-communicating.

This was the unique characteristic of the first New
Testament church to come near the divine ideal – the
church at Antioch. It was not a church that *had* a
missionary society, but a church that *was* itself a
missionary society. The whole church was involved in
the enterprise.

As the Book of Acts covers about thirty years, it would
seem that God desired, at the very beginning of the
Christian era, to demonstrate what He could do in one
generation through obedient men and women.

FOR PRAYER: *Lord, grant that our generation may
not fail You in Your global missionary purpose.*

PAUL'S PERSONAL HANDICAPS

"His letters are weighty and forceful, but in person he is unimpressive, and his speaking amounts to nothing." (2 Corinthians 10:10)

Many missionary leaders would gladly welcome many of the advantages Paul enjoyed. But these advantages were probably more than counterbalanced by the severe handicaps under which he had to work.

More often than not, he had no suitable place in which to preach. Before long he was regarded as a dangerous trouble-maker and the synagogues were closed to him. In order to support himself, and sometimes others too, he had to toil night and day. The wonder is that he found time for effective gospel witness.

He apparently suffered the handicap of being far from impressive physically. "Some say," he wrote, "his letters are weighty and forceful, but in person he is unimpressive."

In an apocryphal writing, *The Acts of Paul and Hecla*, there is the only pen-portrait of Paul extant. In it the apostle is described as "small in size, with meeting eyebrows, with a rather large nose, bald-headed, bow-legged, strongly built, full of grace, for at times he looked like a man, and at times he had the face of an angel".

Though not cast in a herculean mould, Paul displayed incredible stamina, for throughout his ministry bodily suffering, pain and discomfort were routine.

FOR MEDITATION: *Despite his unimpressive physique, the fact that the people at Lystra called Paul "Hermes" (the messenger of the gods) was an impressive tribute to his persuasive speech.*

April 30

ZEAL FOR GOD

"I was thoroughly trained in the law . . . and was just as zealous for God as any of you are today." (Acts 22:3)

Like his Master, Paul was whole-hearted and zealous in all his work for God. As the Lord's family observed His intense zeal, they "went to take charge of Him, for they said 'He is out of his mind'" (Mark 3:21).

King Festus said the same of Paul. "Festus interrupted his defence. 'You are out of your mind, Paul!' he shouted. 'Your great learning is driving you insane'" (Acts 26:24). The worldly mind equates zeal for God with insanity, but in God's sight, it is the highest form of wisdom.

Paul's former intensity carried over into his Christian life, but the Spirit directed it into new and vastly productive channels. The word "zeal" refers to something within that "boils up" – the enthusiasm that irresistibly bubbles up in the heart.

In this quality Paul sought to emulate his Lord. A perusal of his letters reveals that the ideal he cherished for his converts was *a mind aflame with the truth of God, a heart ablaze with the love of God and a will fired with a passion for the glory of God*.

It was the absence of these qualities that brought our Lord's solemn words to the Laodicean church (Rev. 3:14–22). But no such charge could be laid at Paul's door. It is the zealous, enthusiastic leader who most deeply influences his followers.

FOR ASPIRATION: *Lord, I would respond to Paul's injunction: "Never be lacking in zeal, but keep your spiritual fervour."* (Rom. 12:11).

HANNAH – WORDLESS PRAYER

Hannah was praying in her heart and her lips were moving but her voice was not heard. (1 Samuel 1:13)

Strong spiritual leaders often have strong praying mothers. It is not mere coincidence that Bible history frequently records the ancestry of its great men. *Praying Samuels come from praying Hannahs.* Indeed, Samuel was the direct creation of Hannah's wordless prayer.

The traditional shame of her childlessness was crushing her spirit. Her rival, Elkanah's other wife, "provoked her in order to irritate her" (v.6). Tried beyond endurance, she went to the temple and poured out her heart to a listening God. Eli the priest mistook her inarticulate grief for inebriation, and chided her. She protested that her trouble was grief of heart. Some prayers affect us too deeply for formal articulation.

Hannah's prayer was accompanied by a vow. "If you will give me a son . . . then I will give him to the Lord for all the days of his life" (v.11). Now it is not wordless praying!

She kept her promise, and as soon as Samuel was weaned, she presented him to the Lord for life.

Small wonder that Samuel's early life spent in the company of his praying mother made him a man whose ministry was bathed in prayer.

FOR CHALLENGE: *How often do I, like Hannah, ask God for the seemingly impossible?*

May 2

MOSES – STEADFASTNESS IN PRAYER

His hands remained steady till sunset. (Exodus 17:12)

"The Amalekites came and attacked the Israelites . . . Joshua overcame the Amalekite army" (vv.8,13). Between these cryptic sentences stands a third: "I will stand on top of the hill with the staff of God in my hands" (v.9), Moses said.

Here is a pictorial presentation of God's missionary strategy – chosen men interlocked with the foe in the valley, a chosen man exercising his authority in prayer. No contact was apparent between the two groups, yet their functions were inextricably linked. In the fluctuations of battle, the key to victory was in the hands, not of the fighters on the field, but of the intercessor on the hill.

Prayer is more potent than armies. It was the weaponless hands of prayer that controlled the issues of battle. "As long as Moses held up his hands, the Israelites were winning, but whenever he lowered his hands, the Amalekites were winning" (v.11).

Holding aloft our hands in prayer can be exhausting work. The inactivity of praying on the hill is a greater test of spiritual stamina than battling in the valley.

When Moses' hands grew heavy, his two octogenarian friends held them up. When he could no longer stand, he sat. *He must not fail Joshua in the valley.* Joshua must fight as though there were no uplifted rod on the hill. Moses must pray as though there were no drawn sword in the valley.

FOR CHALLENGE: *The issue of many a spiritual battle in a distant land lies in the hands of intercessors at home.*

EPAPHRAS – WRESTLING IN PRAYER

Epaphras . . . is always wrestling in prayer for you.
(Colossians 4:12)

Epaphras, Paul's fellow-prisoner, cherished an intense solicitude for the Christians at his native Colosse, and the neighbouring Lycus Valley. ''From my own observation,'' Paul wrote, ''I can tell you that he has a real passion for your welfare.''

Prison walls could not restrain the flight and freedom of the soul of this spiritual giant. Denied personal contact with his loved flock, he could still exercise on their behalf the most potent of all ministries. His concern for their spiritual advancement expressed itself in agonizing prayer – for that is the very word used. No mere passive and benevolent desire, this praying. He took it seriously.

The picture is of a perspiring wrestler straining every muscle, summoning every last ounce of strength as he contends in the games. Epaphras prayed to the point of exhaustion – *''always''* wrestling for you''.

His prayers were not concerned with the trivial. As he prayed, his soul soared in aspiration for his friends. He prayed that they might stand without wavering in the face of seduction and opposition – no easy task in a licentious pagan city. He pleaded for their spiritual maturity, that they might go on to perfection, standing perfect and complete. He asked that they might have spiritual discernment and conviction.

It was Epaphras' kneeling that kept the Colossians standing.

FOR MEDITATION: *When God plans to send revival blessing, He lays a burden on the hearts of those who make themselves available to Him.*

May 4

NEHEMIAH – EJACULATORY PRAYER

The king said to me, "What is it you want?" Then I prayed . . . and I answered the king. (Nehemiah 2:4–5)

True patriot that he was, Nehemiah's heart was deeply distressed at the desolation of his beloved Zion. Like other spiritual men, he turned his heart burden into prayer. "I wept . . . and prayed." And what a model prayer it was, combining adoration, confession, argument and petition (1:5–11). The sheer impossibility of his desire being granted – leave of absence from the side of a despotic tyrant for four months – did not daunt his faith. He was sure of God.

God can never resist faith. As Nehemiah prayed, God worked in the King's heart, and suddenly the prayed-for opportunity came (2:1–6). Between the king's unexpected question and Nehemiah's daring request, he found time for ejaculatory prayer – "So I prayed . . ." He was granted leave, and full provision for the expedition. Prayer had invaded the realm of the impossible.

Nehemiah's plan of campaign for the restoration of the city wall was simple. *He prayed as he worked and worked as he prayed.* "So I prayed . . . so we rebuilt the wall." Did his enemies mock and hinder? He uttered an ejaculatory prayer and kept on building (4:4–6). Did they threaten attack? "We made prayer and set a watch."

Prayer was no substitute for earnest endeavour and prudent preparation, and work was no hindrance to prayer. He did not reserve his prayers for special occasions. They pervaded all occasions. Practise ejaculatory prayer!

FOR MEDITATION: *Nehemiah worked no miracle, saw no spectacular vision, but his prayers secured spectacular results.*

May 5

HEZEKIAH – SIMPLICITY IN PRAYER

And Hezekiah spread it [the letter] out before the Lord.
(Isaiah 37:14)

Simplicity is not necessarily stupidity. A person may be childlike without being childish. Indeed, faith is always characterised by simplicity.

Hezekiah, king, soldier and poet, was artless in his relations with God. Rabshakeh and his hosts were surrounding Jerusalem. He was using every wile to shake the morale of the people. When confronted with a taunting and blasphemous letter from Rabshakeh, Hezekiah's spontaneous reaction was to commit the matter to God. ''He spread it before the Lord.'' *Here is the simplicity of faith!* As though God could not read the letter when rolled up! But his was a simplicity that moved the heart of God.

Hear the sequel. The angel of the Lord smote 185,000 Assyrian soldiers. Mighty armies are powerless before the feeble breath of prayer.

To ask God to reconsider and revoke His decree of death presented no insuperable problem to this man of simple faith (38:1–3). When Isaiah told him that he would die, his faith was not staggered. He turned to God in prayer. And God reversed His decree.

Think of the height to which his prayer soared. Not only did he have no promise of healing as a basis for faith, but he had the decree of God that he would die. In spite of this, he pressed his plea, and God responded magnificently.

FOR MEDITATION: *The man who knows God may even reverently challenge His decrees.*

JABEZ – AMBITION IN PRAYER

"Oh, that you would bless me and enlarge my territory . . ." (1 Chronicles 4:10)

There can be ambition in prayer that is pleasing to God. He is not honoured when we present only minimum requests. Because we are coming to the throne of a great King, we should honour him by bringing worthy petitions. Granting them will not strain His resources.

Jabez is an example of ambitious praying. That his praying met the conditions of divine approval is attested by God's response – "and God granted his request".

Despite the hereditary handicap hinted in his name (sorrowful), *his prayers lifted him far above his contemporaries.* "Jabez was more honourable than his brothers." He alone is singled out for mention.

His intensity of aspiration is evidenced in the opening clause – "Oh, that . . ." He would be content with no ordinary blessing. He appealed for an extension of his boundaries. He was not "content to fill a little space" for God when he could fill a bigger one. With true realism he asked God's help to equip for these larger responsibilities.

God is still looking for men and women whose ambition expresses itself in such a prayer.

FOR PRAISE: *Father, I thank you that to the man of faith handicaps need not handicap and limitations need not limit.*

ABRAHAM – LOGIC IN PRAYER

Abraham approached [the Lord] and said: "Will you sweep away the righteous with the wicked?" (Genesis 18:23)

The processes of prayer and answer are not irrational. Indeed, God encourages argument in prayer. "Present your case," says the Lord. "Set forth your arguments" (Isa. 41:21). We are invited to muster and present the strongest possible arguments for our petition, and press it with logic and vigour.

Confronted with the imminent doom of Sodom, home of his nephew Lot, Abraham does just this. His first recourse is to God with whom he shared great intimacy. In the intensity of his desire, he mixes audacity with argument and petition with pleading.

Mark *his holy daring* as he intercedes, his growing confidence as he marshals his propositions: "Will you sweep away the righteous with the wicked?"

He argues that such action would compromise God's character and tarnish His honour. As God graciously responds, Abraham returns again and again with larger requests – yet tempering his boldness with reverence. He ceased his suit when he reached what he considered to be the irreducible minimum of the righteous in Sodom. He ceased pleading before God ceased answering.

FOR MEDITATION: *Even when our prayer seems to meet with no response from God, we can rest on Abraham's question: "Will not the Judge of all the earth do right?"* (Gen. 10:25)

May 8

ELIJAH – FAITH IN PRAYER

Elijah was a man just like us. He prayed earnestly that it would not rain, and it did not rain. (James 5:17)

God's man for the hour is the one who has mastered the prayer of faith. Because of his prayers, Elijah flamed like a meteor across the midnight of Israel's apostasy. Though he was just like us, he was of unlike passion in prayer. He threw all the fiery forces of his nature into his praying. Before ever he crashed on to the stage of Israel's history, he had graduated in the school of prayer.

Who else had the serene faith to expect God to stop the course of nature at his word? Who else had offered prayer that rent the sky with heaven's vindicating flame? (1 Kgs. 18:38). *His prayers had prevailed in private before he put God to the test in public.* His faith created the atmosphere in which God could work His miracles. The divine response to his prayer demonstrated to the nation that God was God, and brought them on their faces in awe before Him (18:39).

Elijah's prayer had the divine promise of rain on which to rest (18:1). But he had no promise of fire. Yet he knew God so well that he dared to so commit Him that He could not fail to respond without compromising His own character and existence. When he prayed for rain, he did not require the confirming assurance of sight. He could believe God without any evidence to the senses. This is the prayer of faith.

FOR THANKSGIVING: *Father, I thank You for men of faith like Abraham and Elijah who encourage me to ask for the seemingly impossible.*

DANIEL – CONFLICT IN PRAYER

*"Do not be afraid, Daniel . . . your words were heard
. . . But the prince of the Persian kingdom resisted me
twenty-one days."* (Daniel 10:12,13)

Elijah was a brilliant meteor in Israel's firmament,
whereas Daniel was a fixed star. For over seventy years,
and through five reigns as prime minister of mighty
Babylon, he wielded a prodigious influence. The record
compresses his secret into few words: "Three times a day
he got down on his knees and prayed" (6:10).

The tyrant king could not compel him to bow to his
golden image. The jealous courtiers could not keep him
on his feet when the time for prayer arrived.

It was his praying that broke the Babylonian captivity, and
his praying was not uncontested. His invisible adversaries
opposed the answering of his prayer (10:13).

Daniel learned that invisible forces rule the world, that
the course of global events can be influenced by the
persistent praying of one man. The angel Michael assured
him that his prayer was heard the moment he uttered it,
though the answer was delayed three weeks.

Prayer is often a contest between angels who minister and
demons who hinder. Sometimes the answer to our prayer
is delayed through invisible spiritual activity.

FOR MEDITATION: *When we pray the prayer of
faith, unconsciously we send both angels and
demons scurrying.*

THE PRAYING CHRIST

Very early in the morning, Jesus . . . went off to a solitary place, where he prayed. (Mark 1:35)

It is an astounding thought that so completely did our Lord renounce the independent exercise of His divine powers, that He became dependent on His Father for all. As we do, He received His daily needs through the medium of prayer.

While bodily posture is secondary to the attitude of the soul, it is instructive to note that at times Jesus prayed while *standing*, just where He happened to be at the moment. At another time, He *knelt*, while on another occasion He *fell on His face*. While posture is not everything, it is something.

Much of His prayer life was concealed, even from His intimates, but sufficient is recorded to stimulate our emulation.

He prayed in secret, and He told His disciples to engage in secret prayer behind closed doors. Secret prayer brings its own reward.

He prayed in company with others, frequently taking some of His disciples apart for prayer. His instruction in this exercise, both by precept and example, kindled a desire to know more of the art. ''Lord teach us to pray,'' they asked. His longest prayer (John 17) was prayed in the presence of His disciples.

The majesty and solitude of the mountainside had a strange fascination for Him. There He enjoyed a solitude not only of place but of spirit that it was difficult to find elsewhere.

FOR PRAYER: *May my sense of inadequacy cause me to be more prayerful and dependent on You.*

May 11

CHRIST'S PRAYER HABITS

Jesus went out to a mountainside to pray, and spent the night praying to God. (Luke 6:12)

Great crises were preceded by prayer. It was "while he was praying" that the Holy Spirit descended on Him. His selection of the twelve disciples was made only after He had spent the night in prayer. The Transfiguration scene took place "as he was praying". It was after a season of prayer that He unburdened His heart concerning His impending suffering and death.

Great achievements were preceded by prayer. His feeding of the four thousand, of the five thousand, walking on the water, raising Lazarus, were each the outcome of prayer.

Great achievements were followed by prayer. When confronted by great crises or demanding tasks, we turn instinctively to prayer. But once the crisis is past, the tendency is to revert to our own wisdom or ability. But after one of the most successful days of His ministry, Jesus "departed into a mountain to pray".

Great pressure of work was a call to extra prayer. Jesus' life was exceptionally busy and He worked under constant pressure. At times He had no leisure even for meals. But the pressure of the multitude was never permitted to crowd out prayer. We are apt to advance pressure of business as a reason for *not* praying.

Our Lord *died praying*: "Father, into your hands I commit my spirit."

FOR PRAISE: *I praise You, Lord, for setting the example in praying, and for giving the Holy Spirit to help me in prayer.*

May 12

WHEN JESUS SANG

*When they had sung a hymn, they went out to the
Mount of Olives.* (Matthew 26:30)

This precious fragment is preserved for us by both
Matthew and Mark. We should not otherwise have
known that Jesus sang under the very shadow of the
cross. What serenity and inward triumph are reflected
in this revealing sentence! The Son of Man approaches
the sorrows of Gethsemane, the shame of Gabbatha and
the suffering of Golgotha with a song on His lips. Anyone
can sing in the sunshine, but *to sing in the shadows is a
rare accomplishment.*

Jesus had eagerly anticipated this Last Supper with His
loved disciples. Gathered around the festal board, they
had recalled the first Passover when God liberated Israel.
How poignantly the realisation that the paschal lamb
would soon find fulfilment in His own death would
sweep over Him. So now He transmutes the Passover
feast into the Lord's Supper.

What a thrilling male chorus they must have made as they
left the table, for it was customary to sing Psalm 118. But
what the Jews sang with blinded eyes, Jesus sang with
open vision. Since He was the leader of the feast, it would
be for Him to raise the tune. Think of the implications
of Psalm 118:24 as He sang it on the way to the cross:
*"This is the day the Lord has made; let us rejoice and be glad
in it."*

FOR WORSHIP: *Lord, I worship You for Your life of
complete dedication to Your Father's will, and
for this glorious expression of it.*

THE SINLESS CHRIST

In him was no sin. (1 John 3:5)

The sinlessness of Christ was an almost undisputed tenet of the Christian faith for many centuries, but this is not so today. It is contended by some that the presence of a sinless man among universally sinful men, would be as much a miracle in the moral realm as would a virgin birth in the physical realm. But in spite of this improbability, *if sufficient evidence is adduced, is it reasonable to reject it*?

Sinlessness in Jesus was not a merely negative quality of innocence, as it was in the first Adam. Jesus was tempted as we are, but the conflict left Him immaculate. This is the consistent testimony of Scripture. There is not one statement of Scripture which, if consistently interpreted, can be made to imply less than sinlessness for our Lord.

Four affirmations by different New Testament writers are unequivocal in their testimony: "In Him was no sin" – essentially (1 John 3:5). "He did no sin" – actually (1 Pet. 2:22). "He knew no sin" – experientially (2 Cor. 5:21). "Tempted . . . yet without sin" (Heb. 14:5).

The challenge He flung out to His carping critics still remains unanswered: "Can any of you prove me guilty of sin?" (John 8:46). His sinlessness was unimpeachable or they would have brought a charge against Him. Even hell could bring no accusation. "The prince of this world is coming. He has no hold on me," Jesus claimed (John 14:30).

FOR MEDITATION: *The sinlessness of Jesus was not merely a neutral quality of innocence as it was with the first Adam.*

THE MANLY CHRIST

"Behold the Man!" (John 19:5 RSV)

Jesus was not only a man, He was a manly man – the crown and glory of humanity. He combined in Himself the gentler graces of womanhood and the virile virtues of manhood. Unfortunately the former have received stronger emphasis.

Think of *His resolute physical courage.* He knew more of peril than most, yet He faced it without the slightest timidity or fear. Though He knew Jerusalem meant for Him suffering and death, yet He "resolutely set out for Jerusalem" (Luke 9:51).

His intrepid utterances marked Him out as a man of great moral courage. He is a strong man who will voluntarily speak words which will inevitably incur painful consequences. The Lord never, from fear of possible suffering, withheld one word given to Him by the Father.

His courageous silences were as eloquent of His strength as were His fearless words. A strong man may be recognised by his silence. Jesus knew when to speak and when to hold His peace. However strong the provocation, He never stooped to self-vindication, much less retaliation. Before the craven Pilate and the taunting Herod, both of whom possessed the power of death, He maintained a majestic silence.

FOR PRAISE: *O Lord, I praise You that in every circumstance and in testing hours, You showed Yourself a manly man.*

CHRIST – REALLY HUMAN

The man Christ Jesus (1 Timothy 2:5)

While we must not divorce the humanity from the deity of the Master, we should draw all the comfort and help that we can from the fact that He took part in historic manhood, and was made "in the likeness of sinful man" (Rom. 8:3). His humanity was real and not feigned.

Details of His *human ancestry* are preserved in the Gospel records. The names of His brothers are given and His genealogy on both sides of the family are tabulated.

He was normal in *human appearance*. Mary at first mistook Him for the gardener. The woman of Samaria noted nothing unusual in His appearance.

So far as the elements of His *human constitution* were concerned, He possessed the normal faculties of man. He spoke of His body, soul and spirit. He invited His disciples to handle Him and satisfy themselves of His real humanity.

He evidenced the *sinless infirmities of mankind*. He was hungry, weary, craved human sympathy and wept. He died!

In His incarnation he became subject to *human limitations* – part of the mystery of His great self-humiliation. He submitted to the ordinary laws of human development, and acquired knowledge through the ordinary channels open to other boys. He even renounced knowledge of certain future events. We can appropriate Pilate's words, *"Behold the Man!"*

FOR PRAISE: *Lord, I thank You that You took part in historic manhood. Deliver us from allowing Your real humanity to hide Your full deity.*

THE KEY DOCTRINE

"You are the Christ, the Son of the living God."
(Matthew 16:16)

Is any other question so far-reaching and important as, "Who was Jesus? Is He, or is He not, God?"

If Jesus is not God, then there is no Christianity, and we who worship Him are nothing more than idolators. Conversely, if He is God, those who say He was only a good man are blasphemers. More serious still, if He is not God, then *He* is a blasphemer in the fullest sense of the word. The deity of Christ is the key doctrine of Scripture. Reject it, and the Bible becomes a confused jumble of words without any unifying theme. Accept it, and the Bible becomes an intelligible and coherent revelation of God.

In the final analysis our belief in the deity of Christ is rooted in our faith in the inspired Scriptures. We believe Him to be the Son of God because we accept the teaching of Holy Scripture and its statements about Him.

The very basis of Christianity is that God was "manifest in the flesh" (1 Tim. 3:16 RSV). If that assertion can be overthrown, then the whole superstructure of Christianity crashes to the ground, and we are bound to assume that Jesus was either a shameless impostor or that He suffered from a delusion. In either case, He is disqualified from being a Saviour, and is not the Second Person of the divine Trinity.

FOR THANKSGIVING: *Lord, I thank You that I can echo Peter's grand confession, and worship You as Son of God.*

May 17

SEVENTH DAY OR FIRST DAY?

On the first day of the week, we came together to break bread. (Acts 20:7)

Some Christians are confused by the diverse views on sabbath observance.

Sabbath-keeping is expressly stated to be not obligatory on Christians. "Therefore, do not let anyone judge you . . . with regard to . . . a Sabbath day" (Col. 2:16).

There are a number of reasons why we observe the Lord's Day and not the sabbath. After His resurrection, Jesus met with His disciples on the first day (John 20:19), and as though to confirm that day, He met with them again a week later (20:26). This was the birth of the Lord's Day.

It was on the first day of the week that the Spirit descended to constitute the Church (Acts 2). On the first day of the week the church in Troas met to break bread (Acts 20:7). Following the resurrection, the Passover was superseded by the Lord's Supper. Even so did the Jewish Sabbath give place to the Lord's Day – the Old Covenant was superseded by the New.

It is significant that in the New Testament *each commandment of the Decalogue is reiterated and expanded, except the fourth* relating to the Sabbath. Why this omission? Paul classes the Sabbath as an integral part of a disappeared law which Christ nailed to His cross (Col. 2:14).

We may well rejoice in the liberty which the gospel has brought us and refuse to allow anyone to replace the yoke of bondage from which the cross of Christ has delivered us.

FOR MEDITATION: *We observe the Lord's day as a day of rest and worship, not because we must, but as an expression of love and obedience.*

AMBASSADORS FOR CHRIST

We are therefore Christ's ambassadors. (2 Corinthians
5:20)

One of the most impressive metaphors Paul used to
illustrate the privilege of his ministry, is that of
ambassador for Christ.

An ambassador is *a diplomatic minister of state of highest
rank* – one of the highest honours a country can bestow.
Paul delighted to use this term of himself.

An ambassador has both privileges and responsibilities. First,
he actually represents his absent king or president, whose
honour is in his hands. He does not go abroad at his own
expense – all the resources of his country are behind him.
He has personal fellowship and access to his sovereign.
While on national business, his personal safety is
guaranteed. It is not difficult to relate these privileges to
an ambassador of the King of kings.

On the other hand, *he must have no associations that would
compromise his country*. He must keep in constant contact
with his sovereign, and must live and conduct himself
in a worthy manner. He is expected to watch over the
interests of fellow-citizens in that country.

*He has no right to add to or subtract from the message of
his government*; nor need he apologise for his message.
He is to represent his government's viewpoint, not his
own.

It is not difficult to make a pertinent application of these
responsibilities to the ambassador of Christ. Do we
qualify for the post?

FOR MEDITATION: *The missionary goes as Christ's
representative, the embodiment of His teaching,
the demonstrator of His ethics and the upholder
of His Name and reputation.*

UNION WITH CHRIST

Do you not know that your bodies are members of Christ himself? (1 Corinthians 6:15)

One of the most important doctrines relating to the inner spiritual life, is that of the believer's vital union with Christ. Yet many Christians do not know that they have been grafted into Christ and are vitally united to Him. It is as a result of this union, that everything He achieved by His life and death becomes ours.

There is *the figure of marriage*. ". . . that you should be married to another . . ." (Rom. 7:4 KJV). This is the highest and most intimate union known to man, and is a picture of Christ and His Church.

Then there is *the figure of the body and the head*. "Do you not know that your bodies are members of Christ?" The picture here is of mutual dependence through sharing the same life. The least important member of the body shares the life of the head.

Jesus employed *the figure of the vine and branches* (John 15:5). The vine and branches are one. Neither can exist independently of the other. The sole responsibility of the branch is to receive from root and stem the life-giving sap.

Jesus is the Vine, root, stem, branch, flower and fruit. I need not worry about how to get the sap out of the vine into myself. Jesus simply said: "Abide, remain in me." Then fruit-bearing is automatic.

FOR MEDITATION: *The secret of our Lord's incredibly fruitful life was His unbroken contact with His Father.*

THE POWER OF CHRIST

I will boast about my weaknesses . . . so that Christ's power might rest on me. (2 Corinthians 12:9)

It is a truth of Scripture that whatever Christ is, He is for us by virtue of our vital union with Him. He is the reservoir of divine omnipotence, from which we can draw for our ever-recurring needs.

It is instructive that the Greek word *dunamis*, or inherent power, is never predicated of our Lord by the writers of the Gospels. Nor in the Scripture record does He claim its exercise. It is the word *exousia*, or authority that is used of Him, e.g. "All authority in heaven and on earth has been given to me" (Matt. 28:18).

In fulfilling His earthly ministry, Jesus never exercised or drew on His *inherent power*, but used only the authority delegated from His Father. This can bring us ordinary mortals much comfort. We are often daunted by the thought that Christ had powers and resources that are not available to us. But that is just where we are wrong.

Although He possessed limitless inherent power, He voluntarily refrained from using it, and restricted Himself to exercise only the authority His Father had delegated to Him. "I can of my own self do nothing," was His astounding claim (John 5:30 KJV).

So instead of being discouraged by His deity, we can be encouraged that He chose to be continually dependent on His Father for power to do His will.

FOR ENCOURAGEMENT: *Christ's miracles were not performed by innate power, but in dependence on the Holy Spirit.*

THE LORDSHIP OF CHRIST

*For this very reason, Christ died and returned to life
so that he might be the Lord . . . (Romans 14:9)*

It is tragic that many Christians who verbally
acknowledge Christ's Lordship, do not concede it to Him
in practice. They are willing to accord Him the position
of constitutional Monarch, so long as they can remain
prime minister. Like Peter, they reserve the right to say
"Not so, Lord," to Him (Acts 10:14).

Do we ever say "Not so" to Him – when He calls us
to pray, to witness, to service? To such, Jesus says, "Why
do you call me 'Lord, Lord,' and do not do what I say?"
(Luke 6:46).

We cannot accept Christ as Saviour while wilfully *rejecting
Him as Sovereign*. A. W. Tozer, with his usual pungency,
said, "It is altogether doubtful whether anyone can be
saved who comes to Christ for His help, but with no
intention of obeying Him."

Christ's reign in our hearts is to extend to all areas of
life. Disobedience vitiates all our pious professions of
recognition of His Lordship.

How can we recognise His Lordship? By making a break
with the rule of "other lords" (Isa. 26:13). By decisively
renouncing all known sin or disobedience. By enthroning
Christ in the heart. By depending on the Holy Spirit, for
"No-one can say [*keep on saying*] that Jesus is Lord *except
through the Holy Spirit*" (1 Cor. 12:3).

FOR MEDITATION: *Disobedience vitiates all our
pious professions of recognition of His Lordship.*

WE DO NOT LOSE HEART

We do not lose heart. Though outwardly we are wasting away, yet inwardly we are being renewed day by day. (2 Corinthians 4:16)

In this paragraph, Paul shares with the Corinthian believers his own experience of God's upholding power.

The expression "we do not lose heart" is derived from military life and could be rendered, "we do not act as deserters and cowards"; we do not defect from positions of trust even if they involve danger, because we have learned the secret.

True, the outer man which belongs to the seen and temporal, is wasting and decaying, and suffers wear and tear. With advancing years, physical vigour wanes, and beauty takes wings. Old age and death advance with relentless step, and those whose lives are bounded by the seen and temporal, are filled with dismay. "But", Paul replies, "we do not lose heart!"

Note the paradox: our outer man *decaying*, our inner man *renewed*. The inner man is rejuvenated in the divine beauty parlour. Each new day brings a fresh provision of divine strength. Here is a cheering revelation. By a divine alchemy, the very forces which destroy the outer, are harnessed by God to promote the inner. This renewal goes on day by day. There are no idle days with the Holy Spirit.

This was the reason Paul viewed with equanimity the wasting of his body through persecution, disease and hardships, and enabled him to say, "I glory in tribulations" (Rom. 5:3 KJV).

FOR THANKSGIVING: *Lord, I thank You that the Holy Spirit can use adverse circumstances to mature and strengthen me.*

COMFORTED TO COMFORT

*The God of all comfort . . . comforts us . . . so that
we may be able to comfort . . .* (2 Corinthians 1:3,4
RSV)

One of the great preachers, sensitive to the needs of his
generation, declared that if he could live his life over
again, he would devote more time to the ministry of
comfort and encouragement.

Isaiah described the mission of the Messiah as being
to the poor, the broken-hearted, the captives, the blind
and the bruised, for God is deeply concerned for His
suffering children. He comforts them with a definite end
in view.

The English word "comfort" is an inadequate
translation. This comfort is more than soothing sympathy
– it is comfort that brings courage, and enables us to meet
and triumph over the worst life can bring to us.

It is the personal experience of God's comfort that
qualifies us to comfort others. If we ourselves know no
trouble and affliction, we will have no ministry of comfort
to others. It is one of the consolations of greying hair that,
not having been strangers to sorrow, and to the resulting
comfort of God, we are able to use our experience to bring
similar comfort to others. Are we treating our experience
as a trust?

"It is possible to escape a multitude of troubles, by
living an insignificant life. The range of our possible
suffering is determined by the largeness and nobility of
our aims" (J. H. Jowett).

FOR ASPIRATION: *Lord, give me a ministry of
comfort and encouragement to the hurting
hearts around me.*

SORROW DOES COLOUR LIFE

*Add to your faith . . . perseverance . . . godliness . . .
brotherly kindness . . . love.* (2 Peter 1:5)

Perseverance is a grace in which there are two elements
– active perseverance and passive endurance. Our idea
of patience is usually stolid toughing it out, but it is much
more than that. It is the spirit that not only endures, but
actually triumphs over trials and turns them into glorious
victories. Someone said to a woman who was in the midst
of a great sorrow: "Sorrow does colour life, doesn't
it?" "Yes, indeed it does," was the reply, "*and I intend
to choose the colours.*" This is the idea behind
"perseverance".

Godliness – true reverence for God, reverential trust,
is not a quality innate in man, it must be cultivated. It
results in both God and man receiving their due from us.
If we are determined to be godly, we must be willing to
pay the price in discipline.

Brotherly love is the badge of our discipleship. "By this
all men will know that you are my disciples if you love
one another" (John 13:35).

Love is the crown and culmination of all. It is the queen
of graces – the sovereign preference of one person for
another. Jesus claimed the supreme place in the affections
of His followers. When this is conceded, there is an
abundance of love in the heart which will flow out to
others.

FOR PRAYER: *Lord of love, work in me a brotherly
love that will overleap prejudice or aversion.*

HEAVENLY ADDITION

Add to your faith goodness . . . knowledge . . . self-control. (2 Peter 1:5)

Peter urges us to supplement our faith with *goodness* or *virtue*, which is that virile, manly strength which inspires to resolute action. It carries the idea of excellence. It is not a merely passive quality, but issues in a life of courageous service and effective witness. It is the inflexible determination to do right and choose God's will, no matter how strongly the tide is running in the opposite direction.

Knowledge is here not theoretical knowledge alone, but practical knowledge born out of personal experience. It does not refer to general culture or even intellectual knowledge of theological truth, but is the insight into what is right and wrong, the discernment of how we ought to act in the light of what we know.

Self-control is the ability to rule oneself, body and spirit – discipline. It extends over the whole of life – emotions, passions, desires and imaginations. Jeremy Taylor described self-control as ''reason's girdle as well as passion's bridle''.

Our bodily appetites, which are part of our humanity, are beneficent when controlled, but ruinous when in command. But strong though they are, they can be controlled by the indwelling Holy Spirit, whose fruit is self-control (Gal. 5:23). Apart from His enabling, one part of our nature cannot control another part which is in revolt.

FOR PRAYER: *Blessed Spirit, work in my life so that I will become expert in these heavenly mathematics.*

WEAPONS OF WARFARE

The weapons we fight with have divine power to demolish strongholds. (2 Corinthians 10:4)

What are the spiritual weapons we can use in our warfare with Satan?

The cross. We pay lip-service to the cross, and even wear it as a talisman or symbol. But do we in practice use it as a spiritual weapon? When facing spiritual problems, do we rely more on conference than on the cross? Do we pay more attention to organisation, methods, techniques, than to the conquering power of the cross? Do we bring the cross on to the field? There is nothing the devil fears more than the intelligent application of the power generated by the cross and resurrection.

The truth, a weapon which, wielded in the power of the Spirit, will reduce the stoutest stronghold of sin and error. The adversary has no answer to the truth of God, for the entrance of divine truth into the heart gives light and dispels his erroneous conceptions. It is like a hammer, demolishing resistance, or a sword, discerning the thoughts and intents of the heart.

All kinds of prayers (Eph. 6:18). We are to engage in prayer of every kind, whether worship, confession, thanksgiving, petition or intercession. Especially must we engage in that kind of prayer which claims and releases the power of the cross. It is prayer that gives the edge to truth, and prepares the soil of the heart for the reception of the good seed of the Word.

FOR PRAYER: *Lord make Your cross so real to me that I can sing with fervour:*

> *In the cross of Christ I glory,*
> *Towering o'er the wrecks of time.*

WARFARE WITH SATAN

The weapons we fight with are not the weapons of the world. (2 Corinthians 10:4)

In his classic, *The Holy War*, Bunyan wrote: *"Mansoul's matchless wars no fables be."* He was very conscious of the truceless warfare in which the followers of the Lamb are inevitably embroiled. Few who have been engaged in spiritual warfare in heathen lands will quarrel with Bunyan's description.

There are those who doubt the existence of a personal and malignant devil, but the *fact* of the battle proves the *existence* of the foe, and the fierceness of the fight is an index of his might.

This warfare is *real, not imaginary*. His encounter with the devil in the desert was very real to Jesus, and the conflict was not confined to those forty days.

The warfare is *spiritual, not worldly*. "We do not war after the flesh" (v.3) — on the plane or after the methods of the natural man. It can be waged only on the spiritual plane and with spiritual weapons.

The warfare is *intangible*, not against flesh and blood. It would be more satisfying if we could grapple with our foe. There is satisfaction in making contact. We can reach and move people only by spiritual means.

The warfare is *interminable*. It began in Eden and will end only when Satan is finally bound. Meanwhile, let us "resist the devil and he will flee from us" (Jas. 4:7).

FOR PRAYER: *Lord make real to me the implications of the fact that Satan is the second most powerful being in the universe.*

THE DEVIL'S SCHEMES

Take your stand against the devil's schemes.
(Ephesians 6:11)

There is a tendency in contemporary society to discount our Lord's teaching on the existence of the devil. Instead of there being a personal God and a personal devil, many say there is only impersonal good and evil. But the language of Scripture cannot be made to fit an impersonal force or influence. There is a uniform conception of a personal tempter who is able to inflame the base tendencies of our hearts with his incitements to evil. In the scriptural view the devil is the personification of evil as God is the personification of all that is holy.

The consistent theme of the Bible is the conflict between the hierarchies of heaven and hell. The key to an understanding of the world situation is the recognition that *these two thrones are at war*. Satan's objective is nothing less than the elimination of God and the usurpation of His throne.

Victor Hugo said that a good general must penetrate the brain of his enemy. Today it must be acknowledged that on this subject the majority are spiritual illiterates – a condition that pleases the adversary. *He knows that there is no ultimate victory for him*. The pronounced sentence has only been postponed, not cancelled.

FOR ACTION: *Spend some time studying the person and activities of Satan – but in the light of his defeat at the cross* (Col. 2:15).

PERSONALITY NOT OBLITERATED

I live, yet not I, but Christ liveth in me. (Galatians 2:20 KJV)

Christ will never force His way into a human personality. He will bring every influence to bear on a life, short of violating the personality. Before his conversion, Christ was anathema to Paul. But when on the Damascus road he surrendered to Him, his whole being was indwelt and irradiated by Christ.

Paul's personality was not obliterated by that indwelling. He did not become any less Paul. Indeed, he became more and more the Paul God intended him to be – a chosen vessel to the Lord.

We need not fear making the fullest surrender to Christ, for *He enhances and ennobles personality*, imparting qualities and gifts which are absent, and brings into activity powers and possibilities that have been latent. True, he became a different Paul, but a greater and better one.

Christ lived in Paul in the sense that from within the citadel of his yielded personality, He reproduced His own radiant life. It was still characteristically Paul who is seen in his letters.

Through consistent communion with Christ he became less and less like the Saul of his persecuting days and more and more like the Christ with whom he companied.

FOR THANKSGIVING: *Lord, I thank You for the fact that You respect and make use of human personality, yet do not breach free will.*

LIFE IS SOMEONE ELSE

I have been crucified with Christ, and I no longer live,
but Christ lives in me. (Galatians, 2:20)

What is the talisman enfolded in these simple words, "To
me, to live is Christ" (Phil. 1:21)?

Christ was the Source of Paul's life. Christ does not
impart life as something separate from Himself. "Christ
who is our life" are Paul's words (Col. 3:4). When a heart
is opened to Him in true repentance and surrender, He
Himself comes in and communicates His own life. And
abundant life is in view – not that of an emaciated
convalescent, but of a virile footballer.

Christ was the Mediator of his spiritual life. If the words
"Christ lives in me" mean anything, they mean that the
Christian life is Christ living out His holy and wholesome
life in terms of our human life and personality. The new
life which a person receives at conversion is the
indwelling of a divine Person. Christianity is not a creed
to live by. It is a Person who indwells.

Christ living in us *will stimulate and not stultify the
intellect*. With the advent of Christ into the personality,
the mind is better able to apprehend spiritual truth. It will
quicken the affections and emotional life, and fix them on God,
the ethically perfect Being. It will *vitalise the will* which
has become weakened and emasculated by habitual
yielding to sinful impulses.

FOR THANKSGIVING:
> *Lord, Thou hast made Thyself to me*
> *A living bright reality;*
> *More present to faith's vision keen*
> *Than any earthly object seen.*

CHRIST IN US

Do you not realise that Christ Jesus is in you . . .?
(2 Corinthians 13:5)

Is it too elementary to point out that Paul, writing by inspiration, said, "Do you not *know*," not, "Do you not *feel*"? And yet the latter seems to be the sense in which many read this verse. This is *a fact to be counted on*, not *an experience to be sought*. First believe the fact and then you will begin to enjoy the experience. The order cannot be reversed.

When Jesus was on earth, He was *with* His disciples – a blessed experience. But in the Upper Room He said to them: "On that day you will realise that . . . *I am in you*" (John 14:20). This was an experience beyond anything they had known.

When on earth, Jesus could be in only one place at a time, and He could influence His disciples only from without. But with the descent of the Holy Spirit all this was changed. From that day Jesus knew no geographical limitations. By His Spirit He could now dwell with each believer and hold converse with them. They lost His physical presence, but gained His spiritual indwelling. He could now carry on His sanctifying work from within.

Count on His presence in you.

FOR PRAISE: *I praise You for the promised and actual indwelling of the Father, Son and the Holy Spirit in my unworthy heart.*

June 1

ANXIETY IS FAITHLESS

"O you of little faith . . . do not worry." (Matthew 6:30,31)

We are apt to shrug off the worry habit as an amiable hereditary weakness that we will have to learn to live with. But Jesus did not so view it. To Him it was a sinful lack of faith in His Father, and this is no amiable weakness. For "without faith it is *impossible* to please God" (Heb. 11:6).

The author once hung in his office a motto that seldom failed to draw comment. It ran: WHY TRUST WHEN YOU CAN WORRY? Almost invariably visitors would say that the words were the wrong way round – and so they were – intentionally. Their reversal drew attention to the fact that many Christians are more prone to worry faithlessly about their problems, than to trust God to solve them. We trust God for the stupendously important matter of our salvation, and then are strangely timid about trusting Him for infinitely less important concerns.

Trust and worry cannot sleep in the same bed, they are mutually antagonistic. The one negates the other. *If you trust, you do not worry, and if you worry you do not trust.*

"So do not worry, saying, 'What shall we eat? . . . What shall we wear?' . . . Your heavenly Father knows that you need them. But seek first his kingdom and His righteousness, and all these things will be given to you as well" (Matthew 6:31–33).

FOR PRAYER: *Lord, in our troubled world You know how easy it is to become anxious about the future. Keep reminding me that You are still on the throne.*

June 2

FORBIDDEN WORRY

"Do not worry about your life . . ." (Matthew 6:25)

If Mammon tends to be the characteristic temptation of men, perhaps worry is the special besetment of women – although sometimes the lines may cross. The rich worry over what they have, the poor over what they have not. For such a universal problem the Lord had sage counsel to give.

The word translated "anxious care, or worry" signifies a concern for the means of life that has degenerated into worry. Jesus does not denounce prudent forethought, nor does He advocate careless improvidence. It is not concern, but over-concern, that He forbids. The antithesis of worry is not carelessness, or even carefreeness, but confidence and trust in a Father's care. From this the devil seeks to seduce us into the debilitating sin of anxious care.

The tense of the verb is significant. The meaning is, "Stop worrying!" If the habit has you in its grip, stop it! No matter what happens, don't worry!

Worry is needless. Your Father feeds the birds, and you are more valuable than they (v.26). (In any case, worry won't improve the situation.)

Worry is futile. "Who of you by worrying can add a single hour to his life?" (v.27). Worry cannot recall the past, and worry about the present is more likely to produce ulcers and thrombosis than solution to the problem. Since this is Christ's command, *in the Spirit's power it is an attainable goal*.

FOR PRAYER: *Lord, keep my necessary prudent forethought from degenerating into faithless anxiety.*

June 3

FORBIDDEN OSTENTATION

"Be careful not to do your 'acts of righteousness' before men, to be seen by them." (Matthew 6:1)

In this verse Jesus announced a general principle which He proceeded to illustrate by three acts of visible devotion – giving, praying, fasting. These were three specimens of Pharisaic "righteousness", as it was called.

He now warns His disciples of a twofold peril. First, performing acts of devotion "to be seen by men" – ostentation and self-advertisement. Second, failing to maintain in private the standard of devotion professed in public – hypocrisy. They must not do "as the hypocrites do".

That this same principle is applicable to all three activities is seen in the thrice-repeated refrain: "They have received their reward in full." Their professed acts of devotion were a theatrical performance, designed to win the applause of the audience. They looked for applause and received it. The account is closed.

The fundamental lesson of this passage is that *the disciple's life is to be lived primarily in the presence of God* – "Your Father who sees in secret" – and only secondarily before men. While not insensitive to the presence of his fellows, the true disciple sets greater store on the approval of God than on the passing applause of his contemporaries.

FOR PRAYER: *Lord, adjust my motivation so that Your approval means more to me than the praise of men.*

June 4

FORBIDDEN COVETOUSNESS

"Do not store up for yourselves treasures on earth, where moth and rust destroy and where thieves break in and steal." (Matthew 6:19)

In the Orient, wealth was preserved in three main forms – clothing, grain, gold.

Garments as a form of wealth appear as an element in Achan's tragic sin (Josh. 7:21).

Grain as a form of wealth appears in the parable of the rich fool (Luke 12:16–21).

Gold, or precious stones, as a form of wealth are exemplified in the "treasure hid in the field" (Matt. 13:44). There were no safe-deposit boxes in those days!

Realistic as ever, Jesus pointed out that treasure on earth was very vulnerable and precarious. Clothing is subject to the ravages of the moth. Grain can be consumed by rats and mice. Gold can be stolen by thieves. Investments can be lost in stock market crashes!

In view of all these factors, Jesus issued a direction to His disciples – and to us: "Don't *continue the habit of laying up* for yourselves treasure on earth." "If you are doing this, STOP IT!" is the significance of the command.

"To lay up *treasure in heaven* is to do acts that promote or belong to the Kingdom of God; and what our Lord assures us is that any act of our hands, any thought of our hearts, any word of our lips which promotes the Kingdom, is really stored up for us in the divine treasure-house" (Bishop Gore).

FOR PRAYER: *Lord, as I am only trustee and not owner of my possessions, help me to hold them as always available to You.*

June 5

THE FORBIDDEN LOOK

"Anyone who looks at a woman lustfully, has already committed adultery with her in his heart." (Matthew 5:28)

In this permissive age when morals have tobogganed to an all-time low, and incitements to moral laxity assault eye and ear from all directions, we must rediscover and proclaim *the lost standard*. Jesus made no apology for dealing with the sordid aspects of life, nor need we.

Jesus nowhere condemned a natural and normal relationship between the sexes, nor was He speaking of the natural stirring of the God-given sexual impulse. The Bible teaches *purity*, not *prudery*. God made us male and female, and sexual desire is an integral part of our human nature.

The tense and context of the word "looks" in the text indicate, not the involuntary glance, but a purposeful and repeated looking. Looking to incite longing; using the eyes to excite lust.

What Jesus is condemning is the looking at a woman as a possible object for the gratification of desire; as an object to exploit, not as a person to be loved and respected. It is the look which disregards the sacredness of a woman's person.

While the temptation to illicit sex is not in itself sin, it quickly develops into sin when welcomed and given hospitality in the heart.

Rigid self-discipline is the price of moral purity, but it is abundantly worth the cost involved.

FOR PRAYER: *In our sex-saturated society, through Your Spirit work in me Your holiness and purity.*

June 6

FORBIDDEN ANGER

"Anyone who is angry with his brother will be subject to judgment." (Matthew 5:22)

In His exposition of the sixth commandment, "Do not murder," Jesus asserts that murder goes deeper than the overt act, for it is a crime not of the hand but of the heart — in the motive, not in the act alone. Jesus here puts anger, whether nursed in the heart or expressed in contemptuous or passionate speech, in the same category as murder.

It is significant that of two Greek words for anger, one means anger that *flares up* but soon dies down, and the other, anger that *broods and becomes deep-seated*. It is the latter word that Jesus employs here. Anger and contempt are the seed-plot of murder.

There are degrees of anger, and corresponding degrees of retribution:

Malicious anger nursed in the heart, which brings the offender in danger of the judgement of the local council.

Contemptuous speech — the expression of arrogant contempt that despises another. *"Raca"* is a term of contempt expressed in insulting words — the intellectual snobbery that despises the lesser breeds. This person is in danger of judgement by the Sanhedrin.

Uncontrolled rage exploding into passionate speech: "You cursed fool!" The word "fool" here refers to a man's morals. He who thus robs a man of his moral character, is in danger of "the Gehenna of fire". Uncontrolled rage brings on itself an automatic retribution.

FOR PRAYER: *Father, by Your Spirit's power, show those who are addicted to deep-seated anger its sinfulness, and the way of victory over it.*

MAMMON, OR HEAVENLY TREASURE?

"You cannot serve both God and money." (Matthew 6:24)

As Jesus used the word, "mammon" meant "property, earthly goods", or, as in the NIV, "money" – but with the derogatory sense of the materialistic, anti-godly and sinful. In the earthly property which a person gathers, in which he erroneously seeks security and to which he gives his heart, Jesus finds the very opposite of God. Because of the power immanent in possessions, surrender to them brings practical enslavement. So, mammon does not mean wealth *per se*, but wealth become an idol.

The insidious effect of wealth on character is so well known as to need no amplification. It demands one's whole attention, and that ultimately means a divided loyalty, for God demands the whole devotion too. Note that Jesus did not say "you must not", but *"you cannot"* serve God and money.

Money is neutral: there is nothing inherently evil in it. How it is gained, how it is regarded, how it is used – these are the things that determine whether it is mammon or heavenly treasure.

The Christian man of business constantly faces a choice between God and mammon. Often he must choose between profit and principle. A large profit at the sacrifice of a little principle is often the devil's lure.

The best way of breaking the power of the material over our lives, is to devote it to spiritual ends – exchanging it for heavenly treasure.

FOR THANKSGIVING: *Thank You, Lord, that my monetary gifts of love can be transmitted into heavenly treasure.*

LOVE YOUR ENEMIES

If your enemy is hungry, feed him. If he is thirsty, give him something to drink . . . Overcome evil with good. (Romans 12:20,21)
"Love your enemies." (Matthew 5:44)

This illustration of the new standard of Christ's Kingdom imposes on the disciple the impossible requirement of loving the enemy who hates, reviles and persecutes him. This incredible law of love has been termed the concentrated expression of the Christian ethic. Affinity or aversion are alike irrelevant to this exotic species of love.

The Greek word *agape* used here is "the love which loves despite the repulsiveness of its object", and is contrasted with *eros*, which is "love elicited by the attractive qualities of the loved one". It is *moral* love as distinguished from personal affection. It is the attitude of sustained and undiscourageable love towards both friend and enemy. A love which does not demand but gives, and goes on giving, whatever the insult or injury suffered.

This love is not mere emotion, but involves volition and action as well. It must find expression in acts of love for deserving and undeserving alike. It is the love of God as seen in John 3:16. In this verse it is the volitional rather than the emotional element in God's love which is highlighted. The most important thing is not what we *feel*, but what we *will*. To give His Son to such a shameful and agonising death as crucifixion was the last thing God would *feel* like doing.

FOR PRAISE: *I praise You, Lord, for demonstrating on the cross the attitude I should adopt to my enemies.*

THE POWER OF HABIT

Put off your old self . . . Put on the new self.
(Ephesians 4:22–24)

Man is a bundle of habits, and character is made up of habits either good or bad. The old saying is true to life:

> Sow a thought, reap an act.
> Sow an act, reap a habit.
> Sow a habit, reap a character.
> Sow a character, reap a destiny.

Habit-making and habit-breaking are among man's dominant activities. *Every part of life is affected by the kind of habits he forms.* Each day he must choose whether he will obey the dictates of the old or of the new nature.

Habit is defined as "a behaviour pattern acquired by frequent repetition". We can develop habits without any definite acts of the will. An act begins by being occasional, but by frequent repetition it becomes habitual.

Paul employs the figure of *robing and disrobing* to illustrate his point. "Put off your old self . . . Put on the new self."

Forming good habits is the best antidote to the old bad habits. The sinful disposition and habits formed over a lifetime are to be discarded like an old suit of clothes, and this involves a decisive act of the renewed will. In addition, new and holy habits are to be adopted and donned as with a new garment. For this we are promised the aid of God: "It is God who works in you to will and to act according to His good purpose" (Phil. 2:13).

FOR MEDITATION: *It is by persistence and obedience to the requirements of Scripture that godly patterns of life are developed.*

SPIRITUAL ATHLETICS

Train yourself to be godly. (1 Timothy 4:7)

From the frequency with which the Greek games are used as illustrations of the Christian life, it would seem that God desires us to do in the spiritual realm what the athlete does in the physical. The pampered and flabby athlete wins no medals. Paul ran "in such a way as to get the prize" (1 Cor. 9:24).

He imposed a rigorous discipline on his mind, and monitored his mental habits. "Our voluntary thoughts," wrote A. W. Tozer, "not only reveal what we are, but predict what we will become."

Sin has its genesis in the thought-life, so Paul waged war with his thoughts. He made it his constant endeavour to make a prisoner of his fugitive thoughts and bring them under the control of Christ (2 Cor. 10:5). It requires more than strong will-power to bring and keep the mind under control, but "the fruit of the spirit is . . . self-control" (Gal. 5:22–23).

He exercised a strong discipline on his body. "I beat my body and make it my slave so that after I have preached to others, I myself will not be disqualified for the prize" (1 Cor. 9:27). He was in no doubt of his salvation, but there was still time for his body to betray him. So to the end he continued a strict discipline in this area, and made his body his servant. This attitude is worthy of your emulation.

FOR PRAYER: *Lord, may I exhibit the same intensity in training for godliness as the Olympic athlete does for a gold medal.*

June 11

THE FUNCTION OF CONSCIENCE

I thank my God whom I serve . . . with a clear conscience. (2 Timothy 1:3)

In view of the vastly important role which conscience fills, especially in regard to our emotional well-being, it is strange that such scant attention is paid to the function of this persistent monitor of the soul, which distinguishes man from animal.

Conscience is not easy to define. Is it a separate faculty of our moral nature? Is it a divine and therefore infallible endowment, or is it a fallible human mechanism? It would appear from Scripture that it is a special activity of the intellect and the emotions that enables us to perceive moral distinctions, to discriminate between good and evil.

One definition is that it is *the testimony and judgment of the soul which gives approval or disapproval to the decisions and acts of the will* (Rom. 2:14,15). It is the activity of conscience which makes man's sin culpable. The word signifies "knowledge held in conjunction with another", and of course the other is God. It thus makes man a co-witness with God against himself!

Conscience is not an executive faculty, for it is completely powerless to make man do right or cease doing wrong. Its sole responsibility is to deliver its verdict according to its standards, and produce the appropriate emotion. If its verdict is ignored, it can do no more. It is not infallible and must constantly be checked with the Word of God.

FOR MEDITATION: *Conscience is not something we acquire but is part of our essential nature.*

A CLEANSED CONSCIENCE

Holding on to faith and a good conscience. (1 Timothy 1:19)

Paul warns of the peril of failing to heed and respond to the voice of conscience. Conscience has no cure for its own ills, but we should be eternally grateful that adequate provision has been made for the maintenance of its purity and sensitivity.

A mature conscience accepts and rests on the affirmations of the Word of God. It refuses to resurrect what God has forgiven and forgotten. It reposes on God's good faith when He said, "I will forgive their wickedness and will remember their sins no more" (Heb. 8:12).

There is a remedy for a guilty or defiled conscience, but there must be a sincere and honest dealing with sin. The invitation is extended: "Let us draw near to God with a sincere heart in full assurance of faith, having our hearts sprinkled to cleanse us from a guilty conscience . . ." (Heb. 10:22).

John gives further assurance: "If we confess our sins, he is faithful and just and will forgive us our sins *and purify us from all unrighteousness*" (1 John 1:9). To continue condemning ourselves for what God has forgiven is disloyalty to Christ.

How wonderful that the solvent of the blood of Christ applied to the guilty conscience removes every last stain, and leaves the believer with a clean and good conscience, void of offence towards God and man.

FOR WARNING: *An evil conscience results from habitual disregard of the warnings of conscience.*

THE POTTER'S FIRE

When you walk through the fire, you will not be burned. (Isaiah 43:2)

In eastern lands the potter is a familiar figure, with his revolving wheels, malleable clay and skilful fingers, under which the clay is moulded into a vessel of symmetry and beauty.

In Jeremiah's parable (Jer. 18:2–6), the potter's fire is not mentioned, but it is an essential part of his art. Without the fire, the soft, unburnt clay would soon collapse and become a shapeless mass. So God subjects His children to the fires of testing lest their characters become flabby and formless. Lessons learned in the fire are not soon forgotten!

Once the potter has moulded the vessel and painted on it the desired pattern, he encloses it in a fire-resisting case before placing it in a furnace heated to the appropriate temperature. In the fire, the moisture evaporates and unwanted materials are burnt out, while the colour and pattern are burnt in. In this way they are made permanent.

It should be noted that *the vessel does not go into the fire unshielded and unprotected*. Even so, the believer is not alone in the furnace of affliction. He is environed by God. It is only in the fire that the beautiful and concealed colours are burnt in.

There is endless comfort in the divine assurance, "When you walk through the fire . . . the flames will not set you ablaze. For I am the Lord your God" (Isa. 43:2,3).

FOR ENCOURAGEMENT:
When through fiery trials I cause thee to go,
The rivers of grief shall not thee overflow.
The flame shall not hurt thee, I only design
Thy dross to consume and thy gold to refine.

RADICAL CLEANSING

*Who can stand when he appears? For he will be like
a refiner's fire, or like launderer's soap.* (Malachi 3:3)

Two purifying agents are in view in this passage — fire
and soap. The *external* impurities clinging to the gold or
silver ore can be removed by the application of soap and
water, but only fire can reach and remove the *internal*,
hidden impurities — dross, slag, alloy.

So the externals of religion may remove surface stains
from our lives and make us outwardly presentable, but
they are powerless to effect cleansing of the inner
impurities embedded in the subconscious (Mark 7:21).
*Only the fire of the Holy Spirit can penetrate these hidden
depths.* Only He can deal effectively with such deep-
seated habits and ingrained sins.

The refining process is simple, but it demands
considerable expertise. The refiner places the gold in the
crucible, which is suspended over a fierce flame. As it
melts, the impurities are released and come to the surface.
He removes the worthless scum that would diminish the
value of the gold. The purifying process is complete only
when the refiner can see in the molten metal, his own
undimmed likeness.

When we find ourselves in the crucible of testing, we
can take comfort from the fact that it is only because the
heavenly Refiner desires to remove everything that mars
His image in us that He subjects us to the test. The fire
cannot touch our essential personality (Isa. 43:2,3).

FOR CHALLENGE: *Am I willing for the deep inner
cleansing of the Spirit's fire, or am I content with
a superficial application of soap and water?*

THE FRAGRANCE OF CHRIST

*God . . . through us spreads everywhere the fragrance
of the knowledge of him.* (2 Corinthians 2:14)

When we enjoy the sweetness of some fragrant perfume,
how seldom do we consider the cost at which it has been
produced! Thousands of flowers are taken at the height
of their beauty, and crushed in order to capture their
aroma for our delectation.

Some flowers release their fragrance freely all day long,
but others are more selective. Some yield their perfume
only when they are crushed, e.g. lavender and rosemary.
Others become fragrant only under cover of the darkness
of night, e.g. night-scented stock. The aroma of incense
is imprisoned until the flame kindles it.

Does this not find a parallel in the Christian life? Are
not the lives most redolent of the fragrance of Christ,
those who have experienced the dark and crushing
experiences of life? Those who have passed through the
fires and waters of testing and have emerged triumphant?

*The fragrance of Christ flows pre-eminently from His cross
and suffering.* The borrowed fragrance of Paul's life can
be attributed to his experience of the fellowship of those
sufferings. Nor will it be otherwise with us, for suffering
rightly received will produce a sweetness of character that
can be produced in no other way. Such lives are always
unconsciously influential for God.

FOR MEDITATION: *In spreading the fragrance of the
knowledge of Christ, our own lives become
fragrant.*

June 16

THE PRECIOUSNESS OF CHRIST

To you therefore which believe, he is precious (1 Peter 2:7 RSV)

As a lad of sixteen, Charles Haddon Spurgeon preached his first sermon from this text. Could he have chosen a more spacious text?

Christ was *precious to God*. "I was daily his delight" (Prov. 8:30 RSV). "This is my beloved Son, with whom I am well pleased," was God's testimony at Jesus' baptism (Matt. 3:17 RSV). He was inexpressibly dear to the Father. Everything in His walk from Bethlehem to Calvary gave His Father infinite delight.

Christ is *precious to the believer*. "Precious" in the text is a noun, not an adjective. It could be better rendered, *"he is the preciousness"*. An adjective admits of degrees, but not a noun. He is the essence of preciousness.

All the most precious things are hidden in Him — "all the treasures of wisdom and knowledge" (Col. 2:3); "all the fulness of the Godhead" (2:9). We may lose earth's precious things, but we can never lose Jesus, our priceless treasure. Even death serves only to bring Him nearer. He is a jewel of which neither Satan nor death can rob us. He shares our sorrows, lightens our loads, and doubles our joys.

He is precious as Saviour. He not only saves us from our sin, but shares His own life with us. Should this not make Him inexpressibly precious to us?

> What the hand is to the lute,
> What the breath is to the flute,
> What is fragrance to the smell,
>   That is Jesus Christ to me.

FOR PRAISE: *Christ is the complement of every spiritual need of ours.*

THE MEEKNESS OF CHRIST

"I am meek and lowly in heart." (Matthew 11:29
KJV)

In these words Jesus crowned the modest grace of
meekness queen of the virtues. Then, as in our own time,
meekness was regarded as effeminate and servile.

The word was one of the great ethical words of the
Greeks. It was used of the breaking-in of a horse, in which
the animal learned to accept control, and bow to the will
of another. How does this apply to our Lord?

It might be said that *meekness plus lowliness equals
humility*. Meekness is humility towards God, humiliation
towards man. But meekness is not equivalent to
weakness, or to mildness of disposition. Meekness is
strong, but it is strength held in control.

Jesus demonstrated this grace in His boyhood when He
went home and was subject to His parents (Luke
2:41–52).

Without complaint He was willing to perform the
lowliest duties. He made ploughs and yokes for the
farmers, He who made the worlds. He meekly accepted
His Father's plan for His life, even though it involved
exchanging the freedom of the universe for the
restrictions of a carpenter's shop.

Meekness is essentially the attitude that *does not insist
on its own rights*, but is always ready to waive privilege
in the interests of others. Is this grace prominent in our
lives?

FOR PRAYER:
> Love is kind and suffers long,
> Love is meek and thinks no wrong;
> Love than death itself more strong;
> Therefore give us love.

THE LOVE OF CHRIST

The love of Christ . . . that surpasses knowledge.
(Ephesians 3:19)

Love sometimes expresses itself in a seemingly contradictory way. Parental love expresses itself in a wholesome and loving discipline, not in the indulgence of every whim. Not every child appreciates this expression of love. It is the same with the Lord's children.

Christ's love corrects the one whom He loves. Speaking of the young ruler, Mark says, "Jesus looked at him and loved him" (10:21). And what did His love lead Him to do? He discerned the fatal flaw in his life, and dealt with him faithfully. In clinging to his great possessions, the young man sacrificed the greatest possession.

Christ's love allows suffering. "Jesus loved Martha, Mary and Lazarus." Was He soft and indulgent with this favoured family in whose home He was a frequent visitor? No, He was not. He did not intervene to prevent Lazarus treading the vale of death. He did not spare the sisters the heartbreak of seeing him slowly slip away. Did He not care? He delayed His coming "so that they might believe" (John 11:15). He cared so much that He permitted their suffering.

Christ's love cleanses. "Having loved his own . . . he began to wash the disciples' feet" (John 13:1,5). At that moment He was on the way to cleanse their defiled souls with His blood. No task was too menial. He washed their feet with water and their souls with blood from the basin of the cross.

FOR PRAYER:
> *Faith and hope and love we see*
> *Joining hand in hand agree,*
> *But the greatest of the three*
> *And the best is love.*

THE MIND OF CHRIST

Let this mind be in you which was also in Christ Jesus.
(Philippians 2:5 KJV)

The mind of Christ was more than His thinking processes. It was His entire inner disposition and included His thoughts, motives and desires. It is because we reflect the mind of Christ so imperfectly, that we make so slight an impression on the cynical world around us.

In this passage, the mind of Christ is seen operating on two levels.

On the level of deity, Christ did not count equality with God and its attendant majesty, something to be grasped and retained at all costs. He did not greedily cling to His rights as God's equal. Instead He "made himself nothing", veiled His majesty and accepted the limitations involved in assuming human form. He could never be less than God, but He renounced the outward display of His glory, and the independent exercise of His will.

On the level of humanity, "he humbled himself". We have every reason to humble ourselves, but it was not so with Him. He did not demand such a standard of treatment as befitted His dignity. Instead of a palace, He chose a manger; His throne was a carpenter's bench; His university a village school. So low did He stoop in His self-humiliation, that He took the lowest step — death on a cross as a criminal.

His mind was the exact reverse of the worldly mind that revels in position and power, wealth and possessions. *Let this mind be in you.*

FOR PRAYER:
May the mind of Christ our Saviour
Dwell in me from day to day,
By His love and power controlling
All I do and say.

June 20

THE ABILITY OF CHRIST

He is able . . . He is able . . . He is able . . .
(Hebrews 2:18; 4:15; 7:25)

The remedy the writer of the Hebrews letter prescribed for recovery from premature spiritual senility was — *Get better acquainted with Christ,* who, in His capacity as High Priest, secures our access to God, presents our prayers at His Father's throne, and lives to intercede for us. This is the significance of Hebrews 5:4–7. Three of His gracious activities are revealed in this letter.

First, He is *"able to help* those who are being tempted" (2:18). There are two Greek words for "help". One means "to come unsought", the other, "to come in response to a call of need". It is comforting to know that our High Priest knows no limitations. We are often *willing* to help someone in need, but are *unable.* Our Lord is not only willing, but able.

Second, He is *"able to sympathise* with our weaknesses" (4:15). Sympathy is more than mere pity. It means "to suffer together with someone". To enter into the experience of another as though it were one's own. This is a concept entirely absent from Greek thought. Their gods came to earth to enjoy themselves. What a contrast with the Son of God!

Third, He is *"able to save completely"* (7:25). The present tense indicates "a sustained experience resulting from a continuing practice". "He is able to keep on saving those who are continually coming to God." So let us come confidently to the throne of grace.

FOR THANKSGIVING: *I thank You, Lord, that when You were on earth You demonstrated that You were not only* able, *but willing, to help us in our problems.*

June 21

NON-CONFORMITY

Do not conform any longer to the pattern of this world.
(Romans 12:2)

"Do not let the world squeeze you into its mould," is J. B. Phillips' translation of Romans 12:2. We are not to adopt the protective colouration of the chameleon as we move about in different environments. We are not to follow the world's agenda. To speak of a "worldly Christian" is strictly as great an anomaly as to speak of "an honest thief", or "a truthful liar". The words are antithetical, and logically they are mutually exclusive.

The mature Christian will not cover himself with the veneer of this age – *he will be a non-conformist where worldly standards and practices are concerned*. He will not allow the world to dictate what he should do or be.

Instead, he will be "transformed", changed from within. "Cease adapting yourself to this present age, but continue your transformation by the renewing of your mind." This inward renewal will involve a change in thinking and viewing things. Not a sudden metamorphosis, but a process initiated and stimulated by a renewed will, and empowered by the Holy Spirit.

This almost sounds as though Paul is advocating a process of sanctification by self-effort. In fact, he is only recognising that the mind has been affected by the fall, and must be renewed by the Holy Spirit.

FOR ASPIRATION:
> *Let me then be always growing,*
> *Never standing still,*
> *Listening, learning, better knowing*
> *Thee and Thy blessed will.*

FAN THE FLAME

*Do not neglect your gift, which was given you . . .
when the body of elders laid their hands on you.* (1
Timothy 4:14)
Fan into a flame the gift of God which is in you. (2
Timothy 1:6)

At the ordination of young Timothy, Paul and the elders
laid their hands on him, thus passing on the grace-gift
which would equip him as apostolic representative.
Aware of Timothy's weaknesses as well as of his
strengths, Paul gave him a double exhortation:

"Do not neglect your gift." Don't grow careless of the
sacred trust. It was a sovereignly bestowed endowment
of the Spirit – not an external operation, but an inward
grace. Apparently the efficiency of the gift was not
automatic; it could potentially decline. "Don't let it suffer
by neglect," was Paul's advice.

"Fan into flame the gift of God." "For God did not give
us a spirit of timidity, but a spirit of power, and of love
and self-discipline" (v.7). It was not that Timothy needed
a new endowment, but the spiritual fire had burned low.
"Stir up that inner fire", is J. B. Phillips' translation.

Did Paul sense that Timothy's zeal had begun to wane?
A flame does not automatically rise higher. "Keep in full
flame", or rekindle the fire. Put new fuel on the dying
embers.

O that in me the sacred fire
Might now begin to glow,
Burn up the dross of base desire
And make the mountains flow.

FOR PRAYER: *I pray, Lord, that no false fire may
burn on the altar of my heart.*

THE CRIME OF SELFISHNESS

"If I have . . . eaten my morsel alone . . ." (Job 31:17 RSV)

As an Oriental, Job would never have eaten himself, until he had set his best before his guest. It would make no difference if it were his last bite. To have eaten his meal alone when others were hungry around him, would have demeaned him as much as if he were guilty of the heinous sins he mentions in verses 5 to 16 — falsehood, deceit, adultery, injustice, defrauding the poor. In the midst of these he places the *crime of selfishness* — eating his morsel alone — and acknowledges that this deserves retribution. "Let my arm fall from my shoulder, let it be broken off at the joint" (v.22).

This *self-centred spirit* was the crime of the prodigal's elder brother. He saw no significance in the surplus at his father's table (Luke 15:17) and spared no thought for his brother starving in a foreign country. It was the sin of the rich man who callously ignored the need of the destitute Lazarus at his gate (Luke 16:19,20).

We should ask ourselves this conscience-stirring question, *Am I eating my morsel, myself alone* — feasting at the gospel table while others in the far country are perishing for lack of the bread of life?

Jesus did not eat His morsel alone. He went to the cross so that His broken body might become the Bread of Life.

FOR PRAYER: *O Lord, may I never be guilty of hoarding the Bread of Life while millions are starving for it.*

CONTENTMENT, NOT COMPLAINING

If we have food and clothing, we will be content with that. (1 Timothy 6:8)

Most of us shine better when we emerge from difficult circumstances than when we are in them. Paul shone more brightly when he was in the midst of them. What was his secret?

Acceptance instead of rebellion. Anyone can resist or rebel against God, and charge Him with not treating them fairly. "Why should this happen to me?" they protest. The mature Christian accepts the biblical teaching that no circumstance comes into his life apart from divine permission, even though the reason is not immediately apparent. This attitude allows him to discern that the will of God is indeed "good and acceptable and perfect".

Contentment, not complaining. Anyone can complain at what God allows. Only the mature Christian knows contentment in the midst of it. As a nation, the Hebrews were complainers, a fault which marred their history. They have their counterparts in the Church today, and the complainers are usually the ones who cause division and dissension.

Trustfulness, not anxiety. The natural reaction to difficult or threatening circumstances is to indulge in an orgy of worry. But is it not true that times without number the calamity we foresaw never came to pass? And yet we continue our ulcer-producing, peace-destroying habit of worry. Remember:

> *If you trust you do not worry,*
> *If you worry you do not trust.*

FOR PRAYER: *Lord, I would heed Paul's admonitions: "Be content with what you have," and "Godliness with contentment is great gain."*

LEARNING CONTENTMENT

I have learned the secret of being content. (Philippians 4:12)

Our maturity is most accurately reflected in *our attitudes and unstudied reactions to our circumstances*, especially the unexpected and unwelcome ones. Paul's maturity shone brightly in his reactions to his unjust imprisonments. In the inner prison in Philippi, with their feet fast in the stocks, he and Silas sang songs at midnight! (Acts 16:25).

When later he wrote from prison, far from bemoaning his fate, his theme-song was, "Rejoice in the Lord always" (Phil. 4:4). He drew his strength from the knowledge that God was still on His throne, and that he was safe in His Father's hands.

When he said, "I have *learned* the secret of being content in any and every situation," he used the ordinary word for learning at school. The child learns by adding knowledge to what he has already learned. The disciple has to learn in exactly the same way.

Even the Son of God could not go through life while wearing our humanity without submitting to the learning process (Heb. 5:8). Paul's attitude was not that of the stoic or the fatalist, who bow to the inevitable. Rather was it the attitude of glad acceptance: "For Christ's sake, I delight in weaknesses, in insults, in hardships" – the very things we would wish to avoid! And the result? "When I am weak, then I am strong" (2 Cor. 12:10).

FOR PRAYER: *Lord, I find it easier to complain than to be content. Please help me to master this lesson.*

WHEN TEMPTATION STRIKES

> *He [Jesus] was hungry. The devil said to him, "If you
> are the Son of God, tell this stone to become bread."*
> (Luke 4:2,3)

We can gain insight into our adversary's methods from
a study of Christ's representative temptations.

They came *after a time of rich blessing*, when, at His
baptism and the descent of the Spirit, His Father had
expressed unbounded approval of His Son (Matt. 3:17).
"Then was Jesus led into the desert to be tempted by the
devil" (Luke 4:1). After the dove, the devil. After the
blessing, the battle. This is often the sequence, and has
been down the ages.

They came *in an inhospitable environment* – the desert,
among the wild beasts. The fact that we have experienced
great blessing does not alter the reality of returning to
face difficult conditions. Indeed, our circumstances may
change for the worse. We can take courage from the fact
that Jesus proved His Father's care even in the loneliness
of the barren desert.

They came *when His body was weak* through prolonged
fasting. It is easier to meet temptation when we are in
top physical form, but the devil is a dirty fighter. He
delights to launch his fiery darts when we are weary and
under pressure. Natural law still applies even when we
are engaged in the Lord's service, and we should be
careful to guard against a reckless over-expenditure of
physical and nervous energy.

> Tempted and tried?
> There is One at your side!

FOR THANKSGIVING: *Lord, I thank You that You
"suffered, being tempted", so that You could
help me in my temptations.*

AVENUES OF TEMPTATION

"All this I will give you," he [*the devil*] *said, "if you will bow down and worship me."* (Matthew 4:9)

Temptation is the uniform experience of life. "No one is so good that he is immune from temptation," wrote Thomas à Kempis.

A study of the three temptations of Christ indicates that they were representative and cover the whole range of human desire. Temptation assails men along three avenues.

The first is *appetite, the desire to enjoy things*. Satan made his first approach to Jesus on the *physical* plane (Matt. 4:2,3). He stirred up a natural and legitimate desire, but pressured the Lord to go beyond the limits set by God. The focus of the temptation was not on His right to satisfy His hunger, but on His submission to the will of God. Satan was foiled in this attempt.

The second is *ambition, the desire to achieve great things or be somebody* (vv.5,6). This approach was on the *mental* plane. It focused on our Lord's confidence in His Father – putting Him to the test. Jesus replied that for Him this would be presumption, not faith. Once again Satan was defeated.

The third is *avarice, the desire to gain possession of things* (vv.8–10). The temptation in this case was to put things in the place rightly belonging to God. The focus here was on the possibility that He could achieve His purpose without the anguish and agony of the Cross. Once again Jesus unsheathed the sword of the Spirit and routed the tempter.

FOR MEDITATION: *The mature believer is one who has learned how to meet temptation and emerge victorious.*

June 28

ACCEPTING OUR AGE

"So here I am today, eighty-five years old." (Joshua 14:10)

If we are to experience serenity and joy in our closing years, we must gladly accept our age and what it brings as part of God's perfect will. We must resolutely lay ourselves out to maintain a positive, cheerful outlook. Of course, there can be a phoney cheerfulness. But "joy in the Holy Spirit" is a supernatural something that transcends even suffering, pain and increasing limitation.

It should be our ambition to make our last years the best — for God, for our fellows, and for ourselves. Why should they not be the best? God promised "I . . . will do better unto you than at your beginnings" (Ezek. 36:11 KJV).

> What then? Shall we sit idly down and say,
> The night is come; it is no longer day?
> For age is opportunity no less
> Than youth itself, though in another dress.
> And as the evening twilight fades away,
> The sky is filled with stars
> Invisible by day.
>
> *H. W. Longfellow*

Some elderly folk fairly radiate joy, and their very presence is a benediction. They evidence an attractive maturity to which the self-absorbed and self-pitying are strangers. Inward growth is still possible after the physical falls into decay, for all true growth is mental and spiritual.

FOR MEDITATION:
> *It is not the years that make men old,*
> *The spirit may be young*
> *Though three score years and ten*
> *The wheels of life have run.*

June 29

SELFLESS LOVE

"My command is this: Love each other." (John 15:12)

We are not to love our fellows merely because we like them. Aversion and affinity are alike irrelevant. Our love must not be selective because of family or social ties; nor because people are neighbours geographically, but simply because, being redeemed sinners ourselves, we seek to share the love of Christ with others.

Jesus told us that we are to love others even as He loved us. How did He express His love? His was *selfless love*. In even the noblest human love there is always some element of self-interest. We love, in part, because of what it brings to us, the happiness it imparts. Christ's love was disinterested, unselfish, unconditional.

It was *forgiving love*. The only person in a position to forgive, is the one against whom the offence has been committed. Although He was doubted, denied, betrayed, forsaken, our Lord's love was not quenched. When He told Peter that his forgiveness was to extend not to seven offences but to seventy times seven, He was only illustrating the extent of His own forgiving love.

It was *sacrificial love*. Every act of service our Lord performed cost Him something (e.g. Mark 5:30). There was no limit to the sacrifices He made in His lifetime, but the supreme sacrifice was made on the cross. True love gives unconditionally and demands nothing in return.

FOR MEDITATION: *No task is too menial for love. Christ washed the disciples' feet with water, and then with blood from the basin of the cross.*

NO SHORT-TERM DISCIPLESHIP

"Follow me," Jesus said to him . . . and Levi got up, left everything and followed him. (Luke 5:28)

The New Testament makes no provision for short-term discipleship. We are living, however, in days when most involvements are short-term — even the marriage covenant.

Many say they are willing to follow Christ, but on a short-term basis. But this is not acceptable to Him. It is true that the *location* in which we exercise our discipleship may be for a short term, but total and long-term commitment is involved. The short-term disciple usually does not burn his bridges behind him, and seldom quite reaches the point of no return.

A young man recently said to me, "I think I will take a trip to Asia, and look around to see what it is like. If I feel comfortable about it, I might return as a missionary!" He was a short-term disciple. The Great Commission does not make the comfort of the messenger the determining factor. One whose discipleship was so languid and calculating would be no asset to the missionary force.

Samuel Chadwick stated the implications of discipleship in stark terms: "We are moved by the act of God. Omniscience holds no conference. Infinite authority leaves no room for compromise. Eternal love offers no explanations. The Lord expects to be trusted. He disturbs us at will. Human arrangements are disregarded, business claims put aside. We are never asked if it is convenient."

FOR MEDITATION: *Our geographical location may be short-term, but Jesus made no provision for short-term discipleship.*

THE DEVIL IS DEFEATABLE

They overcame him. (Revelation 12:11)

A firm belief in the defeatability of Satan is one of the strongest weapons in the Christian's arsenal. For us to highlight Satan's power without taking into account Christ's victory over him at Calvary, is like speaking of the Napoleonic wars without mentioning the battle of Waterloo.

Although Satan is the second most powerful being in the universe, he is *not omnipotent*. He possesses no power at all independently of God. He has a very effective communications system through his demons, but he is *not omnipresent*. He possesses great subtlety and shrewdness, but he is *not omniscient*. He has to gather his information as we do. He is no match for our omnipotent, omniscient and omnipresent Lord.

James 4:7 has been termed the most incredible verse in the Bible: "Submit yourselves, then, to God. Resist the devil, and he will flee from you." It does seem incredible that this powerful, malignant being who controls hell's legions, who could offer the kingdoms of the world to Christ, will flee before the weakest believer who resists him on the ground of Calvary's victory. But it is gloriously true. We can go into every battle with the assurance in advance of victory.

> Jesus is stronger than Satan and sin,
> Satan to Jesus must bow.
> Therefore I triumph without and within;
> Jesus saves me now.

FOR PRAISE: *I praise You, Lord, for the completeness of Your triumph over Satan on the cross.*

July 2

SATAN'S INCOGNITO

Do not give the devil a foothold. (Ephesians 4:27)

We are in danger of running to one of two extremes in relation to the devil our relentless adversary. One is largely to ignore him, and get on with our work as though he did not exist. The other is to take him too seriously, and make too much of him. Christians in the Middle Ages tended to follow the latter course, and gave the devil a disproportionate place in their preaching. Their morbid fears robbed them of peace and assurance.

But we must neither over-estimate nor under-estimate the power of Satan, nor should we live in fear of him. We are not to be "frightened in any way by those who oppose us" (Phil. 1:28).

If the devil is not successful in making sceptics of us, he will try to make us excessively devil-conscious, so that we see an evil spirit as the actor behind every sickness or adverse circumstance. Demons are blamed for sins that Scripture attributes to our own sinful natures. As James writes, "Each one is tempted when, by his own evil desire, he is dragged away and enticed" (1:14). Instead of reckoning themselves dead to that sin (Rom. 6:11), they resort to the supposed exorcism of a demon by someone else.

Satan's incognito is one of his most useful weapons. It affords him comfort when prominent theologians cast doubt on his very existence.

FOR MEDITATION: *"Satan disappears in his successes, and his triumph is his incognito."*

EMOTIONAL INSTABILITY

*Then we will no longer be infants . . . blown here and
there by every wind of teaching.* (Ephesians 4:14)

Emotional instability is characteristic of both an infant and
an immature Christian. The person described by Paul in
our text, never reaches settled convictions of his own,
convictions so strong that he is willing to suffer for them.

He tends to live in the realm of his own fickle emotions,
and these can be both capricious and tyrannical. Instead
of being motivated by the spiritual principles enunciated
in Scripture, he is moved by his transient feelings. In
facing a decision, his question is not, "Will this please
God?" but, "Does this please me?" His actions are
dictated more by what he feels about it, than by what he
ought to do. Like an infant, he is a slave to his feelings,
and thus lacks emotional stability. He should live more
in the realm of the will, and less in the unstable area of
the emotions. After all, *we are what we choose, not what
we feel*.

Before his transforming experience on the day of
Pentecost, Peter was a classic example of this emotional
instability. One moment he was walking on water, the
next he was sinking beneath the waves. After Pentecost
all this was changed. The marks of immaturity
disappeared and he became Peter the rock, no longer
volatile but stable, the leader of the apostolic band.

FOR PRAISE: *"God created us with emotions so
that we could enjoy Him and His creations."*
(E. W. Lutzer)

July 4

GOD'S GOODNESS AND GLORY

Moses did not know that the skin of his face shone . . .
(Exodus 34:29 RSV)

Communion with God kindled in Moses an intense desire to know Him better. He had asked God, "Teach me your ways" (Exod. 33:13), and God had responded, "I will do the very thing you have asked" (v.17). This encouraged him to make a more bold request, "Now show me your glory" (v.18).

God's answer gave him – and us – an insight into the nature of His glory: "I myself will make all my goodness pass before you, and will proclaim the name of the Lord before you . . . The Lord, the Lord God, compassionate and gracious, slow to anger and abounding in loving kindness and truth; who keeps loving kindness for thousands, who forgives iniquity, transgression and sin; yet who will by no means leave the guilty unpunished" (33:19;34:6,7).

God's goodness and glory are enshrined in His name, in His moral character. Moses did not see the full glory of God in its unveiled effulgence, only the after-glow that He left as He passed by (33:20–23). Some of that glory rubbed off on Moses "When Moses was coming down from Mt Sinai . . . he did not know that the skin of his face shone, because of his speaking with Him." That is still the divine prescription for radiance.

FOR PRAYER: *O Lord, work in me a deeper desire to spend longer in Your presence so that I may better represent You before men.*

BRINGING BACK THE KING

"Why do you say nothing about bringing the king back?" (2 Samuel 19:10)

David had been ousted from his throne through the intrigue of his rebellious son, Absalom. The death of the usurper threw the kingdom into confusion. The hearts of the people turned to their old hero, and they were soon vying for the honour of bringing the king back. But David was not prepared to return unconditionally. Certain things must be put right; and these same matters have their counterpart in our relationship to Christ if He is not reigning in our lives. Here they are:

An Undivided Kingdom. Jealousy had separated Judah and Israel, and David was not prepared to reign over a divided kingdom. Christ has the same rights of kinship and kingship over us. He must see an end to the civil war in the soul.

A Unanimous Request. David refused to force himself on a reluctant people. He used every legitimate means to induce them to invite him back, but it was only when they sent an urgent request that he made a move. "They said to the king, 'Return.' . . . Then the king returned" (v.14).

An Uncompromising Allegiance. Before the kingdom could be established, the leader of the rebellion, Sheba, must be punished, the traitor dealt with. The king must have the full allegiance of his subjects. Before Christ consents to reassume the throne of Mansoul, we must deal drastically with sin.

FOR ACTION: *King of my life I crown Thee now, Thine shall the glory be.*

NOT EXEMPT FROM FAILURE

Even Barnabas was led astray with their hypocrisy.
(Galatians 2:13)

Barnabas was one of the most lovable characters in the Bible. His colleagues nicknamed him "Son of Encouragement". He set a noble example of Christian liberality. He worked loyally with Paul. But being a good man, and full of the Holy Spirit, does not preclude the possibility of failure. This attractive man was not a perfect man. The treasure was there, but in an earthen vessel.

Barnabas and Saul were united in their purpose to ignore the legalistic outlook of the Jerusalem hierarchy, and to identify with the new Gentile believers at Antioch. The sad sequel is recorded by Paul: "When they [*the Judaisers*] arrived, he [*Peter*] began to draw back and separate himself from the Gentiles, because he was afraid . . . By their hypocrisy even Barnabas was led astray" (*vv.12,13*).

Even Barnabas! That was a heart-rending blow to Paul. It was bad enough that Peter should yield to the pressure group from Jerusalem, but that his beloved colleague and senior missionary should join in the defection was the unkindest cut of all.

The seriousness of Barnabas' failure was that not only did he embarrass and desert his colleague, but he insulted the believers at Antioch, and imperilled their Christian liberty.

The lesson of this incident is that *even our strong points need constant watchfulness, lest they degenerate into weakness.*

FOR THANKSGIVING: *Lord, You foresaw all my failures before You saved me. Thank You that, knowing them, You did not disqualify me for Your service.*

THE PRINCIPLE OF APPROPRIATION

Praise be to the God and Father of our Lord Jesus Christ, who has blessed us in the heavenly realms with every spiritual blessing in Christ. (Ephesians 1:3)

In surveying the spiritual blessings of the Christian living in his Promised Land, Paul was so carried away that he burst into the above doxology.

Although Canaan *legally* belonged to Israel by gift from God, it became theirs *actually* only when they appropriated it by walking over it, and thus taking possession. God gave, they must take.

The same principle carries over into the New Testament: "According to your faith [*appropriation*] *will it be done to you*" (Matt. 9:29).

Note that Ephesians 1:3 is not a promise to be claimed, but *a statement of fact* to be believed and acted on. Every spiritual blessing has already been given to us, but we enjoy in experience only those we appropriate and make our own.

A young missionary known to the author was having a great struggle at language school, to master the difficult Chinese language. One day, in despair, he took his large Chinese Grammar, placed it on the floor and stood on it. Then he prayed, "Lord, you said you would give every place that the sole of my foot trod on (Josh. 1:3). My feet are on the Chinese Grammar. Give me the Chinese language!"

His symbolical act of faith did not go unrewarded. Through diligent study and application, he gained such proficiency that some years later he became head of that school.

FOR PRAYER: *Father, forgive my ingratitude in appropriating so few of the spiritual blessings You have given.*

APOLLOS THE APOLOGIST

He vigorously refuted the Jews in public debate, proving from the Scriptures that Jesus was the Christ.
(Acts 18:28)

Apollos' preaching was popular yet courageous, a combination not always present. He did not trim his sails to suit his congregation. He seemed to thrive on opposition and controversy. There was nothing defensive or apologetic about his presentation.

Though not apologetic for his message, *he was an able apologist*. He vigorously refuted the arguments of the Judaisers. "Refuted" is a strong word, and the tense gives the meaning: "He kept arguing them down," or, "He refuted them at every point."

The only other occurrence of the word is in Luke 23:10: "The chief priests and the scribes were standing there, vehemently accusing him." They subjected Jesus to non-Christian vehemence, but Apollos met his opponents with sustained Christian vehemence. He believed his beliefs strongly, and he was prepared to vindicate them to the limit.

His robust defence of the gospel was a great strength to the young church at Achaia, which Paul encouraged him to visit. "He was a great help to those who by grace had believed" (Acts 18:27). It meant much to those young Christians to have such a doughty champion.

He excelled in matching Old Testament prophecies with their fulfilment in Christ. The Jews had no answer when from their own Scriptures he was able to demonstrate that Jesus was the Messiah, for whom they had looked so long.

FOR PRAYER: *Lord, equip me to be a contender for the faith, but deliver me from the sin of contentiousness.*

TALKING AND TEARS

Jesus said to [Martha], "Your brother will rise again" . . .
When Jesus saw Mary weeping . . . Jesus wept. (John 11:23,33,35)

Mary and Martha were overwhelmed with unexpected sorrow. The serious illness of Lazarus caused them to turn to the Great Physician, who was in the north of Palestine. They fully expected Him to hasten to their side, but the days passed and He did not come. They experienced the sorrow of losing their brother, alone. Jesus' seemingly inexplicable indifference deeply grieved them.

When at last He came and Martha went to meet Him, her greeting held a note of reproach: "If you had been here, my brother would not have died" (v.21). But her faith was strong, and it was practical Martha who suggested a possible resurrection. Her conversation climaxed with the magnificent confession: "I believe that you are the Christ, the Son of God, who was to come into the world" (v.27).

When Jesus came to Mary, she uttered the same grief-laden words as Martha, and then melted into wordless tears. Jesus had been able to talk things through with Martha, but Mary was beyond words. How did He deal with her in her sorrow? "Jesus burst into tears" (v.35) – tears of love and sympathy.

With deep understanding, *Jesus ministered to each according to her temperament*. He talked things over with logical Martha. He wept with more emotional Mary. He is not less understanding of *our* temperaments.

FOR PRAISE: *I praise You Lord, that You understand every quirk of my personality, and still love and cherish me.*

DIVINE PROVIDENCE

"Do you understand what you are reading?" Philip asked. "How can I," he said, "unless someone explains it to me?" (Acts 8:30–31)

The timing of Philip's encounter with the Ethiopian eunuch bore all the marks of divine providence. He was reading aloud in Isaiah's prophecy, and as the chariot drew alongside, the Spirit said to Philip, "Go to that chariot and stay near it" (v.29).

The traveller was making no sense out of what he was reading, and readily acknowledged his bewilderment to Philip. Was it by chance that he was that moment reading the chapter which, more than any other, reveals Christ as the suffering Saviour? Was it by chance that the one man in the area who could explain the prophet's meaning was sitting next to him?

Never did a preacher have a more attentive and interested audience than did Philip as he told him the good news about Jesus. In addition to explaining the inner meaning of the cross of Christ, Philip must have explained the place of Christian baptism, for no sooner had he embraced Christ, then he was asking to be baptised. No wonder he went away rejoicing.

The whole incident highlights God's interest in the individual. He goes to endless pains to bring one seeker to salvation. To achieve this end, He will take a prominent church leader away from a revival movement, so that he can meet the need of a single inquirer – *and incidentally bring the gospel to the African continent*.

FOR PRAYER: *Father, teach me the prompt obedience that Philip displayed, lest I miss opportunities for witness which You have planned.*

FIVE TIMES PRIME MINISTER

Daniel so distinguished himself among the administrators . . . by his exceptional qualities that the King planned to set him over the whole kingdom. (Daniel 6:3)

Daniel's biography reads like a modern success story. From his lowly position as a captive exile, he rose from one promotion to another, until he became the ruler of the province of Babylon. Loftier heights of fame and honour it would be difficult to imagine in the world of that day.

As a youth, the prince of the eunuchs gave him the name of Belteshazzar – "he whom Belshazzar favours". But he enjoyed the favour of a God infinitely greater than Belshazzar. The Babylonian king loaded him with gifts and honours. His successor made Daniel third ruler of the kingdom. Under King Darius, "Daniel was preferred above the presidents and princes . . . because an excellent spirit was in him: and the King thought to set him over the whole realm" (6:3 KJV).

After his experience in the den of lions and the glorious vindication of his faith in God, we read: "So this Daniel prospered in the reign of Darius and in the reign of Cyrus the Persian" (v.28 KJV).

Never again is he seen under indictment or in trouble with the princes. What other man has filled with distinction the equivalent position of Prime Minister to five kings, some of whom were of different dynasties?

Here is a success story unique in the history of the world.

FOR PRAISE: *Thank You, Lord, for preserving for our emulation the biography of this man of whom no fault is recorded.*

July 12

MISSIONARY MOTIVATION

The love of Christ constrains me. (2 Corinthians 5:14)

Paul's ambition was essentially selfless and Christ-centred. He was himself the best illustration of disinterested love.

Such consuming ambition could be kindled only by the most powerful of motives, and the apostle indicated some of the factors that motivated him.

First and strongest was the drawing power of the love of Christ. "The love of Christ constraineth me" (KJV). The love that captured and broke his heart on the Damascus road, held him in undisputed vassalage until He met Him whom he had never seen in the flesh. It was this love that nerved him for unparalleled labours and suffering.

Then, too, there was *an inescapable sense of obligation*. "I feel myself under a sort of universal obligation," he wrote. "I owe something to all men, from cultured Greek to ignorant savage" (Rom. 1:14 Phillips).

Paul had *the authentic missionary passion to share a personal discovery*. This all-embracing obligation overleaped all racial barriers and overrode all cultural differences. He felt himself equally indebted to *all* men, since all were included in the scope of Christ's love and sacrifice, and all were capable of salvation.

When this deep sense of obligation and passion to share with the unevangelised our discovery of Christ's salvation grips us, the work of mission will be greatly accelerated.

FOR PRAYER: *Lord, I acknowledge that Your love leaves me no choice but to love You in return. Increase that love.*

FLAMING WITNESS

"He was a burning and a shining light." (John 5:35 KJV)

Our Lord greatly eulogised His forerunner, John the Baptist. But it was to *his flaming witness* that Jesus paid the most striking eulogy: "He was a burning and a shining light."

Why use two kindred words to describe the same thing? The words are indeed kindred but not synonymous. *Shining* indicated that his life brilliantly illuminated the surrounding darkness. *Burning* implied that in the process he himself was being consumed. Because his life was on fire for God, its light was burning and shining.

In His character were combustible elements on which the flame of God could kindle. There are combustible elements in our lives too. Our tongues can be set on fire by hell (Jas. 3:6). We can be inflamed with passion and blaze with anger. The fires of ambition, lust and revenge can consume us. But it was holy fire that flamed on the altar of John's heart. This holy flame quenched the false fires of pride and ambition.

The Eastern lamp was a simple affair — container, oil, wick. And who notices the wick? It is the light that catches the eye. The wick exists to be consumed. If it survives, it has failed in its purpose. There is no such thing as costless spiritual service. Ours is the privilege of offering ourselves as fuel for the flame of God.

FOR THANKSGIVING: *Thank You, Lord, for giving me the honour of being a wick on which the flame of the Spirit can feed as He sheds light in the darkness.*

July 14

PARABLE OF THE TALENTS

*"A man going on a journey, called his servants . . .
To one he gave five talents, to another two talents and
to another one talent."* (Matthew 25:14,15)

The parable of the talents is a parable of stewardship –
not only of money, but of life and its opportunities. We
are to fill our time with loyal service.

God has called us into partnership with Himself and
in the affairs of the Kingdom. In the parable, the amount
entrusted to each servant varied, "each according to
his ability" – five, two and one. (A talent would be
equivalent to about $3000 in our money.)

In applying the parable, while the idea of money is not
excluded, the talent would represent intellectual ability,
musical talent, artistic gifts, practical skills, ability to sing
or preach. These are a trust to be used for Christ until
He returns. The number of talents will vary with the
individual's ability to use them.

God will not hold us responsible for talents we do not possess.
He does not demand an A grade from a B grade student,
nor is He satisfied with a B grade from an A grade
student. We are judged on our faithful use of the gifts
we do possess. It is open to any of us to gain one hundred
per cent on our trading. Each can gain the same reward
(vv.21,23).

Those who have only one talent need to be especially
on the watch. Because they feel they can do so little, they
are tempted to do nothing.

FOR THANKSGIVING: *I thank You, Father, for every
gift and talent You have entrusted to me. Help
me to use them to the limit.*

July 15

LITTLE FOXES ARE CUTE

"Catch for us the foxes, the little foxes that ruin the vineyards, our vineyards that are in bloom." (Song of Songs 2:15)

Little foxes are cute and charming, but they can work havoc in the vineyard where the vines are in bloom. They are intriguing in their playfulness, but in their play they can spoil the forming grapes.

Small sins may be very attractive to us, and seem harmless, but they can be very destructive to the spiritual life. A secret sin, truth disobeyed, devotions neglected, a small root of bitterness in the heart, a secret parleying with sexual sin – these can defile ourselves and others, and mar our fellowship with God. Though they are small, our tongues can spark great conflagrations. "Consider what a great forest is set on fire by a small spark" (Jas. 3:5).

Little foxes grow! In babyhood they are so attractive, but in maturity they become ruthlessly destructive. We should ask God to reveal to us the early beginnings of destructive sin, and by His enabling renounce it for ever.

In God's sight there is no such thing as a small sin – all sins are the same size, for they constitute rebellion against Him.

Is something, however seemingly innocent, spoiling our lives? Has the early bloom of Christian experience faded? The writer of the Hebrews letter exhorted: "Look diligently, lest anyone fail of the grace of God" (Heb. 12:15 KJV).

FOR PRAYER: *Lord, reveal to me the "little" sins which You see in my life, and enable me to hand them over to death.*

July 16

FIRST GO – THEN COME

> *"If you remember that your brother has something against you . . . First go and be reconciled . . ."*
> (Matthew 5:23, 24)

If in the place of prayer the Holy Spirit brings to remembrance the fact that a brother or sister has a valid cause of offence against us, our first responsibility is not to continue the ritual of worship, but to go to that person and effect restoration of the broken fellowship. *"First go . . . then come and offer your gift"* is the invariable order. God is more interested in correct relationships than in gifts. *Reconciliation precedes sacrifice.*

It is impossible to be wrong with our brother or sister and to be right with God. The initiative lies with us.

At the Keswick Convention in England in 1905, Dr F. B. Meyer delivered an address on this text which so moved the audience to action in making restitution, that the post office at Keswick ran short of postal notes and money orders!

Obedience to the injunction of these verses has brought great blessing to individuals and churches. At a conference of pastors in South Vietnam, the author witnessed a movement of the Spirit in which the Holy Spirit worked in great power. The climax came at a meeting when pastors and missionaries went to one another in confession and seeking reconciliation. And the result? In spite of escalating war, the Vietnamese Church doubled in three years.

FOR PRAYER: *Lord, show me if there is some act of restitution that I should perform; but deliver me from the devil's unfounded accusations.*

THE GOLDEN PRINCIPLE

"Do to others what you would have them do to you."
(Matthew 7:12)

In this saying, the Sermon on the Mount reaches is apex.
It is a summary of the law concerning man's relation to
man. It is the full expression of our social responsibility,
the principle of all social conduct.

It is true that others have advocated a similar truth –
Socrates, Aristotle, Confucius – but there is a significant
difference. Between our Lord's teaching on the social
duties of man and that of the others mentioned, there
is a crucial difference. His teaching was *positive and active*,
while theirs was *negative and passive*.

Confucius counselled, "Do not do to others what you
would not wish done to yourself." Rabbi Hillel put it,
"What is hateful to thee, do not to anyone else." Their
teachings smacked of calculated prudence. Jesus'
teaching was active benevolence.

It is easier not to do things, not to injure a person, than
to do something positive. Mere inaction will achieve the
former. It takes firm purpose to say, "I will go out of my
way to be as kind and helpful as I would wish them to
be with me." To observe this principle means loving our
neighbour as we love ourselves, and treating him as
magnanimously as God has treated us.

FOR SELF-EXAMINATION: *Review your life today to
see in what ways you have actively obeyed this
rule.*

THE FORBIDDEN CRITICISM

"Do not judge, or you too will be judged." (Matthew 7:1)

The word "judge" carries with it the idea of censoriousness, or carping criticism. In its strict sense, it means simply "to discriminate" or "to distinguish", and does not necessarily have a bad connotation. Our judging could as easily issue in commendation as in condemnation. We are not to be undiscriminating, but we are to be uncritical, for, taken in its context, the word refers to censorious, sharp criticism. We are not to pre-judge — i.e. to be prejudiced.

Destructive criticism is no Christian employment, and Jesus said it must be permanently abandoned. "Stop criticising," He said. Paul gives the same authoritative injunction: "Let us stop passing judgment on one another" (Rom. 14:13). There are valid reasons for this command.

We do not know all the background. We see the issue, but not all the factors involved. We see the failures, but who can accurately assess the influence of heredity and environment on the failure? We see the fall, but who can measure the intensity of the resistance that preceded it?

Then too, our judgement is fallible. Even if we did know all the facts, would we interpret them correctly? Two people, faced with the same set of facts, often come to diametrically opposed conclusions.

Let us settle it in our minds that it is not for us to usurp the role of judge.

FOR PRAYER: *Lord, give me an unsuspicious and uncritical mind without being too gullible and credulous.*

DISCERNING CRITICISM

"Do not give dogs what is sacred; do not throw your pearls to pigs." (Matthew 7:6)

The same Lord who said, "Judge not," also said, "Make a right judgment" (John 7:24). There is a permissible and necessary criticism as well as a forbidden one. We must *discriminate* between people, and act in the light of our appraisal.

Jesus used "dogs" and "pigs" not in an offensive way, but as typical of certain classes of people – obviously unholy people.

In the Orient the dogs were often repulsive and foul scavengers that might have gorged themselves on remains of the holy burnt-offering. The sacred character of the food meant nothing to them.

Pigs were unclean animals to the Jew, and eating their flesh was an abomination. The term is obviously used of non-Christians.

The priests must not throw that part of the holy sacrifice reserved for them to the dogs. Pearls are not to be thrown to unappreciative pigs who might mistake them for beans or barley.

Jesus is teaching that spiritual treasures are not to be given to those who have no appreciation of them. While we are not to be censoriously critical, we must exercise discretion in our dealings with others. The materialist has little appreciation of the spiritual. *All truth is not appropriate for all persons*, and we need spiritual insight to discern what is right for each.

FOR MEDITATION: *Criticism is a cancer of the soul. We are not praying for a person whom we are censoriously criticising.*

DELUDED CRITICISM

"Why do you look at the speck of sawdust in your brother's eye, and pay no attention to the plank in your own eye?" (Matthew 7:3)

With clear perception Jesus laid bare the insincerity of a great deal of the criticism people indulge in. Those who are lynx-eyed in detecting minor defects in the character of others, are usually incredibly blind to their own glaring faults. A passion to put others right and make them over, may very well be suspect. As someone said, "A blind guide is bad enough, but a blind optician is a still more ridiculous anomaly." Our criticism is so often wrong because our moral vision is blurred by our own faults.

Were it not so true to life, the illustration would be ludicrous. But Jesus used the figure of hyperbole to make his hearers conscious of the extent of their guilt for this very sin. So often we have in our own characters a larger version of the very defect we criticise in others.

The point of the illustration is that *the Lord desires the removal of both the speck and the plank.* His concern is for both men.

Before we are qualified for the delicate task of removing the speck from our brother's eye, we must first deal with the plank in our own. Otherwise our judgement is bound to be prejudiced.

It is often the man guilty of large frauds in business, who is most severe on petty theft among his employees.

FOR PRAYER: *Lord, I acknowledge the fallibility of my judgement and the tendency to bias. Help me to "Judge righteous judgement".*

THE LAW OF RETRIBUTION

"In the same way as you judge others, you will be judged." (Matthew 7:2)

Jesus here draws attention to the law of cause and effect, of action and reaction. Censorious criticism is a boomerang that rebounds on the one who throws it. Our unloving criticism will recoil on our own heads. The measure we use in gauging the faults of others, will be the measure used on our conduct by both God and man. "You wicked servant, out of your own mouth I will judge you," is the principle (Luke 19:22).

Scripture is replete with illustrations of this law. With poetic justice, the wicked Haman swung on the very gallows he had erected for Mordecai (Est. 7:9,10). When Adoni-bezek was captured and punished by the Israelites, he said, "Seventy kings with their thumbs and big toes cut off have picked up scraps under my table. Now God has paid me back for what I did to them" (Judg. 1:7).

There is another, though less important, reason why we should stop criticising. Nothing will make our company less welcome to right-thinking people.

On his large dining table, St Augustine had carved a motto of which this is the English equivalent:

> He who loves another's name to stain,
> He shall not dine with me again.

On one occasion when the table was full of bishops, one of them criticised someone. Augustine just pointed to the motto. That bishop never dined there again.

FOR THANKSGIVING: *Father, I thank You that You are a just as well as a loving God, and that every wrong will be redressed in Your time.*

CHOICE, NOT CHANCE

> *I urge you, brothers . . . to offer your bodies as living*
> *sacrifices . . . this is your spiritual act of worship.*
> (Romans 12:1)

One does not grow automatically into a consecrated life
– it is a matter of choice, not of chance. "I beseech you
. . . that you *present* your bodies" (KJV) – a definite act
of the will.

The consecrated life is a life *dedicated to the will of God*.
We choose the will of God as the rule of our life, even
though we do not know all it may mean. We leave it to
Him to fill in the details, confident that His will is "good,
acceptable and perfect" (v.2). The tense of the verb
"present" signifies a definite act that needs no repetition,
though it may be reaffirmed.

It is a life *separated to the glory of God*. There must be
separation from sin if there is to be separation to God.
It is not the separation of the monastery – it is *insulation*
rather than *isolation*. The determining question in any
action will be, "Is this for the glory of God?"

It is a life *concentrated on the service of God*. This will
always be the result of genuine consecration, which is
not an end in itself. If it does not find expression in holy
activity, it is spurious. Realising that he is to be the
medium of conveying the words of life to a world astray
from God, the disciple devotes himself without reserve
to that sacred task.

FOR PRAYER: *Deliver me, Lord, from a legalistic*
separation. May mine be a separation of love to
Yourself as of a bride to the bridegroom.

SAVIOUR AND SOVEREIGN

"God has made this Jesus, whom you crucified, both Lord and Christ." (Acts 2:36)

We cannot divorce Christ's Saviourhood from His sovereignty. How strange that some desire to accept the immediate purpose of Christ's death, forgiveness, while rejecting its ultimate purpose, holiness!

In too many lives the rebellion of Absalom has been re-enacted, and to all intents and purposes Christ is in exile, driven practically from His throne by the very people He delivered by His cross.

When Garibaldi had delivered Italy from her aggressors at great personal sacrifice, he was hailed as the saviour of the nation. No flattery too fulsome, no praise too extreme for the national hero. One grateful group proposed that he should be placed on the throne. His saviourhood entitled him to sovereignty. Others, though glad enough to enjoy the benefits of his conquest, disputed his right to sovereignty. They desired to retain power in their own hands. For a few days he was actually put in prison and later was banished to the island of Capri.

The crucial question for us all is: *"Is Christ today on the throne of my heart as undisputed sovereign,* or has He, to all intents and purposes, been forced into unwilling exile?" Because He is Saviour, we take from Him the gift of salvation He offers. Because He is Sovereign we give back to Him our whole lives in loyal service.

FOR MEDITATION: *The question is not, Did I crown Christ King of my life in the past? but, Is He in reality on the throne today?*

THE SECOND MILE

"If someone forces you to go one mile, go with him two miles." (Matthew 5:41)

This illustration has its source in a practice of the Persian postal service. The King of Persia used to station mounted couriers at fixed points, to transmit messages one to another. If a man was passing one of these posts, the courier was empowered to compel him to go to another post to perform an errand for the King. But the legal limit for such conscripted service was one mile. He had no power to demand more.

What Jesus said was, "Although he has no power to compel you to go more than a mile, surprise him by cheerfully volunteering to go two!" This totally unexpected attitude will convince him that you are actuated by different and higher motives than others.

For us, the lesson is that *we are not to rest content with doing our bare duty, but to do more*, and to do it in a cheerful spirit. We are not to greedily grasp our legal rights and insist on them but to be as our Lord, "who, being in very nature God, did not consider equality with God something to be grasped, but made himself nothing" (Phil. 2:6).

Nor are we to resent public claims on our time or resources, but rather welcome these opportunities of serving others. We are to "render to Caesar the things that are Caesar's", gladly.

FOR ACTION: *Consider real life situations in which you can practise this command.*

THE ULTIMATE INSULT

*"If someone strikes you on the right cheek, turn to him
the other also."* (Matthew 5:39)

The acuteness of the insult in view here is more apparent
when one realises that to the Jew, being slapped in the
face is the equivalent of our spitting in the face. One
commentator sees in our Lord's remark an element of
humour. "Has someone slapped you on the right cheek?
Then you have another!"

According to the rabbis, a blow with the back of the
hand which would normally land on your opponent's
right cheek, was twice as bad as hitting him with the flat
of your hand. This was therefore *the ultimate insult* – and
one is to turn the other cheek!

In point of fact Jesus did not literally turn His other
cheek when the officer struck Him with his hand. Instead,
He courteously but firmly claimed His legal right to fair
trial (John 18:22,23).

While it is true that Jesus did not obey the exact letter
of His own injunction, by His controlled and dignified
bearing, He did fulfil it in spirit. He did not lose His
temper and vilify the officer, or strike back at him. He
simply asserted His right to fair trial.

The point of the illustration is that the disciple is to be
willing to submit to a second insult rather than to retaliate.
"Better to suffer wrong twice than to do wrong once."

FOR CONFESSION: *Lord, when I remember Your
attitude to insult and injury, I am ashamed of my
reactions.*

RELATIVE PERFECTION

"Be perfect, therefore, as your heavenly Father is perfect." (Matthew 5:48)

This verse has been the subject of much misunderstanding and verbal debate. To understand its meaning it must be borne in mind that these words were spoken in the context of the duty of loving one's enemies.

From the meaning of the word "perfect", and its context, it can be asserted that Jesus was not speaking about abstract philosophical perfection, nor of absolute sinlessness. The perfection here envisaged relates back to the perfection of the Father's love (v.45).

The word *teleios*, here translated "perfect", is used elsewhere of *relative* perfection, as of adults compared with children, and carried the idea of maturity, completeness. A thing is perfect in this sense when it reaches maturity and fulfils the purpose for which it was designed.

A love which embraces friends but not enemies is not perfect, it is immature. Like God who sends sun and rain on good and bad alike, we are to be impartial in our love – omitting no group, loving enemies as well as friends.

Love of this kind is a sheer impossibility apart from divine aid. Only the imparted grace of God can empower us to scale those dizzy heights. With Augustine we are compelled to cry, *"O God, give what Thou commandest, then command what Thou wilt."*

FOR MEDITATION: *An ethically perfect God can have no standard less than perfection. My aim should be that each day might see progress towards that maturity.*

UNEXPLAINED DARKNESS

"I will give you the treasures of darkness." (Isaiah 45:37 RSV)

The believer is nowhere promised that life will be all sunshine. Nor, because he is a child of God, is he granted immunity from "the slings and arrows of outrageous fortune". Land that knows nothing but sunshine becomes a desert. Clouds and storms and darkness must have their place if there is to be fertility and fruitfulness.

In His wisdom God sometimes allows us to pass through a period of *unrelieved darkness*, when no rift appears in the clouds. When it is the result of our own sin, we can see some justification. But at other times we can assign no reason for such an experience.

But *it is not purposeless*. God's assurance to King Cyrus was: "I will give you the treasures of darkness." There are treasures to be won from such experiences that we can gain in no other way. Although the darkness may be thick, it is "the thick darkness where God is" (Exod. 20:21).

The discipline of darkness was not absent from the experience of our Lord. Far deeper than the physical darkness that kindly shrouded His dying agonies, was the soul-darkness that engulfed Him when His Father averted His face while our sins were being expiated. In that darkness Jesus affirmed His faith – "MY God! MY God!" His trust in His Father was unimpaired.

FOR PRAYER: *When I am passing through a dark experience, Lord remind me that it is "the thick darkness WHERE GOD IS".*

THE MARK OF A MAN

The Lord had said to Abraham, "Leave your country . . ." So Abraham left, as the Lord had told him. (Genesis 12:1,4)

When at God's call Abraham left his comfortable and affluent ancestral home to embark on a nomadic lifestyle, *he was no callow youth in search of adventure.* He obediently set out on this second career at the age of seventy-five (Gen. 12:4), in complete ignorance of his destination. "By faith Abraham obeyed" (Heb. 11:8).

It would have been a traumatic experience for a much younger woman than Sarah, to break up her luxurious home – Ur of the Chaldees was a highly civilised city and her husband a wealthy man. To leave her treasures behind and take with her only such things as were appropriate to a nomadic life must have created considerable apprehension, and required faith and courage of a more than ordinary degree. In taking that tremendous step, both Abraham and Sarah displayed a maturity that pleased God.

Dietrich Bonhoeffer could have had Abraham in mind when he wrote: "It is the mark of a grown-up man as compared with a callow youth, that he finds his centre of gravity wherever he happens to be at the moment. And however much he longs for the object of his desire, it cannot prevent him staying at his post and doing his duty."

Abraham fully measured up to this standard.

FOR MEDITATION: *Since God has pledged Himself never to test His children beyond their ability to bear it, Abraham's testings were really God's vote of confidence.*

ABOVE THE CIRCUMSTANCES

In all our troubles, my joy knows no bounds. (2 Corinthians 7:4)

It is all too possible that, even after we have gained victory over our *besetting sins*, we may be laid low by our *circumstances* – illness, bereavement, anxiety, financial reverses, tragedy, old age, marital or family problems.

It would be unrealistic to deny the poignancy of the suffering such circumstances generate. But biblical history and the experience of a host of contemporary Christians demonstrate how frail and fallible men and women just like ourselves, have been able to soar above their imprisoning circumstances.

While we genuinely desire to grow in the knowledge of God, most of us insist on drawing up our own curriculum. *We want to dictate our syllabus of studies.* But our kind and all-wise Father will not pander to our weak desirings. He loves us too well to allow us to cheat ourselves out of His highest and best blessings.

Was it not in the searing flames of the furnace that the Lord came down and walked with His three youthful servants? Note that the new revelation of God came to them *inside* the fiery furnace (Dan. 3:24–25).

> He placed thee 'mid this dance
> Of plastic circumstance,
> Machinery just meant
> To give thy soul its bent;
> Try thee and turn thee forth
> Sufficiently impressed.
>
> *Robert Browning*

FOR MEDITATION: *Hudson Taylor said, "There should be only one circumstance to us in life, and that circumstance is GOD."*

REDIRECTED AMBITION

Our hope is that . . . our area of activity among you will greatly expand, so that we can preach the gospel in the regions beyond you. (2 Corinthians 10:16)

The superintending providence of God in the preparation of a leader is seen in the way in which Paul's intense natural ambition was redirected into spiritually reproductive channels, which were diametrically opposed to those of former days. His new ambition found a fresh centre in the glory of Christ and the extension of His Kingdom. *He nailed his old ambition to the cross.*

He cherished two major ambitions. The first was *to win the smile of the Lord.* "So we make it our goal [ambition] to please him" (2 Cor. 5:9). Personal approval from Christ was his sufficient reward for any service or suffering. This ambition goaded him along the path of faithful and sacrificial service.

Paul's second ambition was related to his career: "It has always been my ambition *to preach the gospel where Christ was not known*" (Rom. 15:20). It has been said that he suffered from spiritual claustrophobia – the fear of being confined in an enclosed space. He was in the grip of an insatiable passion for advance. He was haunted by the regions beyond. His vision knew no horizons. Kipling could have had Paul in mind when he wrote:

> Something hidden, go and find it,
> Go and look behind the ranges,
> Something lost behind the ranges,
> Lost, and waiting for you – GO!

FOR PRAYER: *If my ambition is centred on myself, I ask, Lord, for the courage to nail it to the cross.*

THE IDEALISM OF YOUTH

"Teacher, what good thing must I do to get eternal life?" (Matthew 19:16)

A rich young ruler came to Christ with a question to which he had found no answer. He was an attractive man, and when Jesus saw him, He loved him. In this passage we see:

The idealism of youth. "What do I still lack?" He wanted the best life had to offer. His question might be either pathetic despair or proud complacency – probably the former, which is a thoroughly contemporary attitude among young people today.

The emptiness of youth. Despite an outwardly upright life, he felt only an empty shell. He possessed so many *tangibles* – youth, wealth, position – but he was short on *intangibles*. The main youth problem today is *frustration*, one of the root causes of delinquency.

In answer to his question, Jesus listed five provisions of the Law, relating to man's duty to his fellow-man. The young ruler's protestations that he had always kept these revealed his lack of self-knowledge and of the sweep of Scriptures.

By the Lord's demand that he go, sell all and give to the poor, He showed him that he had broken the first commandment – his wealth had become his god. Jesus challenged him to show his love for his neighbour through his pocket. Go – sell – GIVE – come – follow.

The despair of youth. He went away sorrowful because he was unwilling to part with what stood between him and eternal life.

FOR WARNING: *O Lord, forbid that my possessions should ever become idols that displace You in my heart.*

August 1

TEMPTED IN ALL POINTS

> *We have . . . a high priest . . . who has been tempted in every way, just as we are − yet was without sin.* (Hebrews 4:15)

What exactly is implied in this statement? Does it mean that Jesus experienced every kind of temptation experienced by men and women of all ages? Obviously, no. For example, He did not experience the temptations peculiar to the space age.

Does it not mean rather that temptation assailed Him in its full force along every avenue in which it can reach human nature? The incidentals may differ, but *temptations are essentially the same in all ages*. It simply means that Jesus was tempted in every part of His humanity, as we are.

Nor need it be assumed that these three temptations were the only assaults the devil made during the forty days. These were but samples, or climaxes. He was tempted during the whole forty days, but He was so occupied with His spiritual crisis, that food was unimportant. It was at the end of these forty days that He became hungry, and then followed these three representative temptations.

The record implies that in each case Jesus heard the temptation from within, but *He did not open the door to the tempter*. In this way He gained a stunning victory, the benefits of which can be shared today by every tempted soul. Because He was victorious, we who are united to Him can share His triumph.

FOR SELF-EXAMINATION: *Lord, in the hour of temptation, do I trust the Spirit to call to my mind an appropriate, powerful word from God's Book as You did?*

August 2

THE LURE OF APPETITE

"If you are the Son of God, tell these stones to become bread." (Matthew 4:3)

Temptation can come to us along three main avenues. All other temptations are only variations of these. The first avenue is:

Appetite – the desire to enjoy things, referred to by John as "the cravings of sinful man" (1 John 2:16).

Since Jesus was hungry after forty days of fasting, Satan made his first approach on the physical plane – in the realm of legitimate appetite. Why not use His inherent power to gratify His lawful desire? The temptation was so plausible that few would have detected in it a satanic attack.

The whole point of the test focused on *the Lord's submission to the will of His Father*. But He refused to employ His divine prerogatives to gratify His normal desires, for that would have been satisfying them in an illegitimate way. He preferred remaining ravenously hungry to moving out of line with His Father's will. He would await His Father's word and provision. Had He yielded and provided Himself with bread by a miracle, His call to discipleship would have been out of the question for those of us who possessed no such powers, but must earn our daily bread by the sweat of our brow. He expressed confidence that His Father would supply bread in His own way and time. And of course, He did.

FOR PRAYER: *O Lord, give me victory in the realm of normal appetite. Enable me to "walk in the Spirit and not gratify the desires of the sinful nature".* (Gal. 5:16)

August 3

THE LURE OF AMBITION

"If you are the Son of God, throw yourself down."
(Matthew 4:5)

The second avenue along which temptation can reach us is:

Ambition – the desire to achieve things, to be somebody.

The scene changes. Satan takes Jesus up to one of the parapets of the temple overlooking the deep Kidron valley, hundreds of feet below. The focus of this temptation was on *Christ's confidence in God*; and the devil buttressed his temptation with a misquotation from Scripture. Jesus was challenged to prove His faith by putting God's promise to the test: "He will command his angels concerning you to guard you in all your ways" (Ps. 91:11).

The Master's reply revealed that for Him to act thus would be *not faith but presumption*, for "It is written, 'Do not put the Lord your God to the test'." "Stunting" was not one of the ways of God.

Note the repeated use of "it is written" in Jesus' replies to Satan. He knew how to wield the sword of the Spirit. He would not presumptuously walk into danger unless in the will of the Father. He refused to attempt to dazzle people into faith. He would not establish His kingdom by display and outward show.

Foiled again, Satan withdrew to plot another approach.

FOR PRAYER: *Lord, I would share Paul's ambition: "We make it our ambition to please Him."* (2 Cor. 5:9)

August 4

THE LURE OF AVARICE

The devil . . . showed him all the kingdoms of the world and their splendour. "All this I will give you if you will bow down and worship me." (Matthew 4:8,9)

Satan's first approach had been on the *physical* plane, his second on the *mental* and now his third is in the *spiritual* realm – ceding to him a place that belongs to God alone.

Avarice – the desire to obtain things. He takes Jesus to a high mountain. Apparently in a vision, the glory of world-domination was brought vividly before the Son of Man. It is noteworthy that Jesus did not challenge Satan's claim of power to give the kingdoms of the world.

Jesus had indeed come to obtain all the world of power and glory, but He would receive it only in the Father's way and time. And His Father's way included death on a cross. He perceived that Satan was offering Him the crown without the cross. The focus of this temptation was *the possible evasion of the cross by a compromise* with him.

For the third time the Lord drew the sword of the Spirit. "Away from me, Satan! For it is written: 'Worship the Lord your God, and serve him only' " (v.10).

Having failed to storm the citadel of Christ's loyalty to His Father, the adversary "left him, and angels came and attended him".

> For us baptised, for us He bore
> His holy fast and hungered sore,
> For us temptations sharp He knew,
> For us the Tempter overthrew.

FOR PRAISE: *Lord, I praise You that because You suffered, being tempted in all points as we are, You can succour us in our temptations.*

August 5

AFTER THE DOVE, THE DEVIL

At once the Spirit sent him out into the desert, and he was in the desert for forty days, being tempted by Satan. (Mark 1:12)

These words indicate that in the temptation of Christ the initiative was on the side of the divine, not the diabolical. After the approval of heaven came the assault of hell. After the dove, the devil. After the blessing, the battle. This is commonly the order in Christian experience. *The fact that Jesus was filled with the Spirit did not exempt Him from the rigours of temptation.*

An objective reading of the relevant passage leaves no room for doubt that there was a personal agent in the temptation. Not a personification of evil, but an evil person. The Lord was not engaged merely in an inner conflict with His own desires and ambitions, but in a desperate struggle with the external enemy of God and man.

The place where the Last Adam met and vanquished the tempter is in striking contrast to that in which the first Adam succumbed to Satan's subtlety – the arid desert, not the lush Eden. This fact strikes at the fallacy that our environment is the cause of our sin.

Since Jesus was alone in the wilderness, He alone could have given an account of what transpired there, probably on an occasion when He was opening His heart to His intimates. We should be grateful to Him for preserving this record of His victory over the devil.

FOR THANKSGIVING: *Lord, I thank You that "greater is he that is in you than he that is in the world."* (1 John 4:4)

A PASSION FOR SOULS

When Jesus saw the crowds, he had compassion on them. (Matthew 9:36)

"A passion for souls", as a former generation termed the compassion believers should have for their fellow-men, is rare in our day. The majority of Christians appear to feel not the slightest responsibility for the eternal welfare of their fellows. The thought that they are their brother's keeper does not seem to cross their minds. If they can ensure their own future, that is the end of their concern.

Dr Rowland V. Bingham, Founder of the Sudan Interior Mission, referring to this lack of concern for the spiritual welfare of others, had this to say: "Today this consciousness seems to have almost died out. The ethical veil of society, the cloak of self-righteousness, or the thin veneer of legal morals, are impenetrable to the natural sight. When accompanied with the rosy flush of youth, the glitter of prosperity and the joys of home and social life make it hard to realise that in the midst of all these are lost souls. *Christians, as a whole, do not act as though they believed anyone was lost.*"

Many subscribe to an orthodox creed concerning the punishment of the impenitent, but there is a world of difference between mental assent and active compassion.

Our Lord's concern for people was so real that He not only wept salty tears, but He gave His life for them.

FOR MEDITATION: *A passion for souls is one outcome of a passion for Christ. Count Zinzendorf said, "I have one passion, it is He, He alone."*

August 7

SHOULD CHRISTIANS FAST?

"When you fast . . . when you fast . . ." (Matthew
6:16–17)

In the New Testament, fasting is nowhere enjoined on
the disciple. It is a matter on which there is complete
liberty. Yet the fact remains that prayer with fasting has
been the practice of many of the greatest saints.

There is no *merit* in the fasting itself. It does not follow
that so much fasting will produce so much in prayer
answers or spiritual results. There is no *quid pro quo*. It
is not an end in itself, only a means to an end.

One obvious value of fasting is that it assists us to "keep
the body under" – *a practical acknowledgement of the
supremacy of the spiritual over the sensual*. Those who
practise it in a spiritual manner for spiritual ends, state
that the mind becomes unusually clear and vigorous and
there is increased power of concentration.

From the occasions with which it is associated, it would
seem that fasting was the outcome of preoccupation with
matters of deep concern. Nowhere does it appear to be
premeditated or prearranged.

Fasting was the outcome of (a) the challenge of a special
temptation; (b) a deep yearning after a closer walk with
God; (c) a great burden for the spread of the gospel in
regions beyond; (d) spiritual travail for the upbuilding
of the Church; (e) the exigencies of a stubborn problem.

FOR PRAYER: *Father, show me if there are things
in my life other than food from which I should
fast.*

O TO BE LIKE HIM!

*We . . . are being transformed into his likeness with
ever increasing glory, which comes from the Lord who
is the Spirit.* (2 Corinthians 3:18)

Transformation into the likeness of Christ is both our
responsibility and the Spirit's ministry. It is not
automatic, but involves moral endeavour on our part. We
are not only to passively "let go and let God", but we
are to "put on" and "put off" certain things, and this
involves an activity of the renewed will.

As we "behold the glory of the Lord", in active,
expectant faith, the Holy Spirit progressively effects a
change in our characters. We behold in silent, adoring
contemplation. He works into the fabric of our lives the
graces and beauties which we see in Christ.

In achieving this, He first *reveals to us things in our lives
which are unlike Christ*, and therefore must go. This
experience is not pleasant, but it is essential. They must
be "put off", and we alone can do this. But the Spirit
not only reveals what must be discarded, He enables us
to do it. "If *by the Spirit* you put to death the misdeeds
of the body . . ." (Rom. 8:13). We are not left to our own
unaided efforts.

He also *reveals the graces and blessings that can be ours*,
and enables us to appropriate them. There is no grace
which we behold in the character of Christ which may
not be ours in increasing measure as we look to the Spirit
to produce it.

FOR MEDITATION: *The purpose of God's sovereign
choice of us is that we should be "conformed
to the likeness of His Son".* (Rom. 8:29)

August 9

KNOWING THE HOLY SPIRIT

"The Spirit of truth . . . you know him . . ." (John
14:17)

In answer to Paul's enquiry, "Did you receive the Holy
Spirit when you believed?" some disciples of John
replied, "No. We have not even heard that there is a Holy
Spirit" (Acts 19:2). Not many church members would
return such an answer today. They know there is a Holy
Spirit, but conceive of Him as an influence or intangible
power. They do not think of a real, divine Person who
can be known, loved and worshipped.

Others know a great deal *about* the Holy Spirit, but do
not *know* Him in the sense implied in the text. It is one
thing to know about a celebrity, but quite another to know
him or her personally.

The difference is like knowing all about food, even
possessing it, and eating and enjoying it. One is
intellectual apprehension, the other is knowledge gained
by experience. It is not knowing *about* God that brings
eternal life, but knowing Him (John 17:3), surely a vital
distinction. But there is no reason why seeking to know
about Him should not lead to our getting to know Him
personally.

Once the critically important role of the Holy Spirit in
life and experience is grasped, to ignore His gracious
presence or neglect His inner working will be seen as
inexcusable and foolish. So let us get to know Him.

FOR THANKSGIVING: *Father, I thank You for the
glorious possibility of knowing intimately
Yourself, Your Son and Your Holy Spirit.*

THE FRUIT OF THE SPIRIT

*The fruit of the Spirit is love, joy, peace, patience,
kindness, goodness, faithfulness, gentleness and self-
control.* (Galatians 5:22,23)

This attractive cluster of fruit presents a perfect portraiture
of Christ, in whose life it appeared in a profusion never
seen in this world before or since. "The fruits or fruit of
the Spirit are the virtues of Christ."

It delineates, too, the ideal Christian life, for *Christian
character is essentially the fruit of the indwelling Spirit*, who
will not be content until there appears in the life the
virtues and graces of Christ.

The attractiveness of the fruit of the Spirit is enhanced
by the inky blackness of the works of the flesh which Paul
enumerates in the preceding verses. The works of the
flesh outnumber the fruit of the Spirit. "It is a proof of
our fallen state, how much richer every vocabulary is in
words for sin than in those for graces," wrote R. C.
Trench. The works of the flesh are separate acts
performed by man, while the ninefold fruit is the issue
of the Spirit's life within.

To our generation of frenetic activism, it is arresting to
notice that *each of these graces is passive*, and can be
produced in the life of one paralysed from the neck down!
When will we redress the balance? The fruit is what we
are rather than what we do. The test of our spirituality
is the presence of this desirable fruit rather than in
flamboyant gifts.

FOR MEDITATION: *It is not that nine different
persons are to manifest these virtues, but it is
that each person is to have the nine.*

CAN SPIRITUAL GIFTS BE LOST?

God's gifts and his call are irrevocable. (Romans 11:29)

This perplexing problem is sooner or later faced by the Christian worker. He meets people obviously living unspiritual lives, who are exercising spiritual gifts, apparently with resulting blessing. Men who are great preachers or hold high office in the church, yet whose private lives belie their profession, sometimes seem to meet with more apparent success than others whose lives are godly and consistent. What is the explanation?

If spiritual gifts were the outcome of the filling of the Spirit, or if their continuance depended on this experience, they would automatically cease when sin grieved the Holy Spirit. It would seem, however, that they are bestowed at regeneration, and their continued exercise is not dependent on a high plane of Christian living – as in the case of the highly gifted but corrupt and divided Corinthian church (1 Cor. 1:7).

Perhaps some light is shed on the subject by Paul's words in our text. God does not go back on His gifts or call. Marvin Vincent says that, "without repentance" (Rom. 11:29 KJV) means "not subject to recall". Without dogmatism it is suggested that the continued possession of spiritual gifts is no criterion of the spiritual state of the possessor, whether it be oneself or another. It would appear, if this is so, that while sin inevitably affects one's communion with God, it does not necessarily affect the exercise of spiritual gifts to the same degree.

FOR PRAYER: *Lord, save me from presumption on Your grace in the exercise of my spiritual gifts. Enable me to exercise them worthily.*

THE PURPOSE OF SPIRITUAL GIFTS

Try to excel in gifts that build up the church. (1 Corinthians 14:12)

Spiritual gifts are not bestowed for the self-aggrandisement of the recipient, or as evidence of a special enduement of the Spirit. They are given for the edification – building up – of the Body of Christ. The possessor is only an instrument and not the receiver of the glory. *The gift is for ministry to others*, "for the perfecting of the saints". None of them directly concerns character. They are God's equipment and enabling for effective service (1 Cor. 12:4–11).

Paul states that there are "diversities of gifts", but they are mediated by the one Spirit. A musician cannot produce a melody from a single note, or an artist a masterpiece with one colour. So the Spirit's manifold purpose for the Church can be accomplished only by means of several gifts. *No one gift is common to all Christians*, and no one has all the gifts. But no believer has been entirely passed over in the distribution of the gifts. There are no useless organs in the Body of Christ. Each has some useful function.

Frequently the gifts bestowed accord with natural talents and endowments, but they always transcend them. They are supernatural, but make use of and enhance the natural abilities possessed.

Gracious Spirit, Holy Ghost,
Taught by Thee we covet most
Of Thy gifts at Pentecost,
  Holy, heavenly love.

FOR MEDITATION: *The nature of the gifts indicates that they are gifts for service. Not one directly concerns character.*

BLASPHEMING THE HOLY SPIRIT

"The blasphemy against the Spirit will not be forgiven . . . Anyone who speaks against the Holy Spirit will not be forgiven, either in this age or in the age to come." (Matthew 12:31)

If the seriousness of a sin is measured by the seriousness of its consequences, then this is a very serious sin. Many Christians harbour morbid fears of having committed this sin, and are in great distress. In what does it consist?

Bishop J. C. Ryle defines it as "a combination of clear, intellectual knowledge of the gospel, with deliberate rejection of it. It is wilful sin; the union of light in the head and hatred in the heart."

Most evangelical scholars are in essential agreement on the following points:

It is *not a sin of ignorance*, but a sin against spiritual knowledge and light. God has not set a mysterious line over which one may unwittingly cross.

It is *not an isolated act* but a habitual attitude, a sin in character, crystallised in opposition to God.

It is *a sin of the heart*, and not merely of the tongue or the intellect; not an unbidden thought nor an unpremeditated word.

It is *a sin committed in wilful resistance to the strivings of the Spirit*.

Many who fear they may have been guilty of this sin should find comfort in these considerations. Had the sin been committed, there would have been a cessation of sensibility, a spiritual deadness. Conscience would be unresponsive and the Spirit's strivings silenced.

FOR MEDITATION: *Those who are deeply convicted of their sin, and desire to return to the Lord, thereby evidence that they have not committed this sin.*

GRIEVING THE HOLY SPIRIT

Do not grieve the Holy Spirit of God, with whom you were sealed for the day of redemption. (Ephesians 4:30)

We can learn what grieves the Spirit from the context of the command, for it occurs in the midst of a list of sins and actions, all of which cause Him grief. The believer's body is the Temple of the Spirit, therefore the presence of sin grieves its Holy Guest.

To be specific, we can grieve Him *by ignoring His indwelling.* Some Christians live as though there were no Holy Spirit. From Sunday morning to Saturday night they give no thought of conscious recognition to Him. No one appreciates being ignored.

He is grieved *when we infringe His commands.* Only One never grieved Him – He who said, "I always do what pleases Him" (John 8:29). He was able to do this because He entrusted the government of His life to the Holy Spirit. He was instantly and constantly responsive to the Spirit's control.

Since it is the Spirit's purpose to conform us to the image of Christ, anything in which we wilfully depart from the divine ideal grieves Him. The word *wilfully* is used advisedly, for sins concerning which our consciences are not enlightened, do not grieve Him to the same degree as those which are wilfully committed. The Spirit respects our liberty. When we choose to sin rather than obey His will, He suspends His activity, and communion with Christ is broken. But it can be restored on confession.

FOR MEDITATION: *When we grieve the Spirit, we draw the blind and exclude His gracious ministry from our hearts.*

SOLVENT FOR DOUBT

"Are you the one who was to come?" (Matthew 11:3)

To all outward appearance, the sun of John the Baptist's flaming ministry went out in inglorious eclipse — but only to *outward* appearance.

His loyalty to Christ had brought him to prison — an intolerable ordeal for a man of the open spaces. His depression was understandable, and depression too easily generates doubt. At last his faith seems to falter: "Are you the one who was to come," he asked, "or should we expect someone else?" (Matt. 11:3).

Here is an important lesson for those prone to doubt: Do as John did. *Take your doubt directly to the Lord, and ask Him to deal with it.*

John was not the first, and he certainly will not be the last, to be assailed by doubt. The Lord's injunction to him, "Blessed is the man who does not fall away on account of me" (v.6), carries the implication that John had begun to stumble.

When John's disciples came with the question to Jesus, He did not argue, or answer directly. Instead, He performed the miracles that Scripture had indicated would authenticate the Messiah, and told them to report to John what they had seen.

He did not explain His silence and seeming neglect to visit John, as would be expected, but pointed out that blessedness flows from having confidence in Him even in mystifying circumstances.

FOR PRAISE: *Lord, I'm so grateful that You understand my weaknesses, and while not condoning them, forgive and restore me.*

DON'T BE AFRAID

"Do not be afraid . . . Do not be afraid . . . Do not be afraid . . ." (Matthew 10:26,28,31)

Fear is endemic in the world today, and not without reason. It invades every realm and grips young and old alike. On the other hand, it has been asserted that in the Bible there are no fewer than three hundred and sixty-five "Fear nots" – one for every day of the year!

The Lord had been warning His disciples of the treatment they were likely to receive at the hands of the hostile world, and He advanced three reasons why they should not give way to fear.

In the long run *truth will triumph* (vv.26,27). The time is coming when truth and error will be exposed in their true colours.

Men may damage the body but *they are powerless to tamper with the welfare of the soul*. The worst man can do is to destroy the body, while the ultimate disaster is not death but apostasy (v.18). The material as well as the spiritual parts of our nature appear capable of suffering in the eternal world.

Because of *the Father's providential care*. If God cares for the sparrows, the cheapest living thing, how much more will He watch over His children? God's providence extends to minute details – the hairs of our heads. This surely should be a wholesome antidote to fear.

Faith is the infallible antidote to fear.

FOR MEDITATION: *Fear and faith cannot sleep in the same bed.*

OLD TESTAMENT PROMISES

*If you belong to Christ, then you are Abraham's seed,
and heirs according to the promise.* (Galatians 3:29)

In my early Christian life, the promises of the Old
Testament used to be a problem. I had no difficulty in
appropriating New Testament promises, for they were
clearly made to Christians, but the promises of the Old
Testament were made, in the main, to God's people
Israel. It seemed to me that I had no more right to claim
fulfilment of a promise made to Israel, than to open a
letter written to someone else.

The solution came when I read and understood
Galatians 3:29: "If you belong to Christ, then you are
Abraham's seed, and *heirs according to the promise.*" God's
promise to Abraham was that his descendants would be
as numerous as the stars of the sky and the sand on the
seashore. He was to have a heavenly spiritual seed as well
as a physical earthly seed – the earthly Israel, and the
true Israel of God.

Through their union with Christ, who was Abraham's
descendant, believers are indeed Abraham's seed, and
as such they are heirs to the spiritual content of the
promises made to Abraham's earthly seed.

With the apprehension of this great fact, another
milestone was passed and I was now able to turn Old
Testament promises into facts of experience.

FOR THANKSGIVING: *Lord, I gladly add my
testimony to that of Joshua: "Not one of all the
good promises the Lord your God gave you has
failed."* (Josh. 23:14)

FAITH IN OUR FAITH?

"Have faith in GOD." (Mark 11:22)

Is it possible that we are striving to have faith in our faith, rather than faith in our God? Think that through. "Have faith in God" is the divine imperative.

When confronted with some almost incredible promise in Scripture, we are sometimes daunted. "But I haven't the faith to believe for that!" we exclaim. "My faith is not strong enough." To which the pertinent reply is, *"In whom* do you not have the faith to believe?" for faith always reposes in someone. Is it that you are *placing your faith in your faith* to bring the promised blessing? Or are you fixing your faith in your trustworthy God?

Our own faith is a broken reed on which to lean. If it is in this we are trusting, small wonder we receive nothing. It is *faith* in *God*, to which He responds.

If we are worrying whether our faith is right in quality or sufficient in quantity, Satan has successfully deflected it from its objective. All faith which is directed towards God is of the right quality and sufficient in quantity, though it be as tiny as a mustard seed.

Faith's function is simply to link us with the trustworthy God who has promised. But there is a seeming faith to which God is silent − faith which is focused on our own faith. It is God who gives the blessing.

FOR PRAISE:
> *Thou art coming to a King,*
> *Large petitions with thee bring;*
> *For His grace and power are such*
> *None can ever ask too much.*

THE APPROPRIATION OF FAITH

"According to your faith will it be done to you."
(Matthew 9:29)

It is easier to appropriate tangible than spiritual blessings. But are we not constantly appropriating intangible things – love, for example? Love may be lavished without stint, but it is not enjoyed until it is appropriated and reciprocated. Forgiveness may be freely bestowed, but release comes only when it is believed and accepted. The unwavering principle is, "According to your faith" – appropriation – "will it be done to you."

To appropriate is to receive, to take as one's own. The central verse of the Bible is said to be Psalm 81:10, "Open wide your mouth and I will fill it." It pictures a nest of little birds with mouths open beyond belief. Their attitude is the expectation and appropriation of faith. Nor does the mother disappoint them. The fledgling's responsibility is to close its mouth on the mother's provision.

The holiest saint has no greater spiritual resources than we who have been "blessed with every spiritual blessing" (Eph. 1:3). The vast discrepancy in our experience stems from the fact that these men and women have appropriated more blessings than we have.

The wonderful father in Luke 15 divided his estate between his two sons. Despite his glaring faults, the prodigal at least did his father the honour of appropriating his share. The elder brother accused his father of not giving him even a kid. The difference was in appropriation, not in bestowal.

FOR MEDITATION: *Every step that the Israelites took around Jericho was a step of appropriation by faith.* (Josh. 6:2–5)

THE VALIDITY OF FAITH

Faith is being . . . certain of what we do not see.
(Hebrews 11:1)

Faith is no vain exercise. Trusting the eternal God is no misplacing of confidence. Faith finds its validity in three things:

The veracity of the Person in whom it is reposed. God is the true God, and "it is impossible for God to lie" (Heb. 6:18). God's veracity is the expression of truth, both in nature and in revelation. The discoveries of science, in so far as they are verified, are only the unveiling of the veracity of the Creator.

The veracity of the Word which is believed is a second evidence of faith's validity. The Word of God will never betray the confidence placed in it. It is in direct contrast to that of the false prophets who made the people trust in a lie (Jer. 28:15). "My word will never pass away," Jesus asserted (Matt. 24:35). It is no tissue of cunningly devised fables, but a divinely inspired message which has weathered centuries of the most searching scrutiny. The discoveries of the scrutinisers have only served to reveal the veracity of its Author.

Finally, there is *the veracity of the facts believed*. Faith lays hold on three great historic facts. The Son of God came into the world. He died for our sins. He rose from the dead (1 Cor. 15:3,4). These facts are among "those things which cannot be shaken". For two millennia these facts have defied the winds of adverse criticism.

FOR MEDITATION: *Faith is a paradox, in that eternal verities, not accessible to the senses, are more real than tangible, visible and material objects.*

THE ACTIVITY OF FAITH

> . . . *who through faith conquered kingdoms . . . shut the mouth of lions, quenched the fury of the flames.* (Hebrews 11:33,34)

Faith is to the soul what light is to the body. Indeed, it is the spiritual counterpart of all five senses of our physical life, and includes everything represented by them. It is concerned with and gives substance to things unseen (Heb. 11:1). It is on the evidence of faith that we know the reality of things unseen. It provides evidence of the actual existence of spiritual realities, and assures of the certainty of things yet future.

Faith is not passive and inactive, a state of moral indolence. Rather is it the inspiring secret of intense activity. It was through faith that the patriarchs "conquered kingdoms . . . became powerful in battle and routed foreign armies". No passivity here! Their faith was the motivation of their magnificent achievements. A similar faith will move us to attempt great things for God.

Faith brings within our vision the invisible God. It was Moses' faith that enabled him to "persevere because he saw him who was invisible" (Heb. 11:27). The vision of God which faith brought, not only enabled him to endure, but gave him a true perspective of life, and strengthened him for costly renunciation of earthly privileges.

Faith feeds on the pledged Word of God, and flourishes in the atmosphere of His presence. The primary act of faith, constantly repeated, matures into an attitude of faith. The act becomes a habit. The initial step of faith lengthens out into a sustained walk of faith.

FOR MEDITATION: *If we choose faith as the principle of our lives, it will lift us out of the ranks of mediocrity.*

August 22

FAITH AND FEAR

They were not afraid of the King's edict. (Hebrews 11:23)

Fear and faith are spiritual incompatibles. So much so that the one can survive only at the expense of the other. When faith in God enters the lists, fear is routed. The presence of fear is unmistakable evidence of the absence of faith. Between them there is no such thing as peaceful co-existence.

Fear is acutely infectious. It was craven fear that inspired the ten spies to present their adverse report on the Promised Land. "We saw the giants . . . we were as grasshoppers . . ." (Num. 13:33). It was robust faith which enabled Caleb and Joshua to present their minority report. "Let us go up at once and possess it . . . We are well able to overcome" (v.30). Their faith measured the opposing forces, not by their own grasshopper strength but by the omnipotence of God.

Faith, too, is infectious. It was in faith that Moses' parents hid him for three months and were not afraid of the King's commandment. Their supernatural faith overcame their natural fear.

The faith of his parents was communicated to Moses by precept and example. Small wonder that it banished his fear. "By faith he left Egypt, not fearing the King's anger" (Heb. 11:27).

Moses in turn endeavoured to teach Israel the dominance of faith over fear. Unfortunately "the message they heard was of no value to them, because those who heard did not combine it with faith" (Heb. 4:2).

FOR MEDITATION: *In nature the life of parents is imparted to children. It may also be so in the spiritual realm.*

FAITH AND UNBELIEF

See to it that none of you has a sinful, unbelieving heart. (Hebrews 3:12)

The true nature of faith can be learned from its antithesis. *Unbelief* is the absence of faith. *Disbelief* is the denial of truth. Unbelief does not necessarily express itself in blatant disbelief, but the effect is much the same.

Omnipotence is shackled in the presence of unbelief. "He could not do any miracles there . . . and he was amazed at their unbelief" (Mark 6:5,6). Note the "could not" spoken of incarnate Deity! This incident lends credibility to John Wesley's assertion, "God does nothing except in answer to believing prayer." Jesus was ever so willing to act in mercy, but the channel through which His healing power could flow was blocked. Our unbelief is often responsible for the seeming inactivity of God.

Fear is spawned from unbelief. "Why are you so afraid? Do you still have no faith?" (Mark 4:40). Perfect love casts out fear, but can there be perfect love where there is not complete trust?

Spiritual power is short-circuited by unbelief. "Why couldn't we drive it [the demon] out?" "Because you have so little faith," was Jesus' reply (Matt. 17:19,20). They had been invested with authority over all the power of the enemy, but now in the presence of satanic power they were impotent. *Divine power flows only through the reticulating system of faith.*

FOR MEDITATION: *In our intercourse with God, everything depends on the heart, and faith is its natural function. Unbelief is not a frailty but a sin.*

FAITH AND FEELING

Faith comes from hearing the message. (Romans 10:17)

Faith is the *confidence* of things not seen (Heb. 11:1), not the *consciousness* of the unseen. Before we can feel them we must exercise faith concerning them. Faith is the initial act, feeling is the resulting effect. Faith must recognise before it realises, for feelings rest on facts. The facts remain unchanged even when we disbelieve them, but we are robbed of their enjoyment. It is very possible to place more reliance on our fickle feelings than on the facts recorded in Scripture.

Faith comes by hearing the Word, not by introspection or perpetual examination of our spiritual pulse. Constant taking notice of the heartbeat induces disorders of the heart.

The divine order is unfolded in Romans 6:6,11,14. First there is a *revelation* of an objective fact entirely independent of any subjective feeling: "Our old self was crucified with him." Next comes faith's *recognition* of the fact: "Count yourself dead to sin but alive to God." Then follows the *realisation*, the experience, the feeling of the fact: "Sin shall not be your master."

It is essential that we observe the correct sequence. If we desire to have faith, we must first discover a divinely authenticated fact on which it can rest. If we wish to have feelings of joy or peace, we must have faith in the facts on which they are based.

FOR WARNING: *"Following your feelings, doing whatever your animal urges dictate, is the surest way to spiritual ruin."* (E. W. Lutzer)

VICTOR BECAUSE VANQUISHED

> *Thanks be to God, who always leads us in triumphal procession in Christ and through us spreads everywhere the fragrance of the knowledge of him.* (2 Corinthians 2:14)

In this passage Paul thinks of himself as a rebel leader who has taken up arms against the Christ whose Church he has ravaged. But he met more than his match in the encounter. The One stronger than he had vanquished him, stripped him of his armour, and bound him to the wheel of His triumphal chariot with chains of love. It is an alluring picture of one who became victor through being vanquished.

Christianity is a crusading religion. Calvary tells us that God is love, but it also proclaims that two rival thrones are engaged in truceless warfare, in which all His disciples are participants (Col. 2:15).

Though not always apparent, Christ the conqueror is marching through the world in invincible triumph that leads to His universal reign. He leads us, wherever we are, on His triumphal way. On His way He shares His bounty with those who were His enemies (Eph. 4:8).

But there is another side to the picture. It was characteristic of the triumphal procession, that the air was redolent with incense. Paul claimed that wherever he went, Christ diffused through him His own sweet fragrance. As we live in close fellowship with Christ we absorb His fragrance and spread it everywhere.

Is the world sweeter, is the fragrance of Christ more evident, do people love Him because they have detected His fragrance in us?

FOR MEDITATION: *What an exhilarating possibility! We can diffuse the fragrance of Christ in the workplace.*

August 26

PRICELESS TREASURE

We have this treasure in jars of clay to show that this all-surpassing power is of God. (2 Corinthians 4:7)

All the springs of missionary passion are concentrated in three words: *Jesus, priceless treasure*. And, one might add, all the springs of love and devotion too.

The priceless treasure is described in poetic language in the previous verse – "The light of the knowledge of the glory of God in the face of Christ" (v.6). Jesus called the Good News of the Kingdom priceless treasure, but in the ultimate it is Christ Himself – not an ideology to embrace but a Person to adore. Have we lost the wonder of it?

Paul sets in contrast *the very ordinary vessel*, as though to highlight the incongruity of such precious treasure being housed in so commonplace a vessel, yet this was Christ's chosen role. He chose to share the limitations of our "house of clay". God was pleased to display His most precious jewel in a setting of common clay. Does this not impart unique dignity to the vessel?

Despite its privilege, the earthen vessel remains weak and easily marred. *It was the breaking of the earthen vessel of Christ's body that enabled the light of the glory of God to blaze forth*, and the principle is the same for His followers. It is the strategy of God that our human weakness should be a backdrop for the display of His divine power. It is a comforting thought that God does not use us merely in spite of our weakness, but actually because of it.

FOR THANKSGIVING: *God is not confined to the exceptionally clever and greatly gifted for the fulfilment of His purposes.*

August 27

SPIRITUAL OR UNSPIRITUAL?

Brothers, I could not address you as spiritual but as worldly — mere infants in Christ. (1 Corinthians 3:1)

Society has its own standards for classifying people. This may be according to social status, intellectual attainments, bank balance, charm of personality, or a dozen other factors. Scripture knows only three classifications — natural, spiritual, unspiritual (1 Cor. 2:14; 3:1).

The criterion is the way in which one responds to God's Word. *The natural man* lacks both the taste for spiritual truth, and the faculty by which it is learned. Only regeneration can remedy this fatal defect.

The unspiritual Christian, paradoxical though that sounds, has been born again, but has never emerged from the domination of the self-life. He is still a spiritual baby. He is united to Christ by faith, yet not fully satisfied with Christ, and suffers from arrested spiritual growth. He is worldly in outlook and lives very much like other men. In Old Testament language, he lives the unsatisfying life of the wilderness.

The *spiritual person's* life is under the control of the Holy Spirit. Unhindered by carnality, the Spirit can produce in him or her the character of Christ and change him into the same likeness (2 Cor. 3:18). He is no longer a babe in spiritual things but is growing in maturity. He ceases to be self-occupied and shares the truth he learns with others.

FOR SELF-EXAMINATION: *Which am I, spiritual or unspiritual? Am I content to remain unspiritual?*

PRODUCTIVE PRESSURE

> *We were under great pressure, far beyond our ability to endure, so that we despaired even of life.* (2 Corinthians 1:8)

Burdens of heart, acute physical sufferings and hardships were routine for Paul; weariness and pain, hunger and thirst, cold and nakedness, stoning and shipwreck – these were part and parcel of his missionary experience (2 Cor. 11:23–28). He summed it up in one sentence: "Our bodies had no rest, but we were harassed at every turn – conflicts on the outside, fears within" (2 Cor. 7:5).

He worked under constant pressure, yet was not submerged by it, although it seemed to be "far beyond our ability to endure". But the pressure in Paul's life was unusually productive. He learned the reason why God had permitted the pressures to come: *"But this happened that we might not rely on ourselves but on God"* (v.9).

In addition to all the other pressures, was the overarching responsibility for the well-being of the churches he had helped bring into existence. "Besides everything else, I face daily the pressure of my concern for all the churches" (11:28).

Such an intolerable load would have crushed a lesser man. But *Paul had mastered the secret of casting his burden on the Lord* on one hand, *and appropriating His more than sufficient grace* on the other. He did not consider these trials to be unmitigated evils, but valued them as instruments designed to conform him to the image of Christ.

FOR PRAYER: *Lord, grant me the courage to say No to commitments that would generate undue pressure.*

CHAMPION BECOME CLOWN

The Philistines shouted, "Bring out Samson to entertain us." So they called Samson out of the prison, and he performed for them. (Judges 16:25)

Several factors combined to rob Samson of his strength and contributed to his subsequent humiliation.

He carelessly broke his Nazirite vow. His was the sin of hypocrisy. He bore the marks of a Nazirite, but failed to live like one. The Nazirite was to have no contact with death, but he used the jawbone of an ass as his weapon. The locks of his hair were not to be cut, but he weakly yielded his secret to treacherous Delilah.

He persisted in playing with fire. He thought he could safely indulge his sin because God had not withdrawn His power at the first or second lapse. He persisted in disregarding God's red lights. He had grown so accustomed to the co-operation of the Spirit, that he presumed once too often. Descending into an evil atmosphere to indulge illicit passions will inevitably bring its own retribution.

He trifled with the secret of his power. He entered into a relationship purely of the flesh, putting carnal licence before the glory of God. His compromise began with the unequal yoke in marriage. It ended with his head on the knees of his betrayer. The name Delilah means "seductive"!

Samson learned the bitter lesson that there can be no loyalty between the pagan and the man of God.

Obey God's red lights!

FOR MEDITATION: *Samson did not receive a new set of eyes; but God did, upon his repentance, restore fellowship with Himself.*

August 30

THE DIVINE ADVOCATE

"I will ask the Father, and He will give you another Counsellor [Advocate, Paraclete] to be with you for ever." (John 14:16)

The Latin word "advocate" is a close equivalent of the Greek "paraclete", and the figure sheds much light on the work of the Holy Spirit. Both words have the meaning, 'to call to one's side to help", especially against an accuser or judge. This led to the Spirit being called "the Divine Barrister". The ideal barrister of former days pleaded his client's cause, defended his name, and guarded his property.

Such is the work of our Divine Advocate. But on whose behalf does He work? It may come as a surprise that He is *Christ's* Advocate, not ours. Did Jesus not say He would send *another* Paraclete, thus implying that He was one and the Spirit the other? The Son is our Advocate with the Father in Heaven. The Spirit is the Advocate on earth, of the Son. Like the ideal barrister, He represents Christ, pleads His cause, defends His name and protects His interests.

On the other hand we can draw comfort from our Lord's word "another". It means "another of exactly the same kind". Thus the Spirit is Jesus' other Self. He is not a *different* Paraclete, but one of the same kind. In the Person of His Spirit, Christ is constantly at our side to strengthen and help.

In His parting message Jesus prepared his disciples for the treatment they could expect from the world. But He pointed them to the Paraclete by whose aid they would be victorious over the opposition of the world.

FOR THANKSGIVING: *Thank You, Lord, for revealing that the Holy Spirit is just like You.*

August 31

SHOCKED BY OLD SINS

Each one is tempted when, by his own evil desire, he is dragged away and enticed. (James 1:14)

Scripture is realistic in its treatment of sin, whether in believer or unbeliever. It recognises that sin is a continuing problem, even for the believer. He is not forever done with sin when he is converted, because he never gets beyond the reach of temptation. True, he has experienced the joy of forgiveness. He revels in the assurance that his guilt has been removed, but he is nowhere promised exemption from the lure of temptation or the possibility of sinning.

Has the reader never been shocked by the unexpected revival of old sins, or at sudden attacks of the devil who has no respect even for our holiest hours? And those are only surface manifestations. What lies hidden in the depths of our subconscious mind?

The Master Psychologist gives His diagnosis: "From within, out of men's hearts, come evil thoughts, sexual immorality, theft, murder, adultery . . ." (Mark 7:21).

Then how is it possible for a God who hates sin and requires purity to continue to have dealings with a sin-prone mortal? The answer is, that in the multi-faceted death of His Son, provision is made for a cleansing so deep, so radical, so continuous, that a believer can walk in unbroken communion with Him (1 John 1:7,9).

FOR PRAYER: *Father, although the revival of old sins shocks us, it does not surprise You. Thank You for the cleansing blood.*

September 1

LAST WORDS

Jesus called out with a loud voice, "Father, into your hands I commit my spirit." (Luke 23:46)

Last words are always impressive, especially when they come from the lips of one dearly loved. The atmosphere of the approaching end charges them with added solemnity and meaning. In the light of eternity, the trivial is usually abandoned.

Because they were His last words and spoken under such tragic circumstances, the Seven Sayings from the pulpit of the cross are of special significance. In them Jesus laid bare His inmost soul, and in them exemplified the spiritual principles He had been teaching. They are a luminous interpretation of His sufferings and sorrows.

It is significant that He spoke seven times from the cross — *a complete interpretation of the stupendous event* that was being enacted. Each of these sayings is an ocean of truth compressed into a drop of speech, and warrants close and reverent study. It is to be expected that utterances on a cross would be staccato, and yet that monstrous monument was transformed into the most eloquent pulpit of the ages.

> While they nailed Him to the cross,
>   Pardon for His foes He pled;
> Ere His spirit took its flight,
>   Unto God He spoke and said,
> "Father into hands of Thine,
>   I commend this soul of mine."

FOR PRAISE: *Lord, I praise You for showing me how to face the hour of death.*

September 2

FORGIVENESS

"Father, forgive them, for they do not know what they are doing." (Luke 23:34)

Jesus has been acquitted by the highest tribunal of the land, yet He is now impaled on a cross, the most shameful punishment to which a criminal could be subjected. He has been seized by rude hands, stripped and laid on its rough beams. The spikes were callously driven through His quivering flesh.

While they are engaged in their grim task, the lips of the victim are seen to move. But what is He saying? For whom does He pray? For Himself? No. He is "making intercession for the transgressors" – *"Father, forgive them."* His first word was a word of prayer.

His hands can no more perform acts of love for friend or enemy. His feet can no longer carry Him on errands of mercy. But one form of ministry is still open – He can still pray.

Note His petition – "Forgive them". Here is love triumphant over evil. He might justly have left His murderers to their doom. Instead, His heart overflowed its banks in prayer. Jesus is putting His own precept into practice – "Pray for those who despitefully use you."

Hear His plea – "They do not know what they are doing." It seems as though He is trying to find some extenuating circumstance which might lessen their guilt. He recognised degrees of guilt. Judas and Pilate knew what they were doing, and they were excluded.

FOR PRAISE:
Hark, He speaks, and still the hovering breeze
Wafts His last breath to all approving heaven:
"Forgive them, for they know not what they do."

September 3

ASSURANCE

"I tell you the truth, today you will be with me in paradise." (Luke 23:43)

> Three men shared death upon a hill
> But only one man died;
> A thief, and God Himself
> Made rendezvous.

Three men are hanging on three crosses. Two of them are robbers. And the One on the centre cross, what was His crime that He should be in such company? Even before He died, one of the criminals said from deep inner conviction, "This man has done nothing wrong."

A sudden change of attitude comes over one of the robbers who had been abusing Jesus. He turned to Him and pleaded, "Lord, remember me when you come into your kingdom."

The thief's prayer contained *a confession of Christ's Deity* – "Lord". His faith had only a small content of knowledge, but he saw in Christ One worthy of his devotion. A spark of faith had been kindled in his heart.

He expressed *a confidence in Christ's Saviourhood* – "Lord, remember me." He dared to include himself in the wide embrace of Christ's prayer for forgiveness. Had He not power to save, why ask to be remembered?

He had *a conception of Christ's Royalty*. His faith pierced through the appearances of the moment, and was richly rewarded. Hear Christ's assurance. What certainty! "I tell you the truth." What speed! "Today." What glory! "In paradise." What company! "With me!"

FOR MEDITATION: *This saying is a deathblow to the dogma of soul-sleep and the doctrine of purgatory.*

September 4

DEVOTION

When Jesus saw his mother there . . . he said . . .
"Dear woman, here is your son," and to the disciple,
"Here is your mother." (John 19:26, 27)

It is significant that Jesus does not now address Mary as "Mother", but uses the courteous title, "Woman", a highly respectable mode of address. It is the equivalent of our "Lady". Jesus was gently breaking the truth to her that henceforth the special relationship between them no longer obtained. He must have no rival in His mediatorial ministry.

In every relationship Jesus was the pattern Man. As child and as man He had honoured His father and mother. His last thought was to make provision for His widowed mother. He could no longer make provision for her Himself. His brothers were still unbelieving. He had nothing to bequeath to her.

Mary would find a congenial home with John, the disciple who deeply loved Him. These two, of similar temperament and united by a common love, would derive great comfort from their recollections. It would appear that John was wealthy and could make ample provision for her needs. Tradition has it that they lived together for twelve years in Jerusalem, and that John refused to leave the city as long as she survived. In this way *Jesus left an example for all whose parents are still living*.

FOR WORSHIP:
> *And come, ye sons, behold the Christ,*
> *The noblest son of earth!*
> *In death's dark hour He looks in love*
> *On her who gave Him birth.*

September 5

DERELICTION

Jesus cried out in a loud voice, "Eloi, Eloi, lama sabachthani?" — which means, "My God, My God, why have you forsaken me?" (Matthew 27:46)

The first three words from the cross wre concerned with men. Now Jesus addresses Himself to God. For the previous three hours His Father had shrouded the sun in kindly darkness, during which His soul had been exposed to the merciless assaults of the powers of evil. Infinitely worse than that, He had for the first time experienced the averted face of His Father. At the end of the sixth hour, He broke the silence with the shuddering cry of desolation.

The mysterious darkness was no eclipse, for the moon was at its furthest point from the sun. He almost invariably addressed God as His Father, but here, as *"My God"*. Though forsaken, His faith did not suffer eclipse.

Why? Never before had this word, cry of a baffled heart, crossed His lips, nor did it ever again. He was *forsaken* that we might never know that experience. He had been forsaken by men, even His intimates, but never by God. Who can plumb the depths of His anguish? For the first time an eternity of communion had broken. The wrath of hell had broken over His soul, but now it was the wrath of heaven as He bore the sins of the world! Why should God forsake His sinless Son? There was only one explanation. He was taking my place — and yours.

FOR WORSHIP:
Eli, Eli, Lama Sabbachthani! Deep-echoed woe,
Eli, Eli, Lama Sabbachthani! O who can know,
Or who the depth of anguish can divine,
That broken heart, that thrilling cry of Thine?

September 6

AGONY

Knowing that all was now completed, and so that the Scripture would be fulfilled, Jesus said, "I am thirsty." (John 19:28)

The previous word from the cross was a word of spiritual anguish; this was the sob of physical agony. He who began His ministry with gnawing hunger, closed it with raging thirst. Only two syllables in the original, but compressed into it the most intense agony. The Maker of heaven and earth with parched lips!

It was *an exclamation of physical agony* – the supreme physical pain of the crucifixion, a burning fever that consumed Him.

It was *an evidence of His real humanity*. God does not thirst. The Man Christ Jesus did thirst, for He was "God manifest in the flesh". Sufferers in all ages have been able to take comfort from the fact that their God did not insulate Himself from the sufferings of His people. "In all their afflictions He was afflicted."

It was *an example of fulfilled prophecy*. It was only "that the Scriptures might be fulfilled", that this cry escaped His lips.

It was *an exhibition of self-control*. Only once did a cry of pain escape Him during the excruciating ordeal, and then it required His Father's expressed will to open His mouth.

It was *an expression of spiritual thirst*. He knew an even more intense thirst. Did He not thirst to be thirsted after? He is still athirst for the fellowship and devotion of those for whom he thirsted on the cross.

FOR MEDITATION: *"Surely He has borne our griefs and carried our sorrows."*

September 7

TRIUMPH!

Jesus said, "It is finished." With that he bowed his head and gave up his spirit. (John 19:30)

The two previous words from the cross voiced its tragedy. This saying shouted its triumph. The three English words, *It is finished*, are but a single word in the Greek. It has been called the greatest single word ever uttered. For the Lord it meant:

Suffering was ended. It was doubtless a sigh of relief that an eternity of anticipation was over, that never again would He experience His Father's averted face. The cup of suffering had been full for Him, but having drained it, He held it up inverted when He said, "Finished!" and not a drop trickled down the edge.

Shadows became substance. The temporary types and shadows of the Old Covenant had all been fulfilled. The sacrifices of irrational creatures which could never remove sin had reached their culmination. Never again need one drop of sacrificial blood be shed, for He had offered *"one sacrifice for sins for ever"*.

The Father's will was fulfilled. Of all mankind, Jesus alone could say, "It is finished." He alone could review His whole life approvingly.

Satan was defeated. The moment of Satan's seeming triumph was the moment of his defeat. "The Seed of the woman" dealt him a death blow.

Redemption was accomplished. Every obstacle to man's fellowship with God had been removed.

Hallelujah!

FOR PRAISE:
> 'Tis finished — the Messiah dies
> For sins, but not His own;
> The great redemption is complete,
> And Satan's power is overthrown.

September 8

CONFIDENCE

Jesus called out with a loud voice, "Father, into your hands I commit my spirit." When he had said this he breathed his last. (Luke 23:46)

With awe we approach the watershed of the eternities. The eternal Son of God dismisses His spirit. But before He took leave of earth, He uttered His last word from the throne of His cross, and not in subdued tones, but with a loud, triumphant voice. Only eight words, yet they enshrine a rich vein of truth.

His death was voluntary. The word "commend" could be translated "lay down". Had He not said, "I have power to lay it down"? Matthew said, "He dismissed His spirit", an act of His will. Transcendent joy must have flooded Him as His spirit rose from the miasmas of earth to the pure celestial air.

His trust was unshaken. His trust had not been impaired by the awful experience of the cross – no craven fear, but an attitude of calm assurance.

> Father, into hands of Thine,
> I commit this soul of mine.

The secret of our security. He had assured the penitent thief of a place in paradise – death is not the end of all.

As our Lord closed His eyes in death, His spirit reposed in the strong hands of His Father, as restfully as a babe on its mother's breast. His final act of committal was a genuine act of faith.

Who would be afraid of death when it means our spirits are in His hands?

FOR PRAISE: *Redemption was now completed, awaiting only the resurrection as God's seal of final acceptance of Christ's sacrifice.*

FAITH INVOLVES A RISK

Abraham, when called . . . obeyed and went, even though he did not know where he was going. (Hebrews 11:8)

Faith feeds on the promises of God. The conscious presence of God is the atmosphere in which faith thrives. But in the malarial swamps of man's doubts and questionings, it wilts and dies. It is fed and flourishes as a result of time spent in God's presence.

It develops best when all props are removed, for *the exercise of faith always involves a risk*. Where no risk is involved, no faith is necessary. It increases as it responds to the requirements and challenges of the Word of God.

Contrary to popular belief, faith is not always fostered best by great encouragements and swift answers to prayer, much as we appreciate them. It thrives more in the midst of difficulties and conflicts, when all secondary supports have been removed.

It grows with the greatest speed *when we believe our beliefs and doubt our doubts*. The surest way to arrest its growth is to doubt our beliefs and believe our doubts. Faith always involves an act of the will, and we must choose the path we will pursue, the high road or the low.

FOR MEDITATION: *Faith never knows where it is being led, or it would not be faith.*

September 10

UNDER FIRE

About midnight Paul and Silas were singing hymns.
(Acts 16:25)

Paradoxically, faith sings while still in prison. Its song of praise antedates its release, as in the case of Paul and Silas. Faith can fight effectively even when bound in chains (see Tim. 2:9).

It can flourish in the midst of trial and tragedy, but cannot purchase immunity from these experiences for the Christian. The prophet Habakkuk affords a shining example of the triumph of faith under fire.

Stationed on his rural watchtower, he was perplexed by the problem of unanswered prayer and an apparently inactive Providence. The prosperity of the wicked and the afflictions of the righteous seemed out of keeping with his conception of the nature of God.

Relief came when he received a word from the Lord: "The righteous will live by his faith" (Hab. 2:4). With this assurance, he was able to meet stark tragedy with a song in his heart. Hear the sublime strains of faith:

Though the fig tree does not bud, and there are no grapes on the vines, though the olive crop fails and the fields produce no food, though there are no sheep in the pen and no cattle in the stalls, *yet I will rejoice in the Lord, I will be joyful in God my Saviour.* (3:17,18)

Through his faith in God, the prophet was able to face and survive even tragedy and heartbreak.

FOR EMULATION: *Since Habakkuk had God, he had all, and could face tragedy and heartbreak.*

September 11

THE BEATITUDE OF SIGHTLESS FAITH

"Because you have seen me, you have believed: blessed are those who have not seen and yet have believed."
(John 20:29)

Thomas believed because he was presented with the evidence he demanded – the nail-prints in Christ's hands. But the Lord was too faithful to allow an important lesson to go unmastered. Very gently Jesus said: "Blessed are those who have not seen and yet have believed." He stressed the superior blessedness of believing without seeing.

There is much that we may learn from the experience of Thomas about the Master's method with doubting hearts. No believer is immune to the ravages of doubt. *Even after having genuinely believed, it is still possible to have intellectual problems.* But Jesus did not exclude the doubter from the apostolate. Nor did He blame him for having a melancholic disposition; or chide him for desiring satisfying evidence on which to base his faith. He knew that it was not the unbelief of the atheist or agnostic, but the doubt of a soul in travail.

The intellectual climate of our day has exalted the question mark into the category of an absolute virtue. *Belief tends to be crucified and doubt canonised.* But this attitude finds no support in the teaching of Christ. He puts no premium on mental dishonesty, nor does He suggest there is any virtue in doubt.

The beatitude Jesus pronounced on sightless faith was not an exaltation of credulity, but He did indicate the necessity of a leap of faith.

FOR MEDITATION: *This beatitude is for those who believe, not those who doubt. There is no virtue in doubt.*

COOKING OR COMPANY?

Martha was distracted at all the preparations that had to be made . . . Mary sat at the Lord's feet. (Luke 10:39,40)

At the feast in Martha's Bethany home, Jesus would have preferred Martha's company to the sumptuous meal, and He made that clear when He gently chided her: "Martha, you are worried and upset about many things, but only one thing is needed. Mary has chosen what is better" (v.41). It is suggested that Jesus was referring to the single combined dish that would have provided an adequate meal, and yet left her time to join Mary at His feet. A little economy in food and labour would have paid handsome spiritual dividends.

In spite of Martha's petulant protest (v.40), *Jesus refused to rebuke or redirect Mary to the kitchen.* While not undervaluing Martha's labour of love, He made it clear that man does not live by bread alone. Nor did He suggest that Martha should do exactly what Mary had done. But He did commend Mary for choosing her priorities wisely, and putting the more important things first – the spiritual before the temporal.

God gave to each sister, as He gives to us, the distinctive talents that would best enable her to discharge her responsibility to the Kingdom. There was no need for one to be envious or critical of the other, simply because their devotion to Christ found expression in different ways.

FOR MEDITATION: *We could well emulate Martha's diligence and hospitable spirit, but not at the expense of not sitting at Jesus' feet.*

THE MYSTERY OF SUFFERING

"Though he slay me, yet will I hope in him." (Job 13:15)

Job's domestic picture was one of relaxed and happy communication and conviviality (1:4). He displayed deep solicitude for the moral and spiritual welfare of his family, and made regular sacrifices for his children in case they had "sinned and cursed God in their hearts" (1:5). But he was to be tested by terrible and unexplained disaster.

Overnight the scene was reversed. At one stroke flocks and herds, servants and sons and daughters were swept away (1:13–19). The hour of crisis reveals the true man. Caught totally unawares, Job reacted as a man who knows and trusts God. "He fell to the ground and worshipped". In the midst of mystery, his sublime faith in God found expression in a classic affirmation: "The Lord gave and the Lord has taken away; blessed be the name of the Lord (1:21 RSV).

His noble reaction to tragedy won the approval of God, but aroused the hostility of Satan. One of the important insights we gain from the drama that ensued, is that events on earth may have an unsuspected background in the heavenly realm. Job's relation to the spirit world and his accessibility to spiritual forces outside himself are assumed.

The saga closed with Job vindicated before his friends and Satan, and blessed with double what he had before. His fortunes were restored when he prayed for his friends (42:10).

FOR PRAYER: *Lord, give me the confidence which Job expressed: "I know that you can do all things, no plan of yours can be thwarted."* (42:2)

September 14

DWARFED BY A GREAT FATHER

Isaac went out to meditate in the field in the evening.
(Genesis 24:63)

It was Isaac's misfortune to be dwarfed by a great father, Abraham, and a brilliant though devious son, Jacob. That misfortune left scars on his personality. He became a follower rather than a leader. Living as he did for forty years under parental domination, he failed to develop the wholesome independence of character so necessary to a mature individual.

The very qualitites that made his father great stunted Isaac's growth and produced a rather colourless personality. Not for a moment would we denigrate a godly parentage, but everyone has to meet and do battle with his or her own weaknesses, no matter how noble their parents.

After Abraham's hand was removed by death, his enemies soon discovered the weakness and passivity of his son and heir. The Philistines exploited these to the full, forcing him to retreat into the hill country, and stopping the wells Abraham had dug. The problem was not so much that Isaac was poor-spirited, as that *when faced with alternatives of victory or peace, he always opted for peace.*

A revealing sidelight on his character is thrown by Genesis 24:63. ''Isaac went to meditate in the field in the evening.'' He devoted the beautiful evening hour to devout meditation and prayer. He revelled in the solitudes of nature, enjoying fellowship with nature's God.

FOR WARNING: *Most of us have weak spots. With Isaac, food came first and blessing second.* (Genesis 27)

September 15

THE VENTURE OF FAITH

By faith Abraham, when called to go to a place he would later receive as his inheritance, obeyed and went, even though he did not know where he was going.
(Hebrews 11:8)

A step of faith always involves a *calculated risk*. It is *not blind credulity, but calm confidence.* The heroes of faith had their portraits hung in God's Hall of Fame because they were prepared to stake everything on His faithfulness.

A party touring the mint in Philadelphia, viewed the process in which molten metal was poured into the coin moulds. The workman said to one man, "Sir, I suppose you know that if you dip your hand into a bucket of water, I could pour the molten metal into your hand and it would not burn you? Perhaps you would care to try?"

"No, thank you," said the man, "I will take your word for it."

Presently his wife came along and the workman repeated his offer. "Certainly, certainly," she said. When the experiment was safely concluded, the workman turned to the husband. "Sir, I suppose you would say you *believed* me, but your wife *trusted* me." Hers was a faith ready to venture on the veracity of the workman.

Abraham ventured all on the faithfulness of God. Faith does not demand to know where it is being led. He prepared to sacrifice Isaac, not knowing *why* God asked it of him and *how* He would redeem His promise. He *trusted* God.

FOR EMULATION:
> *Faith, mighty faith the promise sees*
> *And looks to God alone,*
> *Laughs at impossibilities*
> *And cries, "It shall be done."*
>
> Charles Wesley

September 16

WHEN WEAKNESS IS STRENGTH

"When I am weak, then I am strong." (2 Corinthians 12:10)

There is an arresting difference between God's thoughts and man's concerning weakness and inadequacy. We are inclined to consider them a justifiable excuse for shrinking from the difficult task. God advances these very qualities as reasons for tackling it. *We maintain that we are too weak. God asserts that to be the very reason He chose us*: "God chose the weak things of the world to shame the strong" (1 Cor. 1:27).

An important spiritual principle is involved here, which must be mastered by all who wish to be their best for God. God is not confined to the exceptionally clever for the accomplishment of His purposes. Indeed, He can use them only as they abandon reliance on their purely natural abilities. All through history God has chosen and used nonentities because their unusual dependence on Him left room for the display of His power. When they are content to be nothing, He can be everything.

"It is a thrilling discovery to make," writes James S. Stewart, "that always it is upon human weakness and humiliation, not human strength and confidence, that God chooses to build His Kingdom; and that He can use us, *not merely in spite of our ordinariness and disqualifying infirmities, but precisely because of them* . . . Nothing can defeat a church or soul that takes, not its strength but its weakness, and offers it to God to be His weapon."

FOR PRAYER: *Help me, Lord, to abandon reliance on my purely natural abilities, and to be joyously dependent on You for spiritual effectiveness.*

THE ESSENCE OF PRIDE

God opposes the proud, but gives grace to the humble.
(James 4:6)
Haughty eyes and a proud heart . . . are sin.
(Proverbs 21:4)

These words, and others like them, express the hatred, the revulsion, the antipathy of God to pride and arrogance. It is an abomination to Him (Prov. 16:5). Can we condone and tolerate what God says He hates? God opposes the proud, and holds them at a distance. The only meeting-place between a proud heart and God is ''a broken and contrite spirit''.

Pride is a deification of self. It arrogates to itself the honour which belongs to God only. It thinks more highly of itself than it ought to think. The word ''proud'' signifies literally, ''one who considers himself above other people''. It was the sin of Nebuchadnezzar which brought him down to the level of the beasts.

Pride is characterised by independence of God. It was at the heart of Adam's sin. Instead of being dependent on God, he desired to be as God, and brought the race to ruin. It desires to be beholden to neither God nor man. In striking contrast, the Son of God said, ''By myself I can do nothing'' (John 5:30).

Pride involves a certain contempt of others. Like the rich man of the parable, pride prays: ''God, I thank you that I am not like other men'' (Luke 18:11). It relegates every other mortal to a minor role in life. It uses other people as a backdrop to display its own brilliance.

FOR MEDITATION: *It is a striking fact that pride heads the list in every catalogue of sins compiled by the Church.*

FIREPROOF FAITH

"The God we serve is able to save us from it [the fiery furnace], and he will rescue us from your hand, O king. But even if he does not . . . we will not serve your gods." (Daniel 3:17,18)

God does not treat everyone alike. These three young men were not concerned with God's treatment of others. They had their dealings direct with Him. We quickly run into spiritual trouble if we look around at God's dealings with others.

Do we, like these young men, have a "But if not . . ." in our spiritual vocabulary? *Do we have this third resource of faith?* Is our faith fireproof?

If war should come and son, daughter, husband, sweetheart be taken from our side, do we have a "But if not" to carry us through our fiery furnace? If financial reverses are experienced? If ill-health overtakes us? When old age enfeebles us? When bereavement strikes? When desire for a life partner is not granted? If our Christian work does not meet with the success we expected?

Let us emulate the dauntless faith in a loving, caring God of the noble three, who maintained their confidence in Him in the face of seemingly unrewarded faith. *"But if not, we will still go on trusting God."* They did not fall into self-pity or unbelief. We may not always understand God's dealings at the time, and He does not always explain Himself.

"You do not realise now what I am doing, but later you will understand," was the Lord's promise (John 13:7).

FOR PRAYER: *If persecution or adversity comes, O Lord, I would have a "but if not" in my vocabulary.*

September 19

INVINCIBLE WEAPONS

They overcame him by the blood of the Lamb and by the word of their testimony: they did not love their lives so much as to shrink from death. (Revelation 12:11)

The weapons the Christian soldier uses in the warfare between God and Satan are spiritual, not material. Before detailing three invincible weapons at our disposal, a voice announces: ''The accuser of our brethren has been thrown down . . . and they overcame him'' (v.10).

The judicial weapon – ''the blood of the Lamb''. This weapon derives its potency from Calvary. The secret of victory over Satan lies not in our innate powers, but in our union with Christ in His victorious death and resurrection. The phrase ''the blood of the Lamb'' is not a mystic charm. It is the expression of an intelligent, active faith in Christ who, by shedding His blood, atoned for our sins and defeated Satan.

The evidential weapon – ''the word of their testimony''. The exercise of faith in the victory of Christ is to be followed by witness to His Word which announces His victory. Grounded in the Word, our testimony becomes a sword in the Spirit's hand.

The sacrificial weapon – ''They loved not their lives even unto death.'' Our word ''martyr'' comes from the Greek here rendered ''testimony''. It is the testimony of one who has the martyr spirit which is mightily effective. To him, life is of secondary importance when compared with the outcome of the battle and the victory of his Lord. His supreme concern is to see Satan defeated and Christ triumphant, even if his life is sacrificed in the process.

FOR MEDITATION: *The martyr witness in life and by tongue to the power of the blood, is more of a barrier to Satan than a wall of fire.*

September 20

THE PANOPLY OF GOD

Put on the full armour of God, so that you can take your stand against the devil's schemes. (Ephesians 6:11)

The believer has no inherent power to overcome the attacks of the evil one. It is useless to have strong armour without if we are weak within. We must "be strong in the Lord and in His mighty power" (v.10).

Four things are noteworthy about this armour:

It is not our armour we are to put on, *but God's.* We have nothing of our own that will afford us sure protection from our wily adversary. Only the armour that God supplies will prevail.

This armour is *of value only when we fight an external foe.* It is powerless and utterly ineffective in dealing with the flesh, the traitor within the citadel of man's soul. The only way to deal with the flesh is to mortify it.

God makes *no provision for armour for the back.* He expects the soldiers in His army always to be on the offensive. He lends no encouragement to flee when the battle grows fierce.

We need *the whole armour of God.* If we put on every piece except one, we leave an Achilles' heel, a vulnerable spot which will enable Satan to inflict defeat on us.

> Stand, then, in His great might,
> With all His strength endued;
> And take to arm you for the fight,
> The panoply of God.

FOR ACTION:
> *Gird your heavenly armour on,*
> *Wear it ever night and day,*
> *Ambushed lies the evil one,*
> *Watch and pray.*

September 21

SATAN'S POWER LIMITED

The Lord said to Satan, "Very well, then, he is in your hands; but you must spare his life." (Job 2:6)

While we must not underestimate the might and malignity of Satan, we must be careful not to fall in the opposite error and overestimate it. Fear can paralyse.

Scripture nowhere ascribes to the devil the divine attributes of omniscience, omnipotence and omnipresence. The fact that he is a created being means that his power is limited. While he can be in only one place at a time, he is able to achieve a "limited omnipresence" through his vast host of minions.

Any power and authority he wields is not inherent but derived from God. "There is no authority except that which God has established" (Rom. 13:1) – and this includes the devil. In his testing of Job he could go no further than God permitted.

Although Scripture recognises him as "the god of this world", the devil is not supreme. Even in the matter of temptation he does not have free hand (1 Cor. 10:13).

Contrary to popular conception, *there is nothing to indicate that he is able to foretell the future infallibly*. He has to gather his information as we do, but he has the advantage of highly organised hosts of evil but obedient servants at his call.

We are encouraged not to be "frightened in any way by those who oppose you" (Phil. 1:28), for "greater is he that is in you, than he that is in the world" (1 John 4:4).

FOR MEDITATION: *We should not overestimate Satan's power, but neither should we underestimate it. "His craft and power are great."*

September 22

THE TARDINESS OF GOD

When God saw . . . how they turned from their evil ways, he had compassion and did not bring upon them the destruction he had threatened. (Jonah 3:10)

We are always in a hurry to have our desires granted, our prayers answered. But God refuses to be stampeded into premature action. Our impatience is often the outcome of an undisciplined spirit, or an imperfect knowledge of the facts and their implications. God's seeming tardiness is the reaction of complete knowledge, and perfect control of every contingency that might arise.

In time of war, people with bleeding hearts cry, "Why does God not intervene?" Certainly not because He is *physically* unable to do so. The answer is that *there are things which are moral and spiritual impossibilities to God*. He will intervene when it is morally right to do so.

When He sees a nation bow in humiliation and confession of its national sins, it becomes possible and right for Him to intervene. When wicked Nineveh publicly expressed its repentance, God immediately responded by lifting the judgement. It is not God who is too slow, but man who is too sinful.

Sometimes God is slow in answering our prayers so that we may learn lessons we could master in no other way. It is for us to maintain the attitude of confident faith as did Abraham: "With undaunted faith he looked at the facts . . . He refused to allow any distrust of a definite pronouncement of God to make him waver" (Rom. 4:19–21 Phillips).

FOR PRAISE:
Then the thing happened that Jonah knew would fall,
Nineveh repented at his prophetic call,
God in mercy pardoned all — after all.

September 23

THE SNARE OF COVETOUSNESS

"What good thing must I do to get eternal life?" . . .
"Go, sell your possessions and give to the poor . . ."
(Matthew 19:16, 21)

In this passage we detect youthful idealism. The young man wanted the best life had to offer, summed up in the words: "eternal life". Idealism can be hidden under a "hippie" exterior. But this young man tended to view goodness as quantitative. Jesus sought to show him that it is qualitative.

We also see a yearning emptiness. "What do I still lack?" (v.20) might be either despair or complacency – probably the former, which is a contemporary attitude among young people. Despite an outwardly upright life, he felt only an empty shell. He possessed so many *tangible* benefits – youth, wealth, position – but he was short on *intangibles*. One of the main youth problems to-day is frustration.

In answer to the young man's question Jesus listed five commandments of the Law relating to man's duty to his fellows. Interestingly, He omitted *covetousness*, his obvious sin, but added the inclusive love of neighbour (Deut. 5:16–20; Lev. 19:18).

The young man's statement that he had kept the law revealed his lack of self-knowledge. His wealth had become his god. Jesus challenged him to show his love for his neighbour through his pocket: Go – sell – GIVE – come – follow.

He went away sorrowful because he was unwilling to part with what cut him off from eternal life.

FOR MEDITATION: *Jesus was young and so were His disciples. He knows the problems of youth.*

September 24

THE CRUCIAL CONFESSION

"Who do you [Peter] say I am?" Simon Peter answered, "You are the Christ, the Son of the living God." (Matthew 16:16)

This paragraph marks the turning point of this Gospel. The shadow of the cross is creeping over the Lord's ministry, and He begins to prepare his disciples for what lies ahead.

First He asked them, "What are the popular ideas about me? – Whom do men say that I am?" (v.14). Their reply was a startling commentary on the variety and versatility of His character, personality and ministry – John the Baptist, Elijah, Jeremiah, Moses, one of the prophets.

In His second question, Jesus elicited Peter's personal opinion concerning the central fact of the Christian faith: "But what about YOU!" (v.15) This is a question that is still finally pertinent. All the great cults have given the wrong answer to this question, and in that fact lies their condemnation.

Peter's answer, probably as spokesman for the twelve who must often have discussed the subject, was a confession of adoring worship. "You are the Christ, the Son of the living God!" He was not only the Messiah, but God's divine Son.

Christ accepted Peter's magnificent confession, an action which would have been blasphemy had it not been true. He told Peter that his confession was not the result of reason or intuition, but of divine revelation. At a time when opposition was mounting, this avowal must have been balm to the heart of Christ.

FOR MEDITATION: *The discovery of Jesus as Son of God is always a revelation from God.*

September 25

WALKING IN THE SPIRIT

Walk in the Spirit and you will not gratify the desires of the flesh. (Galatians 5:16)

"Walking in the Spirit" does not mean that we will be immune from the pull of fleshly desires. When the Holy Spirit fills us, He takes control of our personality, but He does not dehumanise us. The old desires will reassert themselves, but we can be enabled by the Spirit's strengthening to refrain from gratifying them. We are still on the field of battle, but we no longer fight alone. We have a powerful, though unseen Ally.

A walk in the Spirit will be *a walk in accordance with the Word* the Spirit has inspired. Note the significant parallel between Ephesians 5:18–21 and Colossians 3:16,17. The same results are said to flow from being filled with the Spirit and being filled with the Word. A neglected Bible will interrupt a walk in the Spirit.

It will also be *a walk in obedience to the divine will.* The Lord will not admit to His intimate fellowship those who walk in disobedience.

The crucial point is, who is in control of my life? The self-life with its unlawful desires and tendencies is the citadel of the fleshly principle, and it will continue to dominate until consigned to the cross. When we walk in the Spirit, He ensures our emancipation from the tyranny of yielding to the desires of the flesh.

FOR MEDITATION: *It is one thing to embark on a Spirit-filled life, but quite another to walk consistently in the Spirit.*

KEEP IN STEP WITH THE SPIRIT

Since we live by the Spirit, let us keep in step with the Spirit. (Galatians 5:25)

The Christian's enjoyment of full salvation is dependent on his or her "walking in the Spirit". "Walking" is a familiar Bible term for daily living. In Galatians 5:16, the ordinary word for "walking around" is used. It stands for a person's conduct in ordinary life, his actions at home or in business, at work or play. It denotes activity and progress.

The implication of "walk in the Spirit" is that in our daily life we are habitually to order our lifestyle through the Spirit's guidance. The desirable result will be: "You will not gratify the desires of the sinful nature."

In verse 25, however, the Greek word for "walk" signifies more than mere locomotion: "Since we live by the Spirit, let us *keep in step with the Spirit.*" It signifies a measured walk, marching in file or in step. The idea is that of *concerted action*, or joint effort.

When we set out together with our fellow-believers, we are to let the Holy Spirit be the One who gives the orders, and we are habitually to keep step with each other and with Him.

When these two words are combined, they mean that we are to recognise the Holy Spirit as Guide of our *personal* actions. When we engage in *concerted* action, it is the Holy Spirit who is to order and discipline our combined effort.

FOR ENCOURAGEMENT: *"So I say, live by [walk in] the Spirit, and you will not gratify the desires of the sinful nature."* (Gal. 5:16)

TWO KINDS OF FRUIT

"I chose you . . . to go and bear fruit." (John 15:16)

The life of the maturing Christian will be *fruitful, not barren*. One of the marks of physical maturing is the ability to reproduce oneself, and this is true also in the spiritual realm. This is one of the purposes Christ had for us when He chose us to be His disciples. "You did not choose me," He said, "But *I chose you to go and bear fruit*." A fruitless disciple is a contradiction in terms.

What constitutes "fruit"? Firstly, there is *fruit in character* – the fruit of the Spirit which finds expression in the nine winsome graces of Galatians 5:22,23. Note that these are passive, not active, qualities. All nine can be produced in the life of a person who is paralysed from the neck down. As we grow in maturity, these graces will be manifested in increasing measure.

Secondly there is *fruit in service*. "Even now the reaper harvests the crop for eternal life, so that the sower and the reaper may rejoice together" (John 4:36).

In writing to the Romans, Paul revealed the purpose of his visit: "I planned many times to come to you . . . in order that I might have a harvest among you" (Rom. 1:13). Souls won and lives discipled and encouraged to have a closer walk with God will evidence the disciple's growing maturity.

FOR THANKSGIVING: *Thank You, Lord, that if I abide in You as the branch abides in the vine, I can bear fruit for Your glory both in character and in service.*

September 28

THE ELEVENTH COMMANDMENT

"A new commandment I give you: Love one another."
(John 13:34)

"My command is this: Love each other *as I have loved you*"
(John 15:12).

But can love be commanded? Is it not spontaneous? Apparently it can be commanded, for Jesus commands it here. The answer to the problem lies in the fact that love does not spring from the emotions alone, but also from the will. Erotic and romantic love may be mainly of the emotions, but the *agape* love spoken of here is on a higher level and deeply involves the will. Love for the unlovely and undeserving is not spontaneous. It springs from the will to love, *in spite* of the unloveliness. Affinity or aversion are alike irrelevant.

An examination of the great love text, John 3:16, will support this contention. Was it a happy, pleasurable emotion that prompted God's love for the world? Did He feel a warm glow in His heart at sending His Son to the cross? Indeed, no! By a supreme act of His will He chose to pluck out His heart, to sacrifice His only irreplaceable possession, in order that we might be redeemed.

That is the kind of love He expects us to show to one another. Not sloppy sentiment, but sacrificial love that is expressed towards the unlovable as well as towards the attractive.

Because such love is commanded, it is possible.

FOR PRAYER:
> *Gracious Spirit, Holy Ghost,*
> *Taught by Thee we covet most,*
> *Of Thy gifts at Pentecost*
> *Holy heavenly love.*

AN INTERIOR REVELATION

"God . . . was pleased to reveal His son in me."
(Galatians 1:15)

The Holy Spirit is not content with a mere external revelation of Christ to the believing heart. On the Damascus road, Christ was revealed *to* Paul, to the accompaniment of "a light from heaven, brighter than the sun" which blazed around him and his companions (Acts 26:13). He saw with his physical eyes the ascended Christ, and with his ears heard Him speak. It was no hallucination. But external vision was not sufficient. His transforming experience which turned implacable hatred into adoring worship, must be applied to his heart.

Writing of this experience Paul said, "But God . . . was pleased *to reveal his Son in me* . . ." The words "in me" meant vastly more than "to my intellect". The word has reference to *illumining* grace, which is at the same time both revealing and transforming. The result of that interior revelation of Christ meant for Paul a sense of His presence, intimately, ravishingly near.

Paul had already seen Christ, exalted at the right hand of God, but now He was revealed to him by the Holy Spirit, as dwelling in his unworthy heart. From that moment he could say, "I no longer live, but Christ lives in me" (Gal. 2:20).

FOR MEDITATION: *The inner revelation of Christ to Paul enabled him to say, "To me to live is Christ."*

September 30

WHEN SORROW STRIKES

Godliness with contentment is great gain. (1 Timothy 6:6)

Acceptance of the divine disciplines rather than resenting or rebelling against them, is a clear mark of growth in likeness to Christ. His attitude was, "I delight to do your will, O my God" (Ps. 40:8; Heb. 10:7). We may not always actually enjoy the adverse experience while passing through it – and Scripture recognises that possibility (Heb. 12:11) – but we can and should regard the will of God as being "good, acceptable and perfect" (Rom. 12:2). This statement implies that God's will for our lives cannot be improved on and therefore should be accepted.

As Paul grew in his knowledge of Christ, he testified, "I have learned to be content, whatever the circumstances" (Phil. 4:11). Not that he had always been content, but his increasingly intimate walk with God satisfied him that what God ordained was in his best interests.

When sorrow, tragedy, bereavement strike, it is not always easy to hold this ground, but it is the only way to comfort and peace of heart. Paul enunciated a principle of perpetual relevance when he recorded the word of the Lord that came to him when he was struggling with his painful "thorn in the flesh": "He said to me, *My grace is sufficient for you*, for my power is made perfect in weakness" (2 Cor. 12:9).

FOR THANKSGIVING: *Lord, I thank You that though I grieve, it is not like the sorrow of those who have no hope.* (1 Thess. 4:13)

SHAPING AN INSTRUMENT

Run to and fro . . . to see if you can find a man.
(Jeremiah 5:1 RSV)

"Every great work is but the shadow of a man." One of the fascinating exercises of the Christian life is to study the interplay of divine providence and human personality. God employs an infinite variety of methods in preparing the men whom He has chosen for special assignments. He quietly invades the affairs of men, and weaves His own perfect plan from the tangled strands of human experience.

It has been asserted that God's method in achieving His world purpose, has always been a man. Not always a noble or a brilliant man, but always *a man with capacity for a growing faith*.

When God plans a movement, He first shapes an instrument. When He imparts a vision, He at the same time prepares a man – a man in touch with Him, and sensitive to His guiding or restraining hand. Often, unobtrusively and quite unsuspected by the man himself, God has been training His chosen leader in a specialist school – a school with an unorthodox curriculum, but one admirably adapted to the purpose He had in view. Heredity, environment and education are all made tributary to the divine plan.

> Through men whom worldings count as fools,
>   Chosen of God and not of man,
> Reared in Thy secret training schools,
>   Moves forward Thine eternal plan.

FOR PRAISE: *I thank You, Lord, that I did not choose You, but in Your sovereignty You chose and appointed me.* (John 15:16)

GOD'S WAY UP IS DOWN

"I am gentle and humble in heart." (Matthew 11:29)

These words give us a glimpse into the inmost heart of the One who spoke them. On the lips of anyone else, they would have smacked of conceit. If pride is the great and essential sin, then humility is the supreme virtue. *If humility was the distinguishing feature of the Master, then it must characterise the disciple.*

Had Jesus never spoken a word about humility, His lifestyle and circumstances would have been a silent rebuke to the pride and self-exaltation of the men with whom He associated. Not until He came with His peerless life and teaching, was humility elevated to the level of a primary virtue. Humility as a grace is the creation of Christianity. "Everyone who humbles himself will be exalted" (Luke 14:11).

Andrew Murray indicates the way in which our Lord's humility may become ours: "It is only by the indwelling of Christ in His divine humility, that we become truly humble. We have our pride from another, Adam. We must have our humility from Another, too. Pride is ours, and rules us with such terrible power, because it is ourself, our very nature. Humility must be ours in the same way. The promise is, 'Where' – in the heart – 'sin abounded, grace abounded more exceedingly.' "

Our pride stands abashed in the presence of His humility. One lesson stands out crystal clear: *God's way up is down.*

FOR PRAYER: *Lord, forgive the pride of my heart, and through the Spirit's agency, reproduce in me Your own humility.*

THE CHILD JESUS

And the child grew and became strong; he was filled with wisdom, and the grace of God was on him. (Luke 2:40)

This verse is about all we know of the childhood of Jesus, but the silences of God are as eloquent as His speech. It does not satisfy our curiosity, but sufficient is revealed to assure us of His real humanity and full identity with the human race.

Jesus did not burst on the world stage as a mature adult, but as an infant a span long, in striking contrast to the Greek gods who descended to earth fully grown and well armed. In His incarnation Jesus submitted to the sinless limitations of growth and development inherent in membership of the human race.

His home was in the despised village of Nazareth – a significant element in the divine condescension. There were at least eight members in the family, and in that cramped eastern home, the Lord of glory experienced life at close quarters with sinful men and women.

He experienced normal human development. He was indistinguishable from other children, except that He did not sin. He grew at the same rate as the other boys and laid the foundations for a fine physique. He played in the market place with the other children and attended the same village school. No-one in Nazareth suspected that God was living among them.

FOR MEDITATION:
> *When I am tempted to repine*
> *That such a humble lot is mine,*
> *Within I hear a voice that saith –*
> *Mine were the streets of Nazareth.*

October 4

THE SILENT YEARS

Jesus grew in wisdom and stature, and in favour with God and men. (Luke 2:52)

It is significant that the silence shrouding the early years of our Lord's earthly life is broken only once, and then to record an incident which occurred when He was twelve years old – His visit to the Temple, where He sat at the feet of the teachers of the law.

He had now reached the greatest crisis of His life. What would his attitude be when He returned to Nazareth? "He went down to Nazareth with them and was obedient to them" (2:51). He developed from boyhood to manhood, *demonstrating filial obedience both to His human parents and His divine Father*. Then began eighteen years of hidden discipline and training.

At home He learned the habit of obedience that characterised His attitude to His Father and culminated on the cross. He thus provided a pattern for Christian young people.

It is idle to speculate about the time when Jesus first became conscious of the fact that He was God's Son in a unique sense and had a Messianic office to fulfil. James Stalker said, "I cannot trust myself even to think of a time when He did not know what His work in the world was to be." But where Scripture is silent, it is the part of wisdom to refrain from speculation.

FOR PRAISE:
Yes, here for love of thee, through silent years –
Oh, pause and see, if thou art wise –
The King of kings dwelt in disguise.

THE CARPENTER

"Isn't this the carpenter?" (Mark 6:3)

The life of our Lord has been so idealised by its sacred associations that we are apt to miss some of its most comforting and practical lessons, from fear of profaning its sacredness. His earthly occupation was one of these.

What is the significance of the fact that out of all possible occupations, God chose for His Son the lot of a working man? *Why did the only One who could have chosen any vocation, choose to be a carpenter?* Imagine the consternation of the angels when He who made the heavens, stooped to shape with His own hands a yoke for oxen.

Whatever else this act of condescension signified, it meant that Jesus purposed to identify himself with the common people. It stamped manual labour with ever-lasting honour. It acquainted Him with the feelings of the multitude, and gave Him insight into man's inmost thoughts.

In common with other Jewish boys, Jesus was required to learn a trade. What more natural than that He should be apprenticed to His foster-father and become the village carpenter?

> Think how in the sacred story
> Jesus took a humble grade,
> And the Lord of light and glory
> Worked with Joseph at his trade.

FOR MEDITATION:
> *The yokes He made were true,*
> *Because the Man who dreamed*
> *Was too*
> *An artisan.*

October 6

THE NOBILITY OF LABOUR

"He has done everything well!" (Mark 7:37)

Our Lord's choice and pursuit of the vocation of carpenter can teach us important lessons.

Jesus saw no incongruity in His standing in the saw-pit, laboriously cutting the thick logs into planks. In days when white-collar workers tend to despise those who work with their hands, *the contemplation of the life of Jesus during these years would wither such contemptuous pride*. He was a working man who earned His living as others of His contemporaries – by manual skill. His was no forty-hour week, but a twelve-hour day, doubtless with overtime as well.

If it was not beneath the Son of Man to work as an artisan, then surely it is beneath none of His children. The servant is not greater than his Lord. Because he was no stranger to "the dust and sweat of toil", as the hymn puts it, "sons of labour are dear to Jesus". He has imparted to a life of toil both dignity and nobility. If only they knew it, Jesus is "the working man's friend" who, from experience, is able to sympathise with their lot.

In work, no less than in ethics, His standard would be nothing less than perfection. No second rate work ever left His bench. Near enough was not good enough for our great Exemplar.

FOR MEDITATION: *"The carpenter"* — *what a title for the Lord of glory! Yet He gloried in it.*

October 7

FAITH IS CONTAGIOUS

By faith Moses' parents hid him for three months after he was born . . . and they were not afraid of the king's edict. (Hebrews 11:23)

The secret of the greatness of many men may be traced to their parents, especially their mothers. The faith of Moses' parents made possible all God's subsequent dealings with him. In a very real sense the faith of these two slaves significantly influenced the course of world history. Their faith showed itself in that *"they were not afraid of the king's commandment"*.

Their faith risked the wrath of the king, while their love devised an ingenious way of evading his ruthless edict. God honoured their faith and rewarded their love. As a result, Moses had a godly home and religion, which more than countered the adverse factors of his Egyptian secular education.

In that home he learned two vitally important lessons from his parents: *faith in God*, in an environment of evil and slavery. The godly influences left an indelible impression on his character.

From them, too, he imbibed *a fearless courage*. Their faith had transcended the king's anger, and produced a similar moral courage in their son. Later it was written of Moses: "He forsook Egypt, *not fearing the wrath of the King*" (Heb. 11:27 KJV). Faith ousts fear.

The heritage of a godly ancestry is a boon that should be greatly prized. Faith is contagious — and so is sin! What moral qualities are we communicating to our children?

FOR MEDITATION: *Faith feeds on the pledged Word of God and flourishes in the atmosphere of His presence.*

SAVING FAITH

*It is by grace you have been saved, through faith —
and this not from yourselves, it is the gift of God.*
(Ephesians 2:8)

Faith alone can save, but faith cannot save alone. The spiritual attitude essential for salvation involves repentance as well as faith. These two are simultaneous experiences separable only in thought. Paul said of the Greeks, "They must turn to God in repentance and have faith in our Lord Jesus" (Acts 20:21). These are the negative and positive aspects of the same act.

In repentance we turn from sin. In faith we embrace Christ as Saviour from sin. Faith is the universal condition of salvation because it brings salvation within reach of all. Anyone can believe.

Faith, in the saving sense, is not mere belief in a proposition or acceptance of a creed. It is the bond of union between God and man which brings new life and power. The important thing about faith is that it unites us with God. It is through faith that we become "partakers of the divine nature" (2 Pet. 1:4).

In saving faith our whole spiritual nature is called into exercise. With the *intellect* we recognise the truth of God's revelation concerning our sin and His provision for salvation in Christ's death and resurrection. With the *emotions* we respond to the discovery of God's amazing love and grace as demonstrated in the cross. These two make a powerful bid for the assent of the *will*, without which the spiritual transaction is not clinched.

FOR MEDITATION: *Salvation is not a transaction between God and ourselves in which He contributes grace and we contribute faith.*

FAITH AND SUFFERING

> You . . . have had to suffer grief in all kinds of trials
> . . . so that your faith . . . may be proved genuine.
> (1 Peter 1:6,7)

Faith does not stagger when suffering strikes or sorrow engulfs. Nor does she react to the fiery ordeal as something unexpected and extraordinary. She accepts it as a messenger of God sent to prove her genuineness, and to demonstrate the divine adequacy. Indeed, far from thinking it strange, *faith embraces trial with joy*, since it affords the opportunity of sharing Christ's suffering (4:12,13).

Faith discerns that manifold trials (1:6) are always matched by the manifold grace of God (4:10). "Manifold" means "many-coloured". These complementary phrases indicate that there is no colour in any human situation which cannot be matched by God's more than sufficient grace. And God's colours always match perfectly. "Those who receive God's abundant provision of grace . . . [shall] reign in life" (Rom. 5:17).

"Sorrow and suffering do colour life, don't they?" said a friend to a sorely tried Christian. "Indeed they do," was the reply, "and I *intend to choose the colours*." The answer of triumphant faith.

Faith finds her finest hour when she is hard pressed on every side, for she is then best able to demonstrate the utter sufficiency of God. If she must enter the fiery furnace, then her God walks with her in the flame (Isa. 43:2).

FOR MEDITATION: *"And glad may your soul be even to walk in the fiery furnace with one like unto the Son of Man."* (Samuel Rutherford)

October 10

FAITH AND PATIENCE

Imitate those who through faith and patience inherit what has been promised. (Hebrews 6:12)

Faith is often called on to run in double harness with patience. God nowhere promises that faith will receive all it desires exactly when it wants it. That is why the above exhortation was given. In support of it we read of Abraham who "after waiting patiently received what was promised" (v.15). It may be that our failure to obtain the blessing we seek is through lack of patience as well as of faith.

Between God's promise of a son to *Abraham* and its fulfilment, more than twenty years elapsed — years barren of any sign of God's activity. Faith grows by being tested, and the "father of the faithful" had to master the lesson of believing in the face of discouragement. In God's time his faith was rewarded.

David waited more than twenty years before God's promise of the throne was fulfilled, and during those years his faith was severely tested. Waiting *for* God was more difficult than waiting *on* God, but faith and patience secured the throne.

Jericho's capture was the result of faith and patience. The divine promise was the ground for faith (Josh. 6:2). But faith and patience had to encompass the city thirteen times before the promise materialised. Up to the thirteenth circuit there was not the slightest evidence of anything happening, but with the shout of faith the walls fell.

Waiting is more difficult than believing.

FOR THANKSGIVING: "... *No eye has seen any God besides you, who acts on behalf of those who wait for him.*" (Isa. 64:4)

UNDISCOURAGED OPTIMISM

"My prayer is not for them alone, I pray also for those who will believe in me through their message, that all of them may be one." (John 17:20,21)

Our Lord here extends the sweep of His prayer for His disciples to embrace all who would be won to Him by His followers in coming ages and in other lands.

In these words Jesus voiced His undiscouraged optimism concerning the ultimate success of His mission. It affirmed, too, His faith in the men who had failed Him, but who deeply loved Him.

What tremendous importance Jesus attached to unity among His people! And what tremendous efforts the adversary makes to mar that unity! (vv.11,21–23).

This oneness is possible only to those who have believed in Him, and it is exemplified in the vital and close oneness that existed between Him and His Father.

The beginnings of the answer to this petition were in evidence not many days later, after the descent of the Third Person of the Trinity. Luke records that on the Day of Pentecost, "they were all with one accord in one place" (Acts 2:1 KJV). This does not necessarily imply that there was complete unity of mind or uniformity of practice among them. But there was a deep underlying oneness of spiritual devotion and of spiritual purpose.

It is only when this warm oneness is evidenced in the life of the Church and its individual members, that the world will believe (v.21).

FOR EMULATION: *"How good and pleasant it is when brothers live together in unity . . . for there the Lord bestows his blessing."* (Ps. 133:1,3)

October 12

BURNING, BUT NOT CONSUMED

> *The angel of the Lord appeared to him in flames of fire from within a bush . . . Moses thought, "I will go over and see this strange sight – why the bush does not burn up."* (Exodus 3:2,3)

God spares no pains in preparing His instruments. Moses was sent to undertake a post-graduate course in the desert (Exod. 3:1). Up till then he had been an activist, but during this forty-year course, he learned the fundamental lesson – that *being* is even more important than *doing*.

The even tenor of rural life was interrupted by a singular phenomenon – an acacia bush on fire, yet not consumed. The flames caused Moses to turn aside to see the unique sight. Life's crises seldom announce themselves, and Moses found himself in a life-changing encounter with God. *It was at the burning bush that God snatched Moses from anonymity*.

The symbolism of the burning bush is clear. Fire is a frequent symbol of divine self-revelation. The common acacia became extraordinary by the interpenetration of the fire which irradiated it – transformed by God's presence.

Moses had to learn that in spite of his privileged past, he was only a common bush. It was not the character of the bush but the fire in it which distinguished it. He must learn that any greatness in him would be only the result of the divine indwelling.

FOR MEDITATION: *Most of us find it easier to don our shoes in busy activity than to doff them in humble worship.*

THE GREAT RENUNCIATION

*By faith Moses . . . refused to be known as the son
of Pharaoh's daughter. He chose to be ill-treated along
with the people of God . . .* (Hebrews 11:24)

We have little choice in our heredity or early
environment, but we play a major role in the choice of
a career. Sooner or later we reach a watershed in life when
we must choose one of two roads — a time when our
voluntary choice coincides with God's purpose.

Moses reached this crisis point when he had attained
maturity and could evaluate the factors involved. The
question he faced was: would he selfishly retain his
privileged position as a son of Pharaoh's daughter, or
would he identify himself with his nation in their slavery?
Would he choose pomp, power and glory, or poverty,
obscurity and obloquy?

Four verbs reflect the elements in his great refusal:
esteeming the reproach of Christ greater riches than the
treasures of Egypt (v.26 KJV). He carefully weighed the
pros and cons of the situation.

This led to *choosing* and *refusing*. He *chose* rather to suffer
affliction with his people (v.25), and refused (v.26) to be
called Pharaoh's foster-son. His choosing issued in
forsaking. "By faith he forsook Egypt" (v.27), with its
wealth and pleasure, its pomp and power, and instead
chose affliction, slavery and contempt. *His was one of the
epoch-making "No's" of history!*

And the inspiring motive? Because the discerning eye
of his faith saw "Him who is invisible" (v.27).

FOR MEDITATION: *The great crises in life usually
come on us unannounced. Hence the necessity
of walking close to the Lord every day.*

October 14

WHAT DOES CANAAN SYMBOLISE?

These things happened to them as examples, and were written down as warnings for us on whom the fulfilment of the ages has come. (1 Corinthians 10:11)

Both hymnology and general usage have combined to convey the impression that the River Jordan symbolises death, and Canaan the blessedness of heaven.

Only in a secondary sense is the parallel admissible. The *primary* significance of Canaan is not life in heaven, but "life in the heavenlies". Ephesians is the New Testament counterpart of Joshua, and throws great light on it.

Canaan is not heaven, but a suburb of heaven. It stands for a victorious type of Christian experience that it is possible to enjoy here and now. What is presented *historically* in Joshua, is applied *spiritually* in Ephesians – the exchange of a life of defeat in the desert, for the joy, rest and fruitfulness – albeit with conflict – of life in the Promised Land.

That Canaan cannot be identified with heaven is clear on several counts: (a) Canaan was the scene of many battles, but there are no battles in heaven. (b) Nothing that defiles can enter heaven, but Israel sinned in Canaan. (c) Heaven will know no defeats. Israel did in Canaan. (d) In heaven there is no fear of expulsion, but Israel was expelled from Canaan.

So we are justified in concluding that Canaan does not represent heaven, but a life of victory attainable here and now.

FOR PRAISE: *I praise You, Lord, in anticipation of enjoying the heavenly counterpart of the earthly Canaan.*

THE IMPOSSIBLE SITUATION

Moses answered the people, "Do not be afraid. Stand firm and you will see the deliverance the Lord will bring you today." (Exodus 14:13)

Moses and Israel were confronted by a humanly impossible situation when on their exodus from Egypt they reached the Red Sea. On one side lay the impassable range of Baal Zephon, on the other an impassable waste of burning sand. Behind them were the invincible armies of Pharaoh, and ahead of them lay the impassable Red Sea. They were in a perfect cul-de-sac – no unusual experience for one who had determined to go the whole way with God.

In this unexpected and shattering experience, the morale of the nation dropped to zero. "Was it because there were no graves in Egypt that you brought us to the desert to die?" they complained (Exod. 14:11).

But Moses, the man of faith, stayed himself on God and issued God's order of the day, which to faithless Israel seemed like sheer fantasy: "Do not be afraid" – when there was every cause to fear. "Stand firm and you will see the deliverance of the Lord" – when Pharaoh was rapidly overtaking them.

Moses passed the test of the impossible situation with flying colours and was gloriously vindicated by the intervention of God. His prediction came true: "The Egyptians you see today you will never see again" (v.13).

God delights to shut His people up to Himself and then display His grace and power in achieving the impossible.

FOR MEDITATION:
> *Doubt sees the obstacles*
> *Faith sees the way;*
> *Doubt sees the darksome night,*
> *Faith sees the day.*

October 16

AN EXEMPLARY SECOND-IN-COMMAND

*Then Joshua fell face down to the ground in reverence,
and asked him, "What message does my Lord have for
his servant?"* (Joshua 5:14)

Joshua's public career began as Moses' assistant. His
subsequent history justified Moses' confidence and
choice. He was privileged to accompany Moses to Mt
Sinai, and to share at a distance his chief's awesome
meeting with God. One cannot see the majesty and glory
of God and be the same again.

Here was a man who successfully served two masters.
He was not only Moses' servant, but "the servant of the
Lord" (Josh. 24:29). His service to Moses was served with
great distinction because of his even greater devotion to
God. His epitaph could be coveted by us all: "What the
Lord commanded Moses, Moses commanded Joshua;
and Joshua carried it out without deviating in any
respect" (Josh. 11:15 Berkeley).

It is recognised that, as Isaac Stern said, the second
fiddle is the most difficult instrument to play, but in this
respect Joshua displayed great virtuosity. He began his
career as second to Moses. No sooner had he been called
on to succeed him as leader, than God called on him to
surrender his command and become second to the
Captain of the Lord's armies.

Not everyone is big enough to rejoice in being superseded, but *Joshua preferred to be second-in-command of the
Lord's army rather than commander-in-chief of his own.*

Very few Christian leaders pass this test with
distinction.

FOR MEDITATION: *God in Christ appears in many
aspects to His people, and always in the manner
most suited to the circumstances and need of
the hour.*

THE SHOUT OF FAITH

By faith the walls of Jericho fell . . . (Hebrews 11:30)

The conquest of Jericho was the key to Israel's campaign to possess the Promised Land, and it is replete with spiritual lessons.

On crossing Jordan, Israel was shut in the land with their enemies. Retreat was cut off by the flooded Jordan. Impregnable Jericho guarded the pass into the interior. The simple alternatives were victory or death.

The overthrow of Jericho was *a conquest of faith*. There was no merely natural explanation of the collapse of the walls. No weapons, no assault, no sappers undermining them. Joshua had staked all on the trustworthiness of God.

It demanded *the obedience of faith* on Joshua's part. He must communicate faith to his people – always the leader's responsibility. It involved *the discipline of faith*, for the people were commanded to maintain silence as they circled the city (6:10). They had to exercise *the patience of faith* by marching thirteen times around the city.

Even after the thirteenth circuit the walls did not fall until *they shouted the shout of faith*. It is of the nature of faith that it believes and rejoices in advance of the realisation. Every step had been a step of faith, but the climax came when they shouted.

Note that the shout of faith rose while the walls were still intact (see Mark 11:24). Once again they had risked everything on the faithfulness of God, and their faith received its reward.

FOR MEDITATION: *It is the nature of faith that it believes and rejoices in advance of realisation.*

October 18

THE PERIL OF PRESUMPTION

The men of Israel sampled their provisions but did not enquire of the Lord. (Joshua 9:14)

After the victory at Ai, Israel was once again flushed with success. Their triumphant march caused the surrounding nations to declare a truce, and combine against the common foe.

The wily Gibeonites, however, doubting the wisdom of open conflict with Israel, decided to resort to subtlety. They sent ambassadors who purported to come from a distant land. Their appearance bore out their story — old sacks, old wineskins, old garments and shoes, mouldy bread.

At first, Joshua and his leaders were suspicious, but the evidence was so convincing! If the Gibeonites had lived in our day, they would have won an Oscar. But the Israelites had not mastered the lesson of Ai — they "did not inquire of the Lord".

The story was so consistent and reasonable that Joshua accepted the evidence of sight and his own good judgement. To his dismay, only three days later he discovered that the men were Hivites, his next-door neighbours. The discovery came too late. He had made a treaty with them which God would not allow him to break. As God had warned, they became a constant embarrassment to Joshua.

Satan is more dangerous in his wiles than in his open assaults. The angel of light is more to be feared than the roaring lion. The Church flourished under the persecution of Nero, but succumbed to the flatteries of Constantine.

FOR MEDITATION: *Glorious victory today does not preclude defeat tomorrow, if we are prayerless.*

October 19

THE SPIRIT-CONTROLLED LIFE

Do not get drunk on wine, which leads to debauchery.
Instead, be filled with the Spirit. (Ephesians 5:18)

The word "filled" as used in connection with the Holy Spirit in Acts 2:4 and Ephesians 5:18, frequently carries the meaning of "controlled". In his lexicon, Thayer says, "That which takes possession of the mind is said to fill it." For example, "They were all *filled* with fear" (Luke 5:26). "Because I have said these things to you, sorrow has *filled* your hearts" (John 16:6). The obvious meaning is that fear and sorrow had gripped and controlled their personalities.

Similarly we are filled with the Spirit when we voluntarily allow Him to possess and control our whole personality and bring it under the Lordship of Christ. When we allow Him thus to fill us, He exercises His control from the centre of our personality. He constantly *enlightens our intellects* to appreciate and appropriate divine truth. *He purifies and stabilises our emotions* and fixes them on Christ. He *reinforces our weak wills* to obey the commands of Christ.

Rather than obliterating our personalities, He releases and enhances them. In this way the Holy Spirit infused new life and power into the lives of the disciples to equip them for their world-wide evangelistic task. The formerly timid became bold. The doubter believed. The fire-eating apostle became the apostle of love. Self-seekers became self-forgetful. Have we been obedient to this command?

FOR ASPIRATION: *May I offer no obstacle to the Holy Spirit's exercising control of my thoughts, motives and actions.*

NOT BY MIGHT

"Not by might nor by power, but by my Spirit," says the Lord Almighty. (Zechariah 4:6)

The missionary task of the church will never be achieved by purely human means. *"Not by might nor by power"*, was the Lord's word to Zechariah.

The phrase "not by might" may be rendered, "not by an army", i.e. not by collective power, force of men or means. Sometimes it means "wealth", sometimes "virtue" in an ethical sense, or "valour". But in all its uses the underlying thought is of human resources.

"Power" here also signifies force, but rather the prowess and dynamic of an individual. It is never used in a collective sense. Taking both words together, the phrase would mean that success in the Church's task depends on neither the combined strength of men organised to assist one another, nor on the drive and prowess of any individual.

It depends only and entirely on the agency of the Holy Spirit. And why? Because the task is superhuman, and any resources of men, skill, dynamic, are only human. The Church is a supernatural organism which can be nurtured only by spiritual means.

The great danger faced by the Church today is lest, in the midst of careful planning and improved methods, she forget the superhuman factor without which her task will never be encompassed. It is "not by might nor by power but by my Spirit" that it will be realised.

FOR PRAYER: *Father, restrain me from the pride that causes me to rely on my gifts and abilities and not on the Holy Spirit.*

WHO CALLS THE MISSIONARY?

> *While they were worshipping the Lord and fasting, the Holy Spirit said, "Set apart for me Barnabas and Saul for the work to which I have called them."* (Acts 13:2)

In the missionary call, the initiative is with the Holy Spirit, not with the church or the volunteer. The divine call precedes any activity of church or missionary – *"the work to which I have called them"* was the message of the Holy Spirit. The responsibility of the church was to recognise the appointment of the Spirit, concur with it and act upon it. In this case, the leaders "placed their hands on them" – signifying their identification with them in their enterprise – "and sent them off."

It is worthy of note that the Holy Spirit selected the ablest men in the church for His purpose, and the church made no demur.

The responsibility of the missionary was to respond to the call. In the final analysis, the judgement of the fitness of the prospective missionary lay with neither the church nor the individual, but with the Holy Spirit who took the initiative. The part of the leaders was to be sensitive to His leading, and obedient to His command. The church did not vote on the issue. The candidates were discovered to a group of spiritual leaders while in an attitude of prayer and self-denial.

Unfortunately it has not always been so. Happy the missionary who has a church like that at Antioch behind him or her.

FOR SELF-EXAMINATION: *Have I genuinely faced up to the Lord's commission: "Go and make disciples of all nations"? With what result?*

FALLING OUT OF LOVE

*"You have . . . endured hardships for my name . . .
Yet I hold this against you: You have forsaken your
first love. Remember . . . Repent."* (Revelation
2:3–5)

Memory can exert a salutary ministry! If we love Christ
less than we did in the early days of our new life, He says
we have "fallen". It is true that love is likely to be more
demonstrative in its early stages than later, but as love
matures, it will run more deeply and strongly.

Jeremiah's prophecy has a poignant paragraph: "The
word of the Lord came to me . . . 'I remember the
devotion of your youth, how as a bride you loved me,
and followed me through the desert, through a land not
sown' " (2:2). God remembered with sad joy the glow
of His people's early love for Him, a love which was
sacrificial. But that glow had faded.

This condition had been re-enacted in the Ephesian
church, and now Christ *calls on them to repent* – a change
of mind and attitude – before it is too late. It was not
enough for them to feel badly about having fallen out of
love with Christ, they had to fall in love with him afresh!

He also *calls on them to reform* – "Do the things you
did at the first." They must resume the works they did
in the days of their first love. *Love is a matter of the will*
as well as the emotions. When adjustment is made, love
will return.

FOR ACTION: *Lord, forgive me that my love has
grown weak and faint. I purpose to do the things
I did in the days of my first love.*

October 23

THE TYRANNY OF MEMORY

"I will . . . remember their sins no more." (Hebrews 8:12)

The mysterious power of memory is at once a beneficent and yet a tyrannical faculty. It is fortunate that the passing years often dim the memory of unpleasant events, and leave us with the happier recollections.

Memory can, however, be tyrannical in dredging up and even magnifying the failures of the past. There is much in most of our lives that we would sooner forget. And the worst of it is that we tend to believe that these failures and sins are indelible. The naturalistic psychologist would maintain that strictly, nothing is ever wiped out — that God may conceivably forgive, but He can never forget.

But *God says He can forget*. Hear one of His many pronouncements in this connection: "I, even I, am he who blots out your transgressions . . . and remembers your sins no more" (Isa. 43:25).

"Oh, we shall remember, we all know that," wrote Robert E. Speer. "But we are on such terms with God as though the past had not been. We meet Him without the shame that we must feel if we know that He was remembering, and that as He looked on us, He saw all our past sin. *He does not see it*. He sees only the perfect beauty and purity of Christ, in whom we are, and for His sake He has blotted out all our transgressions."

FOR MEDITATION: *Why should I grieve my loving God by persisting in remembering what He has forgiven and forgotten?*

ARTERIES OR ATTITUDES?

"I have learned the secret of being content in any and every situation." (Philippians 4:11)

It is not without significance that Paul wrote *"I have learned* the secret of being content . . ." He did not say "I have always been content." For him, as for us, it had been a painful learning experience in the school of suffering. But he graduated! It was in the same school that the Son of God "learned obedience" (Heb. 5:8).

Our Lord likened the Christian life to a river that broadened, deepened and gathered volume as it flowed down to the sea — an encouraging picture for the ageing Christian. There is no reason why our closing years should not be as enjoyable, stimulating and fruitful as earlier years, although at a reduced pace.

It is our *attitude* to our circumstances that determines what the outcome will be. It is among those who rebel against their circumstances that unhappiness is found. "I'm not as old as my arteries," said one old man, "I am only as old as my attitudes." He had learned the secret — acceptance of "the good, and acceptable and perfect will of God" (Rom. 12:2).

To accept old age with philosophical realism is the best.

FOR ACTION: *Since old age with its limitations is part of God's "good and acceptable and perfect will", accept it with joy and not with complaining.*

OLD AGE – NEW OPPORTUNITY

*They will still bear fruit in old age, they will stay fresh
and green.* (Psalm 92:14)

With the increased leisure time that retirement years
bring, fresh opportunities open out before us, if we have
the eyes to see them.

There is the priceless opportunity of *systematic study of
the Scriptures* that was impossible during busier years.
Have we not, when faced with spiritual or theological
problems, wished we knew our Bible better? Now the
possibility is ours. Bible correspondence courses can be
studied at our own pace. Many helpful Bible study books
are available.

How often in past years our *prayers* have been hurried
and unworthy. But now we have time to spend with God
and develop a deeper intercessory ministry.

There are *community ministries* in which we may engage,
such as "meals on wheels". People in retirement homes
welcome a visit, for many have few or no visitors.

In *the church* there are a wide variety of services which
an ageing person can undertake. If an offer of service is
made to the pastor, it will be unusual if there is no small
but useful task he can suggest. Much can be done to
alleviate the loneliness of "shut-ins", and such small
services as mowing the lawn or helping with the heavier
housework will be much appreciated. Baby-sitting to help
a hard-pressed mother can be a boon.

Retirement gives opportunity to read carefully selected
books, both secular and sacred. Don't misuse these
precious years.

FOR PRAYER: *Lord, I ask You to show me avenues
of service that will make my declining years
meaningful and fruitful.*

GOD OF THE SECOND CHANCE

"I will restore to you the years which the locust has eaten." (Joel 2:25 RSV)

What new hope and optimistic expectations this divine undertaking would kindle in the hearts of the old people to whom it was addressed! And who of us have no locust-eaten years – years that were barren of truly fruitful worship and service? We can take heart. It is not yet too late.

The promise made to Israel was a restoration of *material* prosperity. But as the spiritual seed of Israel, we are entitled to claim the *spiritual* blessings implied in the promise (see Gal. 3:29).

The locust can assume many forms – opportunities given but not utilised, unworthy motivation, time wasted, unsubdued sins – some such "locusts" may have robbed our lives of the freshness of our earlier Christian experience, as well as depriving God of the harvest due to Him.

"But I have always been told that lost time can never be recovered, that opportunities missed are gone for ever!" you say.

When travelling in southern Taiwan, I was shown verdant rice fields. The farmer told me that formerly he was able to produce only one crop of rice a year. But with the aid of technology, fertiliser and better seed, he now reaped three crops of rice each year from the same land.

It is gloriously possible to make up for lost time. God can give us three spiritual harvests in the one year. The past can't be recalled, but no past failures make future victory less possible.

FOR PRAISE: *Lord, I thank You for not throwing me on the scrap heap when I failed. I give myself to You anew today.*

A SECOND CAREER

"Here I am today, eighty-five years old . . . Now give me this hill country that the Lord promised me."
(Joshua 14:11,12)

Retirement is not a terminus but a junction. For those in good health, the exciting possibility of a new career opens out. The Christian should regard it as a divinely given opportunity for new adventure and achievement, not as an opportunity to gradually wind down.

Another career can be commenced at any time, but to make it a success will demand strong motivation and much determination. A second career is often differently motivated from the first, for it is freely chosen, and there is usually no element of necessity.

Abraham is a luminous example of *one who began a second, exciting career at the age of seventy-five*. He was no callow youth thirsty for adventure when the challenge came: "Leave your country, your people and your father's household, and go to the land I will show you" (Gen. 12:1). It says much for their obedience, that Abraham and Sarah went out "not knowing where they were going".

It must have been a traumatic experience for Sarah to leave her luxurious home in Ur, a highly civilised city, for a nomadic life. It required on the part of both more than ordinary faith and courage. It was in the final stages of his life that Abraham achieved his greatest victory.

FOR THANKSGIVING: *Father, I thank you for the inspiring example of saints of former days. Help me to emulate them today.*

AIDS TO MEMORY

> *Though outwardly we are wasting away, yet inwardly we are being renewed day by day.* (2 Corinthians 4:16)

Some elderly Christians (and younger ones too) are distressed because they are unable to retain or recall what they read in their devotions. They chide themselves, as though it were something culpable on their part. One troubled lady mourned, ''I can't even recall the promises of Scripture!''

That is regrettable, but it is not blameworthy; nor is it irremediable. My father used to carry with him little notebooks in which he jotted down choice portions of Scripture or helpful thoughts on which he could meditate. Why not do the same if memory is faltering?

An aged friend provided me with the most optimistic example of how to enjoy growing old in spite of a faulty memory. He had been a diligent Bible teacher, but now he could no longer recall what he had studied.

''I read a passage in the morning,'' he said, ''and all kinds of new thoughts come into my mind. I think, 'I've never seen that before!' Of course I know I've read it hundreds of times and probably preached on it, but it comes to me now as fresh as it was the first time I read it.''

What a wholesome outlook! Rejoice in the truth of the Scripture and promises you are reading *while you read them*, even if you forget them afterwards. They are still in the Bible and you can turn back to them.

FOR THANKSGIVING: *Lord, I thank You for the possibility of daily spiritual renewal. Help me to appropriate it for today.*

"THAT DISMAL FUNGUS"

*Each of you should look not only to your own interests,
but also to the interests of others.* (Philippians 2:4)

Nothing is easier for the ageing person who is growing increasingly infirm, and experiencing some depression as a result, than to turn inwards and *become self-occupied*. That attitude of mind only exacerbates the problem. It is when, with a firm purpose, we turn away from our own griefs, aches and ailments, and busy ourselves in relieving those of others, that we will find relief from our own.

It was when Job prayed for his friends that the Lord restored his fortunes (Job 42:10). "Taking the griefs of others on my heart inoculates me against my own," was the prescription of one sufferer who had mastered this secret of triumph over adverse circumstances.

When Josephine Butler, one of the greatest social workers of her day, lost her only child, an old Quaker to whom she turned for help in her grief reminded her that there were many other hearts who needed mother-love. He directed her to a certain house where forty young people who had been rescued from moral evil were being cared for. Josephine gave herself with abandon to care for these young lives and as a result was able to rise above her own grief.

> Turn your trouble into treasure,
> Turn your sorrow into song,
> Then the world will know the measure
> In which you to Christ belong.

FOR PRAYER: *Lord, help me live from day to day in such a self-forgetful way that even when I kneel to pray my prayer will be for others.*

October 30

THE TRANSFORMATION AT PENTECOST

". . . The promise is for you and . . . for all whom the Lord our God will call." (Acts 2:39)

After the descent of the Holy Spirit on the Day of Pentecost, there was *a noticeable accleration in the progress of disciples towards maturity*. Before that epochal event, the marks of spiritual immaturity were all too evident. They were just average, ordinary men of their day. All were slow learners (Luke 24:25). They were all self-seeking (Mark 10:37–41). They were paralysed with fear of the Jews (John 20:19). They were ordinary, weak, failing men and women, very like ourselves.

But when at Pentecost "they were all filled with the Holy Spirit" and abandoned themselves to His control, *a startling transformation took place*. The timid became brave and the weak powerful. Doubters became believers, and the selfish, self-forgetful slow learners became avid scholars. Individualists became willing to submerge themselves in team ministry.

They all became vividly conscious of Christ's presence with them, and joy and thanksgiving were keynotes of their corporate life (Acts 2:46–47). In their previous ministry they had caused little stir but now they were accused of "turning the world upside down" (Acts 17:6).

While Pentecost, like Calvary, was an historical and never-to-be repeated event, *it can and should be perpetuated*. The inner power and thrust can be reproduced whenever we are prepared to conform to the laws of spiritual power.

FOR ACTION: *As we habitually honour the Holy Spirit, He will honour our witness to Christ, and set His seal on it.*

OUT OF TOUCH WITH GOD

He [Samson] did not know that the Lord had left him.
(Judges 16:20)

One of the characteristics of human love is its hatred of distance. Once nearness has been experienced, distance becomes intolerable. Love knows no suffering more poignant than being out of touch with the loved one.

If this is true of human love, it is no less true of love to God. Once the disciple has known the surpassing joy of fellowship with Him, he can never be at rest while this relationship is broken. And yet there are many Christians who have grown accustomed to being out of touch with God. And worse still, they have come to regard living at a distance from him as almost inevitable.

But lost fellowship can be restored. The way back is not easy or costless, but it is possible. The seriousness of this condition lies in the fact that our fellowship with God — or the absence of it — affects not only this life, but the life to come. It affects not only our own life, but the lives of those with whom we come in contact.

Only a word, yes, only a word
That the Spirit's small voice whispered, "Speak".
But the worker passed onward unblessed and weak
   Whom you were meant to have stirred
To courage, devotion and love anew,
Because when the message came to you,
   You were out of touch with your Lord.

FOR PRAISE: *I praise You, Lord, that You reciprocate every step I take towards You, and I need never fear rebuff.*

November 1

LET US PRESS ON

Let us . . . go on to maturity. (Hebrews 6:1)

In his commentary on this verse, Bishop Westcott asserts that there are three possible translations, each of which warns against a possible danger that confronts the Christian.

"Let us go on to maturity" suggests the possibility that we may *stop too soon*, feeling that we have reached the goal. Paul ruled out complacency when he wrote, "Not as though I had already obtained all this or have already been made perfect . . . but I press on to take hold of that for which Christ Jesus took hold of me" (Phil. 3:12).

A second possible translation is, "Let us press on *to maturity*". The suggestion here is that we may succumb to *the peril of discouragement*, and drop our bundle. No, we are to heed the warning and *"continue progressing towards maturity"*, as the tense of the verb indicates.

Yet a third alternative translation is, "Let us *be borne on* to maturity". This carries a warning against the peril of *thinking that we are left to do it alone*. The comforting assurance is that in our pursuit of spiritual maturity we have the fullest co-operation of the Triune God.

All three of these possible translations are required to convey the wealth and significance of these six words.

FOR ASPIRATION: *Lord, I would re-echo Paul's words: "Not that I have already . . . been made perfect, but I press on . . ."* (Phil. 3:12)

REVERSION TO INFANCY

Anyone who lives on milk . . . [is] still an infant . . .
Solid food is for the mature. (Hebrews 5:13,14)

The author of the letter to the Hebrews indicted the Hebrew Christians to whom he wrote on three counts. (a) They had become sluggish in hearing God's Word, and in working out the implications of their discipleship (v.11). (b) They now needed someone to re-teach them the elementary truths of the gospel (v.12). (c) They had reverted to spiritual infancy and were unskilled in the Word of righteousness (v.13).

They now had *little taste for the deeper things of the Word* and were content with the ABC of truth – pardon for sin, escape from hell, and hope of heaven. They were still orthodox in belief, but apathetic in translating truth into practice. The writer feels he must rouse them by stern reproof and warning.

Such spiritual immaturity in an older Christian is not an amiable weakness, but a positive sin. Neglect of the culture of the inner life will exacerbate this condition.

We must be careful, however, *not to undervalue the elementary doctrines of the faith*. But the gospel is not only simple, it is profound. It begins with simple truth but progresses towards profound teachings that baffle the deepest philosopher. Milk is appropriate for the infant stage of the Christian life, but "solid food is for the mature". Let us be content with nothing less.

FOR MEDITATION: *We should not underestimate the ability of a new Christian to assimilate some of the deeper truths.*

November 3

PREMATURE SPIRITUAL SENILITY

Though by this time you ought to be teachers, you need someone to teach you the elementary truths of God's word. (Hebrews 5:12)

One of the perils that can overtake the believer is an unduly premature spiritual senility. This disorder is not peculiar to those who are old. It is tragic but true that, if we may coin a word, believers can *unknow* spiritual truth, can lose their spiritual insight. Truths that once gripped and enthralled them, can become a dead letter and leave them unmoved.

The reason behind this possibility is that the apprehension of spiritual truth is not a solely intellectual exercise. It is even more a matter of illumination by the Holy Spirit, the Inspirer and Interpreter of the Word of God. Our relationship with him is therefore of prime importance.

"You have become dull of hearing" (v.11 RSV). They had not always been so, but deterioration had set in, and now they had become unresponsive to the voice of the Spirit. Their hearing had become less sensitive than in the days of their first love, and they had become spiritually apathetic and listless.

This peril of unconscious regression confronts us all. In referring to Ephraim (Israel), Hosea wrote, "His hair is sprinkled with grey, but he does not notice" (7:9). Grey hairs are the first sign of waning virility. They come painlessly and unannounced. Spiritual decline need not be conscious. We should look carefully into the mirror of the Word to see if we have spiritual grey hairs.

FOR SELF-EXAMINATION: *Deterioration begins when we are too busy or too lazy to compare ourselves with the standards of Scripture and bring them into conformity.*

DON'T STOP GROWING!

"I'm just as vigorous to go out to battle now as I was then." (Joshua 14:11)

It was eighty-five-year-old Caleb who was speaking! No retirement from the Lord's service for him. These courageous words came from the lips of a man whose outstanding characteristic was that he never stopped growing. He demonstrated the exhilarating truth that *the greatest achievements of life may take place in old age.*

As a young man he displayed undaunted moral courage. In mid-life he demonstrated unabated consistency in extremely frustrating circumstances. In old age he was still spiritually adventurous.

Caleb's last years were his best, and he provides a glorious illustration of the possibilities of declining years. When Joshua was allocating the land to the people, Caleb made a daring request: "Give me this mountain," he demanded of Joshua. Which mountain? Hebron, where the giants lived! This was not recklessness on his part, but calculating faith.

As we grow older, we tend to lose the spirit of aggression, but not so with Caleb. He entirely cleared his territory of the giants and other Canaanites. What was the secret that enabled old Caleb to succeed where the younger men failed? He tells us: "I followed the Lord my God wholeheartedly" (v.8).

Let us older folk emulate him; take off our slippers, rise from the rocking chair and ask God to give us some challenging spiritual mountain.

FOR EMULATION: *Father, give to those who are ageing the spiritual audacity of the aged Caleb who chose as his inheritance the most powerful stronghold of the enemy.*

November 5

THE INTEGRATED LIFE

We proclaim him, admonishing and teaching everyone with all wisdom, so that we may present everyone perfect [mature] in Christ. (Colossians 1:28)

Spiritual maturity is, in a word, Christ-likeness. We are as mature as we are like Christ, and no more. He was the only fully mature Man. His character was complete, well-balanced, and perfectly integrated. His qualities and capacities were perfectly attuned to the will of His Father. This is the standard, the model God has set before us.

God's purpose for His people is summed up in Paul's words: ". . . so that the body of Christ may be built up until we all . . . become mature, attaining to the whole measure of the fullness of Christ" (Eph. 4:12,13).

The supreme goal of the Church is not evangelism, indispensable though that ministry is. The ultimate goal Paul had in view in his proclamation of the everlasting gospel was: "so that we may present everyone mature in Christ". The end objective of evangelism should be not only to gain converts, but to produce mature Christians.

God's purpose is to produce disciples who reflect the perfect humanity of His son – people who react to the exigencies of life in an adult and not in a childish manner, meeting adult situations with adult reactions. In short, people who fulfil their humanity and become what God designed for them.

FOR ASPIRATION:
> *Be docile to thine unseen Guide,*
> *Love Him as He loves thee;*
> *Time and obedience are enough*
> *And thou a saint shall be.*

A DYNAMIC PROCESS

*We . . . are being transformed into his likeness with
ever-increasing glory.* (2 Corinthians 3:18)

Reaching for maturity is a dynamic process that continues
as long as we live. The Christian life is not as it may seem
to the young Christian, a hundred-metre dash. Rather
it is a twenty-six-mile marathon that will test our spiritual
stamina to the very limit. There is no such thing as instant
maturity any more than there is instant sainthood.

F.W.H. Myers aptly expressed this truth:

> Let no one think that sudden in a minute
> All is accomplished, and the work is done;
> Though in thine earliest dawn thou
>   shouldst begin it,
> Scarce were it ended in thy setting sun.

Maturing is a slow process, both in nature and in grace.
It is achieved only with difficulty, whether physically,
mentally or spiritually. It is a never-ending process, but
it can be accelerated through faithful obedience to the
spiritual laws laid down in the Scriptures. This fact should
save us from discouragement, and provide motivation for
earnest moral endeavour.

After all, as Henry Ward Beecher said, ''The church is
not a gallery for the exhibition of eminent Christians, but
a school for the education of imperfect ones.'' Thank
God, a man can grow!

FOR MEDITATION: *The Holy Spirit is the source of
zeal and diligence in the work of the Kingdom.
Am I experiencing His enduement?*

November 7

THE POIGNANCY OF BEREAVEMENT

Surely he has borne our griefs and carried our sorrows.
(Isaiah 53:4 RSV)

Sooner or later the pain of bereavement will be our lot. Married people should face the fact that one or the other will go through the experience.

It is not morbid to consider this eventuality, for although we cannot prepare fully for it, it is wisdom to learn what we may expect. None of us is really prepared for this unwelcome and unexpected visitation. Our ability to cope with death triumphantly is greatly helped by the support of family and friends, and the vitality of our Christian faith and experience.

Facing the fact that grief and bereavement are bound to come to us eventually, will save us from falling into self-pity or thinking that we are the objects of special judgement. Grief comes to others, and we have no grounds for believing that we will be the exception.

How safe it is to come to him in our sorrow and commit our grief to one who so fully understands and cares! Having committed it to Him, *leave it there*, finally and permanently. The deep hurt remains, but the compensating presence and ministry of "the God of all comfort" will support us in our grief and transform it into triumph – even though the triumph may be tear-bedewed. It is right to express our grief. Jesus wept.

FOR PRAISE: *I praise You, Lord, that You have revealed yourself as a comforting mother to those who sorrow.* (Read Isa. 66:13)

WITH CHRIST – BETTER BY FAR

What shall I choose? I do not know! I am torn between the two: I desire to depart and be with Christ, which is better by far . . . (Philippians 1:23)

Was this not the case with Paul the aged? To him death was not an object of dread, but of tranquil expectation. When the hour of his martyrdom drew near, he faced it with a cheerful serenity: "The time has come for my departure. I have fought the good fight, I have finished the race, I have kept the faith. Now there is in store for me the crown of righteousness which the Lord, the righteous judge, will award to me on that day" (2 Tim. 4:6–8).

Early historians remarked on the courage and joy with which the Christians faced a cruel death. The note of triumph was described by Aristides in AD 125. Writing about a new religion called Christianity, he said, "If any righteous man among the Christians passes from this world, they rejoice, and offer thanks to God; and they escort his body with songs of thanksgiving, as if he were setting out from one place to another nearby."

These suffering saints attained a triumphant approach to death, because they had experienced the power of Christ's resurrection. The stark contrast between their joy, and the hopeless wailing of their pagan contemporaries in the presence of death, proved a powerful evangelistic agency.

The fact is that with advancing years, the things of earth grow strangely dim, and the things of eternity gloriously real.

FOR EMULATION: *Father, when I am called on to face suffering or death, strengthen me to display the courage and serenity of the early Christians.*

November 9

LYRIC AND LANCET

*And now I will show you the most excellent way . . .
If I . . . have not love . . . I am nothing.* (1
Corinthians 12:31; 13:1,2)

In Paul's classic chapter, we are presented with a new concept of love. The standard of what we ought to be is not the Ten Commandments, but the perfect character of Christ. Sin is anything in which we fail to conform to the perfection of Christ, and especially failure to love God and our neighbour.

In this letter Paul deals with failure in the Corinthian church, and this wonderful chapter is one of the instruments he employs. *"The beautiful lyric is thus the lancet,"* said James Moffatt. A lancet is for probing a sore and allowing the offensive pus to drain away. Each quality of love is the perfect answer to some failure in the Corinthian church – and in us too. Envy is the fault of those who feel inferior, and boasting that of those who consider themselves superior. Love is the answer to both sins.

The chapter is a beautiful epitome of the life of Christ. Substitute "Christ" for "love" in verses 4–8, and note how perfectly every quality of love is matched in His peerless character.

If we have the courage to use this lyric as a lancet, we may find it a devastating experience, for it will probe many a secret sore. But *the lancet is only a prelude to the cure*. Read verses 4–8, substituting "Christ in me" for "love"!

FOR MEDITATION: *Since love is the self-imparting quality in the nature of God, should not my life display this quality in greater measure?*

November 10

GIFT AND GIFTS

Now about spiritual gifts . . . All these are the work of one and the same Spirit, and he gives them to each one, just as he determines. (1 Corinthians 12:1,11)

God has given two unspeakable Gifts, His Son and His Spirit, one the source of our salvation, the other the inspirer of our service.

A clear distinction must be made, however, between the *gift* of the Spirit, and the *gifts* of the Spirit. The former was bestowed on the Church in fulfilment of the promise of the Father and the prayer of the Son. The latter are bestowed on individual believers as the Spirit in His sovereignty chooses.

On the Day of Pentecost the Spirit was poured out on the waiting Jewish Christians. Later, in the house of Cornelius, the Gentiles became similar beneficiaries. The *gift* is for every member of the body of Christ without discrimination. The *gifts* are special and distributed individually.

Our hymnology is often at fault in petitioning God to give His Spirit, as though He had never been given. We rightly pray for *a greater manifestation of His power*, but the Gift has already been made to all, once for all.

Every believer has been granted some spiritual gift, but not all have troubled to discover what it is. "Each man has his own gift from God" (1 Cor. 7:7). No-one may demand specific gifts, for the Spirit is sovereign in this area. Spiritual gifts are given apart from merit, and qualify the possessor for some form of spiritual service.

FOR SELF-EXAMINATION: *Spiritual gifts are important, but apart from "the fruit of the Spirit – love" – they are spiritually unproductive. Do I recognise this in practice?*

November 11

IMITATING AND IMITATED

Follow my example, as I follow the example of Christ.
(1 Corinthians 11:1)

Paul modelled his life on his Master's. So sincere was he in this, that he actually had the temerity to urge the Corinthians to copy him as he copied Christ. Which of us would dare to make a similar challenge? It was the quality of Paul's life of unselfish adaptation to others, that gave him the right to do that.

We could well imitate Paul in *his modest self-appraisal*. "Who is Paul but [a servant] through whom you came to believe?" (1 Cor. 3:5). Paul knew his limitations, and did not suffer from an inflated ego.

His generous appraisal of others, was another Christ-like quality that we may well copy. He did not hesitate to delegate responsibility to younger colleagues, and was generous in appreciation. He delighted to associate Titus with him on terms of equality (2 Cor. 8:23).

He demonstrated *a sensitive respect for the rights of others*, and was punctilious in his relationships. "I did not want to do anything without your consent" (Philem. 14). He showed *a similar respect for the convictions of others*. "Not that we lord it over your faith" (2 Cor. 1:24). People of strong convictions are not always willing to concede equal liberty to the convictions of others.

We should copy him in *his insatiable passion for advance* into unreached areas. He prayed for an enlarged sphere so that he might "preach the gospel in the regions beyond" (2 Cor. 10:16).

FOR SELF-EXAMINATION: *Paul modelled his life style on that of Christ, and challenged believers to imitate him. Could I give a similar challenge?*

POOR YET RICH

*You know the grace of our Lord Jesus Christ, that
though he was rich, yet for your sakes he became poor,
so that you through his poverty might become rich.*
(2 Corinthians 8:9)

We are presented here with a striking antithesis — *the
unutterable poverty that was ours*, and *the unsearchable riches
that were His*. Our deep poverty serves as a backcloth to
display the magnificence of His riches.

In all that is of supreme and eternal value, we are
tragically poor. Our poverty may not be financial, but
money is the lowest form of riches. The highest values
in life cannot be calculated in dollars and cents. Indeed,
money has a subtle way of devouring all that is most
precious. *The highest riches are not material*, but moral and
spiritual, and our assets of this nature are pitiful.

In what did Christ's riches consist? He was "heir of all
things". He shared God's glory. To be loved is one of
life's richest experiences, and Christ enjoyed the infinite
love of His Father and of all holy beings (John 17:24).

But how poor He became! In His incarnation He
exchanged heaven's purple for a peasant robe; His
Father's love for the insensate hatred of man. He
relinquished heaven's harmony for earth's discord. He
was denounced as a glutton, a drunkard, a demoniac.
Once He was His Father's delight, but now His face is
averted. "He became poor."

But His poverty secures our enrichment. It would have
been wonderful to receive a few crumbs from His table,
but He makes us joint-heirs with Himself. Wonderful
grace of our wonderful Lord!

FOR PRAISE: Lord, I rejoice that Your temporary
impoverishment while on earth has issued in
heavenly enrichment beyond imagination.

November 13

GETHSEMANE'S SORROW

Then Jesus went with his disciples to a place called Gethsemane, and he said to them, "Sit here while I go over there and pray." (Matthew 26:36)

Eight gnarled and ancient olive trees still mark the place where a mysterious incident was enacted. Only a short while before entering the Garden of Gethsemane, Jesus offered His high-priestly prayer. *But what an astounding contrast between that prayer and the one in Gethsemane!*

Jesus had taken with Him His three dearly loved disciples that they might share His midnight vigil. His sentinels, alas, slept at their post. The Garden was, of course, well known to the traitor, Judas.

Divine inspiration has preserved for us at least six statements, each presenting a different facet of the Saviour's suffering.

He became "overwhelmed with sorrow" (Matt. 26:38). He had always been "a man of sorrows", but now He entered into a sorrow never before experienced – even "to the point of death".

"He began to be deeply distressed and troubled" (Mark 14:33). The words express a confused, restless, half-distracted state.

"He was in an agony" (Luke 22:44 RSVn.). This conveys the idea of struggle. As the powers of darkness closed in, He found Himself in a conflict never before known.

"His sweat was like drops of blood falling to the ground" (Luke 22:44). It was a cold night, but as He prayed in agony, the course of nature was reversed. Instead of rushing to the aid of His breaking heart, the blood forced its way through His pores.

FOR MEDITATION:
> *Forsaken Thou, that I might never cry*
> *"Eli! Eli! Lama Sabachthani!"*

November 14

CHRIST'S ILLEGAL TRIALS

"I have examined him [Jesus] in your presence and have found no basis for your charges against him." (Luke 23:14)

Only eighteen hours elapsed between the arrest and the death of our Lord; and yet how much indignity and injustice were crowded into them. Three trials before the religious authorities, and three trials before Pilate and Herod. *The religious trials were illegal.* Because held before the morning sacrifice, they violated the legal provisions. Then, as today, secret trials were illegal.

The charge of blasphemy against Jesus actually originated with His judges. The witnesses against Him were known perjurers, were not sworn, and their evidence was not consistent. It was required of judges that they be humane and kind, but Caiaphas was abusive and struck Jesus on the mouth before any charge was proved.

Fearing that Jesus might appeal to Pilate, the Jews sought to forestall Him by changing their religious charge to that of sedition. Pilate saw that they desired him not so much to dispense justice, as to confirm their condemnation of Christ. Three times Pilate protested that he found no cause of death, but his efforts to release Jesus were futile, and weakly he bowed to the demands of the bloodthirsty crowd.

On what legal grounds was Jesus condemned? None! He was three times acquitted and yet was condemned to die. The Light of the world had shone with such a searching beam, that a guilty world must extinguish it.

FOR PRAYER: *Father, when I am misjudged and treated unjustly, help me to react as Your Son did.*

November 15

HIMSELF FOR ME

The Son of God, who loved me and gave himself for me. (Galatians 2:20)

In the above words lie the heart of the atonement. It is as true today as when it happened, and it puts in personal terms the great transaction of Calvary. Inexhaustible in depth and meaning it may be, but it is neither irrational nor beyond comprehension when the illumination of the Spirit is present.

In the three simple words, *Himself for me*, is enshrined the great mystery of the ages. The most astute minds of the ages have delved into the inner meaning of the cross, but all have failed to plumb its infinite depths. Like Paul, they have withdrawn with the cry of bafflement, "Oh, the depth of the riches of the wisdom and knowledge of God . . . and his paths beyond tracing out!" (Rom. 11:33).

The sin of the first Adam posed a stupendous problem. How could God let His heart of love have its way without condoning guilty man's sin and violating His own holiness? James Denney answers:

At the cross God took the initiative, and so dealt with sin in His Son, that now He can justify the repenting sinner and not compromise His holy character. The cross is not a compromise but a substitution; not a cancellation but a satisfaction; not a wiping off but a wiping out in blood and agony and death. Thus mercy does not cheat justice.

FOR WORSHIP:
This hath He done, and shall we not adore Him?
This shall He do, and can we still despair?

ALIVE AFTER HIS PASSION

*After his suffering, he showed himself to these men
and gave many convincing proofs that he was alive.*
(Acts 1:3)

The doctrine of the resurrection of Christ is central to the
Christian faith, not peripheral. As Paul said, "If Christ
has not been raised, our preaching is useless, and so is
your faith" ((1 Cor. 15:14). Without it, the crucifixion
would have been in vain, for it was the resurrection that
gave saving value to the atoning death.

Of all the great religions, *Christianity alone bases its claim
to acceptance on the resurrection of its Founder*. If it is not
a fact, the Scripture writers become purveyors of
intentional lies and the Scriptures are unreliable. Paul
makes Christianity answer with its life for the truth of
the resurrection.

Christ's resurrection was *no hallucination*. His resurrection was the last thing the apostles expected. Jesus
appeared ten times in forty days, and then His appearances ceased as abruptly as they had begun.

He appeared in His resurrection body, not in the dusk
but in lighted rooms, visible and tangible. He appeared
in the same body as that in which he had been entombed,
but which possessed new characteristics, and transcended the laws of matter.

Our Lord's life demanded such a climax. If we believe
He was supernaturally conceived, lived without sin, died
a voluntary atoning death, then the resurrection is easy
of belief. Without it, a perfect life would end in a shameful
death, surely an inappropriate close.

FOR MEDITATION: *After all, the supreme proof was
His own presence, alive among them.*

November 17

ELOQUENT GRAVE-CLOTHES

He bent over and looked in at the strips of linen lying there . . . as well as the burial cloth that had been around Jesus' head. The cloth was folded up by itself, separate from the linen. (John 20:6,7)

The way in which John presents the evidence of supernatural intervention contrasts strongly with much apocryphal legend.

When Peter, in his race to the tomb, caught up on the more reverent John, he brushed past him and went into the tomb. He was arrested by the way the grave clothes were lying.

In order to accommodate one hundred pounds' weight of spices, Joseph and Nicodemus must have wrapped Jesus in many yards of linen. Peter and John saw the body wrappings in one place, and the turban-like cloth which had been wound around His head, rolled up by itself.

There was no evidence of the tomb having been desecrated or rifled. Anyone likely to have done this would have had a richer prize in the spices than in the corpse. Nor would they have folded the garments so carefully. If it had been friends, would they not have taken the garments too? All the evidence pointed to a carefully executed transaction without any indication of fear or haste.

The disciples were left with only one explanation that would fit all the facts – supernatural intervention. And the effect on John? "He saw and believed" (v.8). He found his faith stimulated by the grave-clothes lying in their original folds, untouched by human hands, yet emptied of the crucified body.

FOR PRAISE: *That I have a believing mind to accept the Scripture record and appropriate the blessings it promises.*

THE ASCENSION

While he was blessing them, he left them and was taken up into heaven. (Luke 24:51)

The crowning event, the ascension, was not without previous intimations. Jesus had predicted it. "What if you see the Son of Man ascend to where he was before?" He asked His disciples (John 6:62).

The ascension was the logical outcome of the crucifixion. No more fitting climax could be conceived. When He ascended, not a claim of God on mankind was left unsettled, and not a promise left in uncertainty. The ascension was to convince His followers that they need not expect to see Him again. It provided the apostles with a satisfactory account of the disappearance of His body from the tomb.

It was *a divine vindication of His claims to deity*. He had claimed the right to ascend into heaven as His own prerogative.

It was *His inauguration into His heavenly Priesthood* which He exercises on our behalf.

It has blessed implications for us. Though physically remote, He is spiritually near. His life above is the guarantee and the promise of ours. "Because I live, you also will live," He promised (John 14:19). His ascension anticipates our glorification, and leaves us the assurance that He has gone to prepare a place for us.

> He has raised our human nature
> In the clouds to God's right hand;
> There with Him in heavenly places,
> There with Him in glory stand.

FOR MEDITATION: *As soon as Christ's feet left the earth, he embarked on His ministry as our Advocate and Intercessor.*

November 19

A GREAT HIGH PRIEST

We have a great high priest who has gone through the heavens, Jesus the Son of God. (Hebrews 4:14)

From the dawn of human history men have craved a priest who would represent them to God. Job lamented, "If only there were someone to arbitrate between us" (9:33). There has been a conscious universal need of someone who had special influence with God. This resulted in the creation of a priestly order. In Christ this deep, hidden yearning finds fulfilment.

Two great essentials were fellowship with man and authority from God. Jesus fulfilled both requirements. He was linked to us by ties of a common humanity, and He was appointed to act on behalf of God.

As our High Priest, "*He is able to help* those who are being tempted" (Heb. 2:18). We are willing to aid those who need help, but we are not always able. Jesus knows no such limitations.

He is able to sympathise with our weaknesses (Heb. 4:15). He never condones or sympathises with our sins, only with our weaknesses. Having been tempted Himself, He can enter into our experiences.

"*He is able to save completely* those who come to God through him, because he always lives to intercede for them" (Heb. 7:25). The present tense signifies "a sustained experience resulting from a continuous practice". There is no personal problem for which he does not have a solution, no enemy from whom He cannot rescue us, no sin from which He cannot deliver.

FOR PRAISE:
Our great High Priest has gone before,
Now on His Church His grace to pour,
And still His love He giveth.

HIS GLORIOUS RETURN

"They will see the Son of Man coming . . . with power and great glory." (Matthew 24:30)

A consideration of the startling contrasts between our Lord's first and second advents will heighten our appreciation of what His return in glory will mean to Him.

Then He came in poverty and humiliation, now in inconceivable riches and glory. Then He came in weakness, now He comes in illimitable power. Then He came in loneliness, now He comes with innumerable angels and the company of the redeemed.

Then He came as a Man of sorrows, but now with radiant joy. Then in mockery the soldiers placed a reed in His hand as sceptre. Now He receives and wields the sceptre of universal dominion. Then men placed on His brow a crown of acanthus thorns. Now His brow is adorned with the many diadems He has won.

Then He was blasphemed, denied, betrayed. Now every knee bows to Him, acknowledging Him as King of Kings and Lord of Lords.

> O, the joy to see Thee reigning,
>   Thee my own beloved Lord!
> Every tongue Thy name confessing,
> Worship, honour, glory, blessing,
>   Brought to Thee with one accord.
> *Frances Ridley Havergal*

FOR PRAISE: *Lord, I rejoice in the approaching day of Your coronation, when You will "see of the travail of Your soul and be satisfied".*

November 21

SATAN'S FINANCIAL STRATEGY

"Do not store up for yourselves treasures on earth."
(Matthew 6:19)

Since money is one of the essentials of the work of the Kingdom, it is not surprising that the great adversary does all in his power to prevent it finding its way into the Lord's treasury. And for that he has many tricks in his bag.

He encourages us to *overcommit ourselves financially* — purchasing more than we can afford, on time payment, so that there is little over to give to God.

He plays on our competitive instincts and incites us to constantly *upgrade our standard of living*, so that any increases in income are already committed.

He dries up the fountains of generosity in the heart by *suggesting postponement* to some future time. The stifling of a generous impulse today, makes it easier to do the same tomorrow.

He so arranges things that the assets of the generous man become *frozen or over-committed*, so that he is unable to give what he genuinely desires to give.

He encourages people to short-circuit present liberality through what Dr A.J. Gordon called *extra-corpus benevolence* — the postponement of generosity until after death.

Do not let us fall for any of his ploys.

FOR PRAYER: *Father, deliver me from falling for Satan's attempts to deflect God's money which You have entrusted to me, from God's treasury.*

GIVING BEYOND ABILITY

They gave as much as they were able, and even beyond their ability. (2 Corinthians 8:3)

The members of the poverty-stricken colonial church in Macedonia were remarkable people. In striking contrast to their deep poverty and affliction, shone the abounding riches of their liberality. "In a severe test of affliction, their abundance of joy and *their extreme poverty* overflowed in a wealth of liberality" (v.2 RSV).

Despite their limited resources – for they were pioneers – they did not shrink from giving to the point of real sacrifice. They calculated the maximum they could give, and then went beyond it (v.3). With them, the question was not, "How little?" but "How much?" They experienced the beatitude, "It is more blessed to give than to receive" (Acts 20:35).

It is a common tendency in our day of credit cards to spend beyond our means. Have we ever emulated the Macedonians? Paul testified that "according to their ability, and beyond their ability, they gave of their own accord, begging us with much entreaty for the favour of participation in the support of the saints" (vv.3,4).

What an extraordinary picture! *The donor is the one who does the begging!* Since they gave beyond the limit of their means, they were obviously looking to God to supply their other needs. Nor were they disappointed.

FOR PRAYER: *O bounteous Giver, reproduce in our hearts the generous spirit that moved You to give Your best for us.*

NOT TEMPERAMENT BUT LOVE

The disciple whom Jesus loved . . . (John 13:23)

Only three disciples qualified for admission to the innermost circle of intimacy with Christ. What excluded the others?

If *perfection* were the criterion, then Peter the denier and James and John the ambitious place-seekers would have been excluded. But they were included. If it were *temperament*, then surely the volatile Peter, and James and John the fire-eaters, would not have found entrance.

Why, then, did John have the primacy in the group? Because he alone appropriated the place of privilege that was open to all. It was *love* that drew John into an ever-deepening relationship with Jesus. Jesus loved them all, but John alone claimed the title of "the disciple whom Jesus loved". If He loved John more, it was because John loved Him more. Mutual confidence and love are the keys to closer intimacy.

It would seem that admission to the inner circle of intimacy with God is the outcome of *deep desire*. Only those who count it a prize worth sacrificing anything else for, are likely to attain it. If other intimacies are more desirable to us, we will not gain entrance to that circle.

The place on Jesus' breast is still vacant!

FOR SELF-EXAMINATION: *Am I truly willing to pay any price involved in experiencing a deeper intimacy with God?*

SATAN HINDERS MISSIONS

> *"We wanted to come to you . . . we made every effort to see you . . . but Satan stopped us."* (1 Thessalonians 2:17,18)

To prevent the extension of Christ's Kingdom, Satan concentrates powerful forces on hindering missionary enterprise. No sooner had Barnabas and Saul begun their momentous assignment, than they met Satan-inspired opposition from Elymas. With Spirit-given insight, Paul saw behind Elymas the evil one, and administered a stinging rebuke: "You son of the devil, you enemy of all righteousness, will you not stop making crooked the straight paths of the Lord?" (Acts 13:9,10 RSV).

In our text *Paul attributed the repeated frustration of his evangelistic plans to satanic activity*. We cannot attribute all obstructions in our path to Satan, but Paul, through the Spirit, discerned the cloven hoof in these frustrated attempts to build up the Church.

He attacks new converts with unbelievable ferocity, especially after they have made a break with their old life at their baptism. Sometimes he compels a false worship as in shrine worship in Japan during World War II.

He creates apathy towards the missionary obligations of the Church in the sending countries, and dries up the springs of Christian liberality.

He raises antipathy towards missionaries in receiving countries, and endeavours to secure their exclusion or expulsion from the land. The "missionary-go-home" movement, while caused in part by faulty missionary attitudes, was the result of satanic activity.

FOR CONSIDERATION: *Satan prevents young people from committing themselves to missionary work by propagating false conceptions of the missionary vocation.*

November 25

THE ALL-POWERFUL NAME

"You may ask me for anything in my name, and I will do it." (John 14:14)
"In my name they will drive out demons." (Mark 16:17)

The name of Christ is a powerful weapon in the hands of the Christian soldier. One cannot read the triumphs of the early Church without noticing the prominence given to the name of Jesus. *The name stands for the whole person with all his power and resources.* A name on a cheque transforms a scrap of paper into a fortune.

Our Lord has given us the privilege and right to use His name. When we use it, we acknowledge that we are not acting in our own name or authority, but as His personal representatives. The phrase "in the name of Jesus" is not to be regarded as a kind of incantation, or a convenient way to end a prayer. It has power only when accompanied by a living faith in the One to whom it belongs.

Paul knew the power of Christ's name when he met the demon-possessed girl: "In the name of Jesus Christ I command you to come out of her" (Acts 16:16–18).

When the Sons of Sceva, a Jewish exorcist, presumed to use the very same formula – they undertook to pronounce the name of Jesus over those who had evil spirits – instead of the demon coming out, the demoniac turned on them and overpowered them (Acts 19:13–16).

The name of Jesus has power only on the lips of those who own His Lordship and know the victory of Calvary.

FOR THANKSGIVING: *I thank You, Lord, for the privilege of using Your name to draw on the bank of heaven.*

LISTENING IN TO DEITY

After Jesus said this, he looked towards heaven and prayed: "Father, the time has come. Glorify your Son that your Son may glorify you." (John 17:1)

This moment of time, this hour of destiny, had been anticipated by the Triune God since before the foundation of the world. Now it had arrived, and the occasion gave birth to the supreme prayer of the ages. It is largely intercessory and covers the experiences and needs of Himself, His disciples and all future believers.

This was the hour when the massed forces of the devil and of evil would launch their final blitzkrieg against our Redeemer and Representative. Characteristically Jesus met the crisis with prayer. "He looked towards heaven and prayed, 'Father, the time has come.'"

Here is our supreme Exemplar, who in the hour of crisis rested His soul in the fatherhood of God. For what did He make petition? That He might once more experience His pre-existent glory; and the glory of the divine Son cannot be independent of the glory of the Father.

He further asked that His authority to bestow eternal life – which he defined in terms not of duration but of vital knowledge of the Father and the Son – might be recognised by all whom the Father had given Him. As He surveyed His life and ministry on earth, He was able to advance a claim that can be made by no other: "I have brought you glory on earth by completing the work you gave me to do" (v.4).

FOR PRAYER: *Lord, You glorified Your Father by finishing the work He gave you to do. Help me to do the same.*

PRAY FOR WORLD RULERS

I urge first of all that prayers . . . be made . . . for kings and all those in authority. (1 Timothy 2:1,2)

The Church and the individual Christian have a duty to the state beyond mere obedience to its laws. It does not matter whether rulers be good or bad, we are under obligation to pray for them.

"First of all" in this verse means, "first in order of importance". Paul is instructing Timothy in the priorities he should observe in his service — and number one is — PRAYER. And among the important group we must pray for are — "kings and all those in authority". Are we observing this priority?

If our prayers cannot be influential in the area of national affairs, why pray? The exhortation would be an exercise in futility. At the time Paul penned this letter, the king in power was the infamous Nero! But that was no excuse for failing to pray for those in authority. The exhortation holds true for every age and in every land. And it can be effective.

Tertullian, one of the early Church fathers, said: "We pray for ourselves, for the state of the world, for the peace of all things and for the postponement of the end."

These early Christians did not neglect their divinely ordained national and civic responsibilities. Men in public office, whether good or bad, carry tremendous burdens and wield great influence. Their decisions affect the community, the Church and ourselves. *The hands of wicked men can be stayed by prayer.* Therefore pray!

FOR SELF-EXAMINATION: *Do I discharge my duty as a Christian citizen in prayer for ruling authorities?*

PRAY WITHOUT CEASING!

Be joyful always: pray continually; *give thanks in all circumstances.* (1 Thessalonians 5:16,17)

Was this counsel to the Thessalonian Christians merely a counsel of perfection? Did Paul really consider it an attainable ideal to "pray in the Spirit on all occasions with all kinds of prayers and requests" (Eph. 6:18)?

To him this was both a glorious possibility and an actual experience: "Night and day we pray most earnestly that we may see you again . . ." (1 Thess. 3:10).

On God's side, Paul's experience of unceasing prayer sprang from the working in him of the Spirit of Prayer. It was not confined to formal sessions of prayer. Those informal, ejaculatory prayers native to the praying heart, were in his view.

Charles H. Spurgeon once said that he had not known a half-hour for years in which he had not consciously prayed. To him, through disciplined habit, unceasing prayer had become almost instinctive, as natural as breathing.

But prayer is not an exercise of the conscious mind alone. Henry Moorehouse frequently prayed aloud in his sleep. Even in sleep, the ever-burning fire of the Spirit within caused the fragrant incense of prayer to ascend from the altar of his heart.

It is for us to form this blessed habit, to find in God a Friend always within call, to use everything as an occasion for prayer.

FOR MEDITATION: *Because of the Holy Spirit's unceasing intercession for us (Rom. 8:27), it is possible to maintain a consistent prayer life.*

November 29

CREATIVE PRAYING

The God who . . . calls things that are not as though they were . . . (Romans 4:17)

It would appear that in the creation of the world, God acted on the principle of faith. When He said to non-existent light, "Let there be light," there was light. It is the same kind of creative faith which we are called on to exercise. "Faith is being certain of what we do not see" (Heb. 11:1), and this concept opens a limitless realm of possibility.

The scientist Alexis Carrel wrote: "Prayer is a force as real as terrestrial gravity . . . it is the only power in the world that seems to overcome the so-called laws of nature."

In prayer, God places in our hands a kind of omnipotence, enabling us to overcome even immutable natural law. Hear His affirmation: "*Whatever* you ask for in prayer, believe that you have received it, and it will be yours" (Mark 11:24).

Strangely enough, so beset by unbelief is the human heart, that this staggering and all-inclusive promise, instead of stimulating our faith, tends to paralyse it. The mind busily discovers reasons why "whatever" cannot mean whatever. But it does mean exactly what it says. Nothing is beyond the scope of prayer except that which is out of the will of God.

Unbelief has always shackled omnipotence. Faith releases its might, for it rests its weight on the divine warrant of the infallible Word.

FOR MEDITATION: *Faith believes that to the God who "calls into existence the things that do not exist", nothing is impossible.*

THE MASTER PRINCIPLE

> *"Whoever wants to be great among you must be your servant."* (Mark 10:43)

In His answer to the request of James and John for prominent leadership positions in His Kingdom, Jesus enunciated three principles that are still relevant:

There is a sovereignty in spiritual leadership. "To sit at my right hand . . . is for those for whom it has been prepared" (v.40). Our emphasis would probably have been, "for those who are best prepared for it". Places in spiritual ministry are sovereignly assigned by God. No theological or leadership course will automatically confer spiritual leadership or qualify one for spiritual ministry.

There is suffering in spiritual leadership. "Are you able to drink the cup that I drink?" Jesus asked them (v.38). He was too honest to conceal the cost of service in the Kingdom. He needed men and women of quality, with eyes wide open, who would follow Him to the death in His world conquest. Such leadership positions cannot be reached on the cheap.

There is servanthood in spiritual leadership. "Whoever wants to be great among you must be your servant." Greatness comes only by way of servanthood. First place in leadership is gained only by becoming *everybody's slave* (v.44).

Only once did Jesus say that He was leaving His disciples with an example – when He washed their feet! (John 13:15).

Thus the thoughts of suffering and servanthood are linked, even as they were in the life of the Lord.

FOR THANKSGIVING: *Thank You, Lord, for providing a perfect model of servant-leadership. Help me to follow in Your steps.*

December 1

THE DAZZLING VISION

He was transfigured before them. His face shone like the sun. (Matthew 17:2)

This glorious event was one of the most astonishing of all our Lord's experiences on earth. It was the sole occasion on which the full glory of the Godhead was permitted to blaze forth.

For the three privileged disciples who witnessed the display of the divine majesty, it was an unforgettable experience. We can almost sense the awe as Peter and John recalled the scene. "We were eye witnesses of his majesty." "We have seen his glory." The passing years had only deepened their sense of wonder.

This incident undoubtedly meant much to Jesus in the days of His humiliation, when the heavenly voice again confirmed His divine Sonship. He had predicted that He would come again in glory, and now His disciples were given a foretaste of what lies ahead. Now Moses and Elijah, heavenly visitants, converse with Christ about His coming death. This glorious scene would assure them that He was not speaking empty words when He told them He would rise from the dead and meet the saints of old in glory.

How will He come? As He appeared on the Transfiguration mountain – "in power and great glory". *Who will meet Him?* Those of whom Moses and Elijah were representatives – "the dead in Christ"; and "we who are still alive and are left" (1 Thess. 4:16,17). Moses and Elijah departed, and "they saw no one except Jesus".

FOR ACTION: *"Beholding the glory of the Lord, we are being changed [transfigured] into the same likeness."* (2 Cor. 3:18)

December 2

DAILY VISION, DAILY RENEWAL

Inwardly we are being renewed day by day . . . We fix our eyes not on what is seen, but on what is unseen. (2 Corinthians 4:16,17)

This inward renewal is not automatic, we are being renewed only while our gaze is fixed on the things visible only to faith. Preoccupation with the visible precludes the renewal and obscures the glory.

But more than a casual glance is involved. Concentrated attention and a steadfast gaze are required to make the invisible visible. The process of renewal is operative on our behalf only so long as we give our undivided attention to the eternal. "Not seen" here signifies "beyond sight" rather than invisible, that is, the thing which makes faith real. Moses endured as seeing Him who is beyond sight.

The things that are seen seem so solid and satisfying, but in reality they are illusory at best. Though they seem so ethereal, it is the unseen things that are permanent.

It is impossible to concentrate one's whole attention on the seen and the unseen at the same time. It will always be one at the expense of the other, and *we do the choosing*. Which has the ascendancy in our lives, the seen or the unseen? Which exercises the greater influence?

When we keep our gaze focused on the unseen and the spiritual, for us life will not be a reluctant slipping down the slope into the tomb, but a glorious ascent into the immediate presence of God.

FOR MEDITATION: *Am I making things visible and tangible central in my life, or am I fixing my eyes on Jesus?*

THE SUBTLETY OF TEMPTATION

Eve was deceived by the serpent's cunning. (2 Corinthians 11:3)

The first revelation of Satan's character in the Bible is in the role of a deceiver; and he runs true to form in the rest of the Book. The method of his attack on Eve's faith and integrity should alert us to the subtlety of his approach.

He approached her *when she was alone* and without the support of her husband. Temptation is a lonely experience.

He was careful *not to appear in a form that would terrorise* or rouse her revulsion. That would only throw her back in the arms of God. Instead he chose as his instrument an attractive animal.

He did not shock her by suggesting *some blatant blasphemy of God* − only the harmless, pleasant and perfectly natural gratification of a legitimate desire − but out of the will of God.

He gave no impression of his being *the implacable enemy of God*. True, his references to God were denigrating, but not blatantly so.

Satan seduced her into rebellion and disobedience by *playing on her bodily appetites* − "good for food"; her aesthetic senses − "a delight to the eyes"; and aroused in her an unholy ambition − "your eyes will be opened and you will be like God, knowing good and evil".

Thus, in the very first mention in the Bible of our great Adversary, we hear a clear warning of his subtlety.

FOR MEDITATION: *Since Adam and Eve came perfect from the throne of God, with no evil strain, evil must have come from without, from a source other than human.*

December 4

SATAN'S DIVISIVE TACTICS

You are still worldly. For since there is jealousy and quarrelling among you, are you not worldly? (1 Corinthians 3:3)

If he cannot destroy the Church, Satan aims to discredit it, and he has been very successful in this. One of his most successful gambits has been *to disturb the unity of the Church by creating discord and division*. Believers are exhorted to "maintain the unity of the Spirit". The fact is implicit that the unity of the Church is under attack.

He works by *playing on the prejudices, ambitions and jealousies* of church members. He creates parties and factions within churches to fragment them and neutralise their witness. Few attitudes play more into his hands than a critical spirit.

Among church members he often reserves this form of attack for those whom he cannot deceive about the teachings of Scripture. He will cause them to be so ardent in defence of the truth, or their particular interpretation of it, that Christian charity and courtesy are forgotten. The battleground shifts from doctrine to personalities.

Another stratagem is *the subversion of the Church through heresy and cults*. The Church had scarcely been born before the devil began to infiltrate it with emissaries who promulgated false doctrine, especially concerning the Person of Christ.

Paul indicated the source of these heresies: "In later times some will abandon the faith and follow deceiving spirits and things taught by demons" (1 Tim. 4:1).

FOR MEDITATION: *In contrast, "How good and pleasant it is when brothers live together in unity." (Ps. 133:1)*

December 5

SATANIC STRATEGY WITH UNBELIEVERS

> *The god of this age has blinded the minds of unbelievers, so that they cannot see the light of the gospel* . . . (2 Corinthians 4:4)

As head of the kingdom of darkness, the devil adopts the strategy of blinding the minds of the unregenerate. To keep them lulled to sleep, he feeds them wrong thoughts about God, and ensnares them in false philosophies.

He snatches away the good seed of the Word (Matt. 13:4,19). The picture is of birds swooping down and picking up the grain fallen on the hard-beaten path. In the same way, the devil snatches the Word before it can sink into the understanding and be received by faith. It underlines the fact that we should pray *after*, as well as *before*, our witness. The solemn impression of a sermon is dissipated by subsequent idle chatter.

He lulls the unbeliever into a false peace (Luke 11:21,22). The context makes it clear that Satan is the strong man who drugs his victims, and assures them that there is nothing in God to fear, and no judgement to anticipate.

He lays snares for the unwary (2 Tim. 2:25,26). He is the master of subtlety, and adept in concealing his snares. He is too wise a hunter to lay the snares in the sight of his victim.

He mixes truth with error (Matt. 13:25,28). His strategy is to include enough truth to make the error palatable. This is the great danger in the cults of today – employing orthodox language for spreading heterodox doctrine.

FOR CONSIDERATION: *Because of this satanic activity, we are deeply dependent on the ministry of the Spirit in our evangelism.*

SATAN'S POWER CONTROLLED

God is faithful: he will not let you be tempted beyond what you can bear. (1 Corinthians 10:13)

The name "Satan" appears first in one of the oldest books of the Bible — Job (1:6) — where he appears among the angels before the Lord. From this we conclude that, despite his fall, *he still had right of access into God's presence.* But he came with no reverent spirit!

Unknown to himself, Job, whom God eulogised as "a blameless and upright man", became the focus of a test of strength between God and Satan. Satan threw down the gauntlet with his cynical question, "Does Job fear God for nothing?" His suggestion was that God had bought his loyalty by preferential treatment.

God staked everything on Job's loyalty, and He was not disappointed. Through devastating reverses Job maintained his loyalty to God and refused to be lured from faith. Satan retired from the field, vanquished.

Several important truths emerge from this incident.

God has allowed Satan great powers, but they are under divine control. He cannot exceed the limits of divine permission.

He could incite the Sabeans to kill Job's children, and originate a cyclone (1:16,19). He had power to afflict Job with disease (2:7). He confessed that his occupation was "roaming about on the earth", and the expression implies "as a spy".

Thus early in history, God gave insight into what transpires in the realm of the unseen, and some idea of the tactics of our enemy.

FOR ACTION: *"Eternal vigilance is the price of freedom"*, a familiar political and military maxim, is not a whit less appropriate in the spiritual sphere.

December 7

THE MEANING OF PENTECOST

"What does this mean?" (Acts 2:12)

The remarkable and supernatural events that occurred on the Day of Pentecost caused the wondering crowds to ask this question. There is a threefold answer.

It was the fulfilment of a promise. In his flaming sermon, Peter claimed that the promise of Joel 2:28 had now seen its fulfilment: "I will pour out my Spirit on all people . . ." This promise had been supported by a further promise from the Lord Himself (Acts 1:5). Further, it was the promise of the Father to the Son (Luke 24:49). On that remarkable day, these promises were fulfilled.

It was the experience of a power. Although the apostles had enjoyed three years of individual instruction from the Peerless Teacher, their lives were characterised more by weakness than by power and success. But Pentecost changed all that when "they were all filled with the Spirit" (Acts 1:8; 2:4). They were now "full of power".

It was the indwelling of a Person. This was the real heart of the Pentecostal event. Jesus had promised that "the Spirit . . . lives with you *and will be in you*" (John 14:17). This meant nothing less than the personal and permanent indwelling of the other Comforter of whom Jesus had spoken. Not a power, not an influence, not an emanation, but a divine Person who would bring with Him His own powers and attributes.

This, and not the spectacular miracles, was the true focus of Pentecost.

FOR PRAYER: *Lord, I pray that while Pentecost can never be repeated, the blessing and power released then may be more manifest in our churches.*

POST-GRADUATE TRAINING

Moses fled to Midian, where he settled as a foreigner.
(Acts 7:29)

Before he was qualified to lead God's people out of Egyptian bondage, Moses had to undertake post-graduate training. For forty years he had enjoyed luxurious living in a palace, and obtained an unrivalled education in Egypt's famous university – "Moses was educated in all the wisdom of the Egyptians" (Acts 7:22). There his intellect was sharpened and his social graces polished. This fitted him uniquely for ministry to the upper classes. But God's plan for him was the leadership of a nation of slaves. In training for that, he was assigned a period in the solitude of the bleak, barren desert. Up to this time he had been an activist. Now he must learn that *being is more important than doing.*

Paul had a similar experience. He had enjoyed superb academic training under Gamaliel, the famous rabbi. But his fiery spirit must be tempered and a period of theological orientation was necessary. Three years in Arabia afforded him the opportunity of greater intimacy with God.

One important lesson to be learned from these men is that, when God is training us for some form of ministry, He does not shorten or soften the training days. For both men *a period of solitude was an important ingredient in their preparation.*

FOR PRAYER: *Lord, if You learned obedience from what You suffered, help me not to flinch when I have to tread the same path.* (Heb. 5:8)

December 9

DOES IT REALLY MATTER?

"Give to Caesar what is Caesar's, and to God what is God's." (Matthew 22:21)

Does it really matter for whom we vote? For a party or for an individual? What kind of person we elect? Whether we vote at all? These are questions every Christian should consider.

Some conscientious Christians refrain from voting on the grounds that their citizenship is in heaven, not on earth. Others, not without justification, regard politics as a dirty business in which Christians are better not to be involved. Since the Lord said things would get worse in the last days, there is not much we can do about it.

But did not Jesus say above that Christians have a dual citizenship, and therefore have responsibilities to both? Our primary duty is of course to God. But that does not cancel out our civic responsibility.

The prophets were nothing if not vocal on national affairs. Daniel was Prime Minister in five totalitarian regimes.

It is not always realised that one who fails to vote for the party he would favour, in reality casts a double vote. Say the issue was abortion, the party favourable to it would require one vote to neutralise it and one vote to pass it. It does matter whether we vote or not.

FOR PRAYER: *Lord, help me to discharge my civic as well as my Christian duty.*

FAITH A PARADOX

"Blessed are those who have not seen and yet have believed." (John 20:29)

"Seeing is believing," says Mr Worldly Wiseman. "Believing is seeing," affirms the man of faith. The Bible abounds in such paradoxes. A paradox is something apparently wrong and contrary to reason, and yet actually true. Jesus frequently employed this arresting method of conveying spiritual truth. For example, the grain of wheat was unfruitful because it had not died, yet its only hope of living lay in dying (John 12:24).

Moses' faith was evidenced in his "enduring as seeing him who is invisible" (Heb. 11:27). But how can one see the invisible? Faith operates in the realm of the unseen things which cannot be proved mathematically but are true and real. "Faith is being certain of what we cannot see" (Heb. 11:1). It brings the unseen into the realm of personal experience. Faith is being sure without seeing.

Paradoxically, *faith sings while still in prison*. Its song of faith antedates its release, as in the case of Paul and Silas (Acts 16:25). It glorifies God by singing in hopeless situations. It fights effectively in chains. "Remember my bonds," said the enchained yet victorious warrior (Col. 4:18 KJV).

FOR MEDITATION: *Where there is no risk involved in a commitment, faith is unnecessary.*

December 11

WHAT OF THE UNEVANGELISED?

They show that the requirements of the law are written on their hearts, their consciences also bearing witness. (Romans 2:15)

If the unevangelised heathen are "lost", is it merely because of an unfortunate accident of birth? Is the reason one of geography or race? Is it because they have been unfortunate in having been denied the privileges of people in Christian lands? Surely not. If they are lost, it is *not because they are unevangelised*. If the reception of Christ by faith is the condition of salvation and the determining factor in human destiny, can the heathen be held responsible for a choice they had no opportunity to make? Paul asks, "How can they believe in the one of whom they have not heard?" (Rom. 10:14).

Any other conclusion would do violence to the principles of justice which we associate with God, and with our own society at its best. No Scripture asserts or implies that heathen are lost merely because they have not responded to a gospel which they have never heard. Condemnation is for *guilt*, not *ignorance*. Then why are they lost?

Because they are sinful men and women, just as you and I were sinful and lost. All men, whether civilised or pagan, are lost *because they are sinners*. "*There is no difference*, for *all* have sinned and fall short of the glory of God" (Rom. 3:23). The heathen are lost because they have violated their own conscience in doing what they know to be wrong.

FOR ACTION: "*Look eagerly for the coming of the Day of God and work to hasten it on.*" (2 Pet. 3:12 NEB)

THE PERIL OF SYNCRETISM

But there were false prophets . . . just as there will be false teachers among you. (2 Peter 2:1)

That some of the great ethnic religions contain high and noble ethical teaching is true, and some of their leaders were good men. There is common ground with Christianity in some of them, small though it may be. But when the view is advanced that those who sincerely follow their own religion will experience salvation, we are forced to part company.

Syncretism is "a mixture of or an attempt to reconcile different religions". This course is advocated by those who are not comfortable with the seeming intolerance of Christianity. They do not accept the scriptural assertion that *all* men are lost and bound for judgement. Their solution to the dilemma created by their rejection of the authority of Christ and Scripture, is to take the best of all the other religions and make an amalgam acceptable to all.

But the two will not mix! Most of these religions are false in their moral standards, and the good ethical teaching has to co-exist with much that is not only erroneous, but often absurd and repugnant. When many of their books are compared with the Christian Scriptures with their unrivalled ethical standards, the contrast is staggering.

The fatal lack of all other religions is that time has proved they have *no saving power, no fulfilled promise of the forgiveness of sin or the rest of conscience.*

FOR PRAYER: *Father, deliver Your Church from falling for Satan's delusion that there is salvation in any other religion than that taught by Christ.*

December 13

SLEEP, NOT DEATH

He died for all. (2 Corinthians 5:15)
*God will bring with Jesus those who have fallen asleep
in him.* (1 Thessalonians 4:14)

In thinking of the cross of Christ, our emphasis tends to
be too much on its physical aspects – and those were
incredibly terrible – but our Lord repeatedly indicated
that the bodily aspect was secondary. Even death is not
primarily a thing of the flesh. Jesus referred to death as
"sleep", much to the mystification of His disciples.

Of Jairus's daughter He said, "She is not dead but
asleep" (Luke 8:52). Of Lazarus, four days dead, He said,
"Our friend Lazarus has fallen asleep" (John 11:11). But
the disciples were so obtuse that Jesus had to spell it out
plainly: "Lazarus is dead." Our concept of physical
death, Jesus called sleep. Paul used the same metaphor:
"those who have fallen asleep in Jesus" (1 Thess. 4:14).

Jesus Himself did more than "sleep" – "*He died for
all.*" We see Him on Calvary, His face drawn in agony,
His quivering body dripping blood. We hear His last
gasp. But that physical cessation which we call death, He
called sleep. To Him, death meant something infinitely
more terrible. Many of His followers were crucified, but
they did not die, they only slept.

In Gethsemane Jesus had not begun to sleep, but He
had begun to die – "sorrowful, even unto death". The
dreadful cup, the desolation, the weight of a world's sin,
the averted face of His Father, *this was death*. He "tasted
death for every man" (Heb. 2:9). He *died* that we may
never die, only *sleep*.

FOR THANKSGIVING: *Thank You, Lord, for
extracting death's sting and transforming
dreaded death into a sleep from which we awake
in Your presence.*

THE FUTURE IS WITH THE DISCIPLINED

The fruit of the Spirit is .. . . self-control [discipline].
(Galatians 5:23)

It has been wisely said that the future is with the disciplined, for without discipline other gifts, however great, will never realise their maximum potential. Only the disciplined person will rise to his highest powers.

The words *disciple* and *discipline* are derived from the same root. A leader is a person who has first submitted willingly, and learned to obey a discipline imposed from without, but who then imposes on himself a more rigorous discipline from within. *Those who rebel against authority and scorn self-discipline, seldom qualify for leadership of a high order*. They shirk the rigours and sacrifices it demands, and reject the divine disciplines that are involved.

Many who drop out of missionary work do so, not because they are not sufficiently gifted, but because there are large areas of their lives that are undisciplined and have never been brought under the control of the Holy Spirit, one of whose fruits is "discipline". The lazy and disorganised never rise to true leadership.

Many who take leadership courses never attain it because they have never learned to follow. They are like the boys playing in the street. When asked why they were so quiet and were doing nothing, one lad replied, "We are all generals. We can't get anyone to do the fighting."

FOR MEDITATION: *Discipline is the wholehearted "yes" to the call of God.*

December 15

THE ANGER OF CHRIST

He looked round at them in anger. (Mark 3:5)

The anger of Christ and the wrath of God are not popular topics in contemporary preaching. But this neglected aspect of His character is important, for He claimed that He fully revealed the character of God. The concept of the wrath of God is no invention of theologians for their own purposes. No one spoke of it more solemnly than did the Lord of love.

The incident of the cleansing of the Temple (Matt. 21:12,13) demonstrated the unique moral authority of Christ. How could a lone and uninfluential man so thoroughly master the great crowd? Why were the temple guards and chief priests silent? Why did the traders not fight for their livelihood?

In the face of the desecration of His Father's house by rapacious traders and priests, the spirit of Jesus blazed with such holy anger that no-one dared gainsay Him. Where personal injury was involved He would turn the other cheek, but when His Father's interests were in jeopardy, He used an uplifted scourge, and the lightning of a holy anger flashed from His eyes.

Our Lord was angry at times, but His anger was *sinless* because it was *selfless*. Our anger is usually sinful because it is self-centred. Christ's anger was always stirred on behalf of others, not on His own account.

FOR SELF-EXAMINATION: *Is my anger of the kind that is not sinful, or is it self-centred?*

THE INTERCESSION OF CHRIST

He ever lives to make intercession for them. (Hebrews 7:25)

It is not uncommon for the idea of intercession of Christ to be associated with tearful entreaty, or with the erroneous concept of overcoming reluctance on the part of God. But our Lord does not appear as a suppliant before a God who needs to be coaxed into compliance. He does not appear as our Advocate to plead for mercy, but to secure the justice which His sacrifice won for us.

His intercession is not to be conceived as a *vocal saying of prayers*. Rather is it foreshadowed in the Levitical ritual of the Day of Atonement, during which the priest uttered not one word. It was not Aaron who was vocal, but the sacrificial blood he sprinkled on the mercy seat (Lev. 16).

Even so it is the presence of our High Priest before the Father, still bearing in His glorified body the tangible evidence of His finished work, that speaks on our behalf. Charles Wesley expresses the truth in these noble words:

> Five bleeding wounds He bears,
>   Received on Calvary,
> They pour effectual prayers,
>   They strongly plead for me.
> Forgive them, O forgive, they cry,
> Nor let the ransomed sinner die.

His intercession is *without intermission*. He ever lives to ensure that we receive the full benefits He secured for us by His cross.

FOR PRAISE: *I rejoice, Lord, that You were exalted to the Father's right hand, and that Your presence there on my behalf assures me of His acceptance.*

December 17

REACTION TO DISAPPOINTMENT

"Blessed is he who takes no offence at me." (Matthew 11:6 RSV)

The man or woman who is on intimate terms with God does not misinterpret His providential dealings, even though they may not understand them. That was true of King David. He learned to accept his disappointments in a mature way.

Having completed his own magnificent palace, he conceived the noble purpose of building a house worthy of his God. It was to be a magnificent edifice, the crowning achievement of his life. But when his plan was rejected by God, because he was "a man of blood", though he was desperately disappointed, he did not sulk or go sour (2 Sam. 7:1–5,12,13). Instead, he gave his strength and wealth to gathering materials for the house that his son Solomon was to build.

If our ideals and desires are sometimes not realised, this incident has a relevant message for us. David was the forerunner of many disappointed people whose purpose and motives are accepted by the Lord, but whose actual services may be denied or postponed. Although God did not permit David to build the house, he said to him, "Because it was in your heart to build a temple for my Name, you did well that it was in your heart" (1 Kgs. 8:18). The will was accepted for the deed.

FOR PRAYER: *Father, give me the faith and love to accept without murmuring the disappointments You permit.*

MEETING THE WORLD'S HATRED

"I have chosen you out of the world. That is why the world hates you." (John 15:19)

A Christian should not expect sympathy and consideration from a hostile, satanically controlled society. Because he is identified with Christ, he should expect to share some of the hostility He experienced. "If the world hates you, keep in mind that it hated me first" (v.18). Intimacy with Christ inevitably draws the world's hatred. Logically, the enemy of the master will be the enemy of the servant.

In a few terse words, Jesus diagnosed the cause of the world's hatred. Had He not come, they could have gone along comfortably in their sin, but now they had no excuse for their sin (v.22). He had laid bare their hypocrisy, malice and deceit, and exposed their evil designs. Now they hated the Exposer, and included His followers in their hostility.

How were the disciples to meet and overcome this hatred? Through the ministry of the Holy Spirit, the Counsellor and Helper. Jesus did not remove His disciples from the hostile world, but empowered them for witness to it and in it through the power of the Spirit (John 15:26,27; Acts 1:8). The same power is available to those disciples who are the objects of the world's hostility in this day.

FOR PRAYER: *Father, keep me insulated from the world and its allurement, but not isolated from the needy men and women in it.*

December 19

THINGS JESUS DID NOT DO

He committed no sin. (1 Peter 2:22)

The uniqueness of Christ is demonstrated in the things that every other great human teacher has done, but which He did not do.

He spoke no word that needed to be withdrawn or modified, because He never spoke inadvisedly, or fell into the evil of exaggeration. He who was the Truth, spoke the whole truth.

He confessed no sin. The holiest of men and women have been the most abject in their confession of sin and failure. But no admission of failure to live up to the highest divine standards fell from Jesus' lips. On the contrary He invited the closest scrutiny of His life by friend and foe.

He never apologised for word or action. And yet the ability to apologise is one of the elements of true greatness. It is the little man who will not stoop to apologise. But Jesus performed no act, spoke no words that required apology.

He was at no pains to justify ambiguous conduct. His delay in responding to the appeal of the two sisters when Lazarus fell ill was open to misunderstanding, but He was content to leave the unfolding of His Father's plan to vindicate His enigmatical actions.

FOR MEDITATION: It is noteworthy that, unlike Paul, Jesus never asked prayer for Himself, though He invited His intimates to watch with Him.

December 20

MERE INFANTS IN CHRIST

Let us leave the elementary teachings about Christ and go on to maturity. (Hebrews 6:1)

"If I were called on to put my finger on the most pressing need of our age, I would unhesitatingly say, 'maturity'." These words of an old preacher of past days are no less relevant in the wonder-world of the space age. It almost seems as though, as knowledge and technology advance, maturity recedes. Unfortunately this is somewhat true in the Church.

The low level of spiritual life in the Corinthian church occasioned Paul acute distress. The underlying problem was neither heresy nor apostasy, but worldliness and spiritual immaturity. For the length of time they had been Christians, they should have been mature, but they were still plagued with carnality. "You do not lack any spiritual gift," he told them, but they failed to evidence a maturity to match their claims. They majored in the gifts of the Spirit, but were sadly deficient in the fruit of the Spirit. Consequently Paul could address them only as "mere infants in Christ" (1 Cor. 3:1).

In our churches today there are too many adult infants whose spiritual infancy has become unduly protracted. The need for them is to confess their failure to "Go on to maturity", surrender their lives afresh to the Lordship of Christ, and renew their daily period of communion with God through the Word of God and prayer.

FOR MEDITATION: *"God wants our emotional stability to be based on Him rather than on physical or chemical stimuli."* (E.W. Lutzer)

December 21

THE ACID TEST

"It is more blessed to give than to receive." (Acts 20:35)

Because money is so often devoted to sordid ends, talking about it can be secular and sordid. But as with many other things, Jesus lifted it to a higher plane, and showed how it can be transmuted into heavenly values.

Jesus accorded an astounding prominence to money in His teaching. An analysis reveals that it figured in sixteen of His thirty-eight parables, and one verse in six in the three synoptic Gospels has the same theme. Why such prominence?

Because *money is one of the central realities of life* and affects us all from the cradle to the grave.

Because *money is an acid test of character*. One cannot be neutral where money is concerned.

Because of *its potential for good or evil*. Jesus made it clear that man is not the owner, but only a trustee, of his money (Luke 12:42).

It is not one tenth of our money that belongs to God, but *ten tenths*. The point at issue is not how much of *my money* I should give to God, but how much of *God's money* I should retain for the use of myself and my family. We should remember the *ninth beatitude*, "It is more blessed to give than to receive."

FOR MEDITATION: *"One man gives freely, yet gains even more; another withholds unduly, but comes to poverty."* (Prov. 11:24)

CHRIST FORMED IN US

. . . until Christ is formed in you. (Galatians 4:19)

In writing to the Galatian Christians, Paul said, "My dear children, for whom I am again in the pains of childbirth until Christ is formed in you." He had previously travailed for them until they experienced new birth, but he was not content with that. He did not want them to remain in a state of spiritual babyhood, but to go on to maturity.

It is one thing to have Christ *dwelling* in you by His Spirit, but quite another to have Christ *formed* in you. "Christ in you" became a fact in the moment of believing. "Christ formed in you" is a process that continues for a lifetime.

Dr F.B. Meyer illustrated this verse from the hatching of an egg. When the egg is laid, there floats in the midst of a sticky fluid the germ of the chick that is to be – the whole chick, but in embryo. But as the hen turns the eggs twice a day for three weeks, there is less and less of the sticky substance and more and more of the chick that is being formed in the egg. One day there is no more viscous matter, and all is chick. The picture is clear. How much of the sticky-self life there is in us! We should pray:

FOR PRAYER:
> *O Jesus Christ, grow Thou in me,*
> *And all things else recede.*
> *My heart be daily closer Thee,*
> *From sin be daily freed.*

December 23

OUR WONDERFUL LORD

He will be called Wonderful Counsellor, Mighty God, Everlasting Father, Prince of Peace. (Isaiah 9:6)

Wonderful Counsellor. The name given to our Lord in this prophetic passage indicates that He is the source of all wisdom and counsel. The guidance offered by professional counsellors is unreliable, for all earth's advisers are fallible. But if we attend to His voice we will not be led astray.

Mighty God. The fantastically powerful forces at work in the world are controlled by the God who created them. Enthroned above the world, He controls its destiny. He rides in majesty and might, and all His might is operative on our behalf.

Everlasting Father. "Father of eternity" is the correct translation of this title. All His plans and purposes are everlasting, and when we take Him into our lives, all our ways take hold on eternity. He is the uncreated Master of all things, and the Source of life to all. In that title, paternal love and care are marvellously blended with immortal life.

Prince of Peace. This name is the climax of the series. It goes direct to the heart of His earthly mission, for "He made peace by the blood of His cross." He not only made peace, but bequeaths it to His people: He is the true Tranquilliser.

When we turn over our lives into His competent hands, we will experience peace and tranquillity which He alone can impart.

FOR PRAISE:
> *Two wonders I confess,*
> *The wonder of His glorious love,*
> *And my own worthlessness.*

December 24

A VIRGIN BIRTH?

"The virgin will be with child and will give birth to a son." (Matthew 1:23)

The Bible does not require belief in the virgin birth as a prerequisite to salvation. But if it is only a myth or legend as some allege, and not a historical fact, then we are left with a purely human Saviour born of sinful parents, and therefore not a member of the Holy Trinity. It is not the *knowledge* of the fact, but rather *its reality and integrity* that provide the basis for our salvation.

It is possible for a person to be saved without understanding the details of the process, just as a baby may be born of a mother who knows nothing of embryology. The *fact* of the virgin birth is an integral part of the Christian faith.

If there were no virgin birth, *the New Testament record would be proved untrustworthy*, and other doctrines would be thrown in doubt.

Instead of being "blessed among women", *Mary would be branded as unchaste*, and Jesus the illegitimate child of immoral parents. Was God open to such an alternative as this?

Christ's pre-existence would be ruled out, with the inevitable corollary that there was no real incarnation. Nor would He be the Second Person of the Trinity as Scripture asserts.

In the incarnation, Isaiah's prophecy was fulfilled: "The virgin will be with child and will give birth to a son, and will call Him Immanuel" (7:14).

FOR THANKSGIVING: *Father, I thank You for Your eternal plan that climaxed in the birth of Your Son without taint of human sin.*

December 25

THE UNIQUE BABY

"So the holy one to be born will be called the Son of God." (Luke 1:35)

There is a new baby born every minute. What was unique about this one?

He was the only baby *whose conception was not the beginning of His existence*. He claimed, "Before Abraham was born I am" (John 8:58). How could there be an incarnation if there had been no previous existence? To deny the latter makes the former impossible.

He was the only baby *who had no human father*. He was conceived by the supernatural operation of the Holy Spirit (Luke 1:35). A person such as Jesus was, demanded a birth such as Scripture records.

No other baby was *born without taint of sin*. He was "holy, blameless, pure, set apart from sinners" (Heb. 7:26) – free from all moral impurity. Fearlessly He challenged His contemporaries, "Can any of you prove me guilty of sin?" (John 8:46).

He was the only baby *who was more than man*. He possessed two natures – Son of Man and Son of God – yet functioned as a single personality. "He continueth to be God and man, in two distinct natures and one person for ever" (Westminster Catechism).

He was the only baby *who was born for the purpose of dying*. To Him it was self-chosen. No wonder the whole world stops to remember His birthday.

FOR PRAISE:
> *A Son that never did amiss,*
> *That never shamed a mother's kiss,*
> *Nor crossed her fondest prayer.*

December 26

HIDDEN TREASURE AND
PRICELESS PEARL

"The kingdom of heaven is like treasure hidden in a field . . . like a merchant looking for fine pearls . . ."
(Matthew 13:44,45)

Jesus spoke two parables, concerning a man finding treasure and a merchant seeking pearls. *Both parables illustrate the manner in which we come to know God's truth.* Sometimes, like the ploughman, we discover the treasure suddenly and unexpectedly (v.44). Sometimes we find it only after diligent search (v.45). Many exhaust all the philosophies and religions of the world before they personally encounter Christ. When they discover Christ, they find both priceless treasure and incomparable pearl.

The question arises: Is it man who is searching for the Kingdom and its King, or is it God who so loved mankind that He gave all He had for them? The latter interpretation would raise problems. How is the treasure hidden and then accidentally discovered by God? (v.44). What are the other priceless pearls He seeks? How does God sell all? The more natural interpretation would be that *when we find the King, we find something infinitely precious and worthy of any sacrifice*.

The point Jesus was making was that the value of the Kingdom was so great, that *at any price it was a gift*. If we are not willing to renounce *all* for His sake, we cannot be His disciples (Luke 14:33). To obtain the Treasure and Pearl, no sacrifice can be too great (Matt. 16:24–27).

FOR MEDITATION: *Is there any significance in the fact that the man found the treasure in the course of his daily work?*

December 27

THIRD HEAVEN AND THORN

> *To keep me from becoming conceited because of these surpassingly great revelations, there was given me a thorn in my flesh, a messenger of Satan to torment me.* (2 Corinthians 12:7)

In this brief autobiographical glimpse, Paul shares one of his deepest experiences. He tells of being "caught up to the third heaven" (v.3), the realm where God is in full manifestation, and where he heard "inexpressible things" (v.4).

But such an ecstatic experience carried its own dangers, for which God had His own remedy. That Paul was in extreme peril of succumbing to spiritual pride is clear from his own statement. Few things tend to inflate a person with a sense of his own importance more than possession of a great intellect or enjoyment of remarkable experiences. And nothing more surely disqualifies from God's service. So *God brought an equalising factor into Paul's life*, lest his ministry be limited – "a thorn in my flesh".

We should be grateful to Paul for his studied reticence concerning the nature of this thorn, which might have differed from ours. Instead, he concentrated on the unchanging principles involved. "Thorn" conveys the idea of a painful stake on which he was impaled. It had a *deflating effect*, something Satan could exploit.

Our thorn may be some physical or temperamental weakness, some family sorrow. But instead of being a limiting handicap, it can be a heavenly advantage, for God gives compensating grace: "My grace IS sufficient for you" (v.9). Paul accepted the grace, and was delivered from the peril of pride.

FOR PRAYER: *Father, help me, like Paul, to appropriate Your grace which turns a seeming liability into a glorious asset.*

LIFE-GIVING TORRENTS

"Whoever believes in me . . . streams of living water will flow from within him." (John 7:38)

It seems hardly possible that from unpromising lives such as ours God can cause torrents of living water to flow. One of Europe's noblest rivers has its birth in the heart of a glacier. It matters little to God how icy the heart seems; out of that believing heart, He will cause torrents of blessing to flow.

We will never become the fountain-head, but we may be water-courses. Through these ordinary lives of ours God will pour His fullness on others. But before those torrents can reach the thirsty hearts around us, our own thirst must first have been slaked. If we still go to the world or some other source than Christ for satisfaction, the streams will never flow.

"From within him" is the key phrase. The true blessing of the Spirit is always an out-flowing blessing. A Spirit-filled Christian is not self-centred. The Dead Sea remains a dead sea because, while it welcomes the waters that flow into it, it pours out none in return. So when personal happiness and enjoyment are the object of pursuit, life becomes sterile.

Some are content to be like the pitchers the priests dipped into the Pool of Siloam – filled, but soon empty. God's intention is that our lives should know no vacuum, but be a water-course constantly full and overflowing to a world's need.

FOR MEDITATION:
> *Not many rivers flow into the sea.*
> *Most rivers flow into other rivers.*

December 29

CHRIST'S RETURN AND MISSIONS

"This gospel of the kingdom will be preached in the whole world as a testimony to all nations, and then the end will come." (Matthew 24:14)

Since our Lord has not returned, it is, in part, because the supreme task entrusted to the Church has not been completed.

From this and other Scriptures relating to the Second Advent, it would appear that the Lord made His return contingent on the evangelisation (not the conversion) of the world.

There must be some degree of readiness on the part of the Church. "The marriage of the Lamb has come and His bride has made herself ready." (Rev. 19:7).

It should be noted that it is the activity of the Bride which is in view here. There is something the believer should do in anticipation of the Bridegroom's return.

The Church must be complete, for Christ will not come for an incomplete Bride. In Revelation 7:9 John saw "a multitude from every nation, tribe, people and language standing before the throne". The Bride must be completely representative of humanity.

The Church must have completed her task. Can we say this has yet been done? The last stone has yet to be laid, the last soul to be won. Could it be that our tiny contribution to the missionary task may bring in the last soul and thus hasten the Lord's return?

Peter sets out in clear terms what our attitude should be: "You ought to live holy and godly lives as you look forward to the day of God and speed its coming" (2 Pet. 3:12).

FOR PRAYER: *Father, I pray that Your Church may awake to the urgency of the hour and the appalling need of a lost world.*

CHRIST'S SOLITARY THRONE

*"When the Son of Man sits on his glorious throne
. . ."* (Matthew 19:28)

Many who greatly admire the human Jesus, are unwilling to concede to Him *a solitary throne*. Among them was the Indian patriot and mystic, Mahatma Mohandas Gandhi. "I cannot place Christ on a solitary throne," he said, "because I believe God has been incarnate again and again." He would willingly have accorded Him a throne on a level with that of Buddha, Confucius or Mohammed: but a solitary throne? No!

And yet Christ demands nothing less than this, for "He is Lord of all", and "to him every knee shall bow". If we claim pre-eminence for Christ, it is no more than He claimed for Himself.

One of the astounding features of the Sermon on the Mount is the confident manner in which He claimed superiority and precedence over all the prophets who had gone before Him. With utter confidence He challenged and dismissed their interpretations of Scripture and substituted His own. He even had the temerity to make sweeping claims on behalf of God.

He employed a wealth of imagery in relation to Himself that would mark Him out as unique. "I am the good shepherd." "I am the bread of life." So audacious were His claims that we are left with only two options – either He was a deluded megalomaniac, or He was what He claimed to be – the Son of God.

FOR PRAISE:
> *The highest place that heaven affords*
> *Is His by sovereign right.*
> *As King of kings and Lord of lords*
> *He reigns in glory bright.*

December 31

THE NECESSITY OF CHRIST'S RETURN

The Lord Himself will come down from heaven with a loud command . . . (1 Thessalonians 4:16)

There are compelling reasons that lead us to believe that Jesus will return to receive His Bride and usher in the end of the age. He must return:

To redeem His own promise — "If I go, I will come back" (John 14:3). Many other statements of our Lord can be interpreted only in terms of a personal return.

To complete the fulfilment of Messianic prophecies. Luke 4:16–19 is one such. Why did Jesus stop reading in the middle of verse 21? The first part of the prophecy had been fulfilled in His first advent, and the terrible second part awaited His return at the end of the age.

To confirm the trustworthiness of Scripture. Every New Testament writer bears witness to the return of Christ. If He did not return, the trustworthiness of Scripture would be irreparably shaken.

To execute judgement on the impenitent. No-one who accepts the authority of Christ and the authenticity of Scripture can doubt there is a judgement to come. For the impenitent, Christ taught in clearest terms that there is the inescapable prospect of standing before the bar of God.

To complete His work of redemption, which includes "the redemption of the body". In this connection Paul wrote, "We . . . groan inwardly as we wait eagerly for . . . the redemption of our bodies" (Rom. 8:23).

FOR PRAYER: *Lord, may I be among those who look eagerly for Your coming, and work to hasten it on.* (2 Pet. 3:12)

SOURCES OF READINGS
FROM BOOKS BY J. OSWALD SANDERS

At Set of Sun
The Best that I can Be
Bible Men of Faith
Cameos of Comfort
Certainties of the Second Coming
Christ's Solitary Throne
Consider Him
Cults and Isms
100 Days with Matthew
105 Days with John
Doctrinal Studies
Effective Evangelism
Effective Prayer
Enjoying Intimacy with God
Facing Loneliness
Guidelines to Discipleship
The Holy Spirit and His Gifts
The Incomparable Christ
In Pursuit of Maturity
Just Like Us
Just the Same Today
Mighty Faith
Paul the Leader
Prayer Power Unlimited
Private Notes
Promised Land Living
The Pursuit of the Holy
Real Discipleship
Satan No Myth
A Spiritual Clinic
Spiritual Leadership
Spiritual Maturity
Spiritual Problems
This I Remember
What of Those who have never Heard?
Your Best Years

Hodder Christian Paperbacks: a tradition of excellence.

Great names and great books to enrich your life and meet your needs. Choose from such authors as:

Corrie ten Boom	Jackie Pullinger
Charles Colson	David Pytches
Richard Foster	Mary Pytches
Billy Graham	Jennifer Rees Larcombe
Michael Green	Cliff Richard
Michele Guinness	John Stott
Joyce Huggett	Joni Eareckson Tada
Francis MacNutt	Colin Urquhart
Catherine Marshall	David Watson
Jim Packer	David Wilkerson
Adrian Plass	John Wimber

The wide range of books on the Hodder Christian Paperback list include **biography, personal testimony, devotional books, evangelistic books, Christian teaching, fiction, drama, poetry, books that give help for times of need** – and many others.

Ask at your nearest Christian bookshop or at your church bookstall for the latest titles.

SOME BESTSELLERS IN HODDER CHRISTIAN PAPERBACKS

THE HIDING PLACE by Corrie ten Boom

The triumphant story of Corrie ten Boom, heroine of the anti-Nazi underground.

"A brave and heartening story."

Baptist Times

GOD'S SMUGGLER by Brother Andrew

An international bestseller. God's Smuggler carries contraband Bibles past armed border guards to bring the love of Christ to the people behind the Iron Curtain.

"A book you will not want to miss."

Catherine Marshall

DISCIPLESHIP by David Watson

". . . breath-taking, block-busting, Bible-based simplicity on every page."

Jim Packer

LISTENING TO GOD by Joyce Huggett

A profound spiritual testimony, and practical help for discovering a new dimension of prayer.

"This is counselling at its best."

Leadership Today

CELEBRATION OF DISCIPLINE by Richard Foster

A classic on the Spiritual Disciplines.

"For any Christian hungry for teaching, I would recommend this as being one of the most challenging books to have been published."

Delia Smith

RUN BABY RUN by Nicky Cruz with Jamie Buckingham

A tough New York gang leader discovers Christ.

"It is a thrilling story. My hope is that it shall have a wide reading."

Billy Graham

CHASING THE DRAGON by Jackie Pullinger with Andrew Quicke

Life-changing miracles in Hong Kong's Walled City.

"A book to stop you in your tracks."

Liverpool Daily Post

BORN AGAIN by Charles Colson

Disgraced by Watergate, Charles Colson finds a new life.

"An action packed story of real life drama and a revelation of modern history as well as a moving personal account."

Elim Evangel

KNOWING GOD by J I Packer

The biblical portrait that has become a classic.

"(The author) illumines every doctrine he touches and commends it with courage, logic, lucidity and warmth . . . the truth he handles fires the heart. At least it fired mine, and compelled me to turn aside to worship and pray."

John Stott

THE HAPPIEST PEOPLE ON EARTH by Demos Shakarian with John and Elizabeth Sherrill

The extraordinary beginnings of the Full Gospel Business Men's Fellowship.